Back From Betrayal

Advance Praise for
Back from Betrayal

"Dr. Jennifer Schneider has added so much new material to this 4th edition of *Back From Betrayal* that it is truly like a whole new book. She makes a compelling case for presenting a range of information and healing alternatives for partners of sex addicts, emphasizing both trauma recovery and recognizing ways to heal the self-sabotaging thinking and patterns of behavior that can often accompany relational trauma. A researcher herself, Dr. Schneider is very inclusive in her point of view, and she uses a conversational style to impart complicated information. Really, a compassionate gift for the field of sexual addiction treatment, whether you are yourself a partner of a sex addict, or a therapist for such partners."

— **Sharon O'Hara MFT, CSAT**-Supervisor, Clinical Director of the Sexual Recovery Institute in Los Angeles.

"*Back from Betrayal* was groundbreaking as the first book to address the experience of a sex addict's partner and it remains one of the best resources. This fourth addition beautifully weaves together the two "camps" of viewing partners – from a lens of the trauma experienced from being in relationship with a sex addict; and from the perspective of a partner's underlying woundedness and coping mechanisms that often came from her (or his) family experiences long before connecting with the sex addict. Dr. Schneider masterfully illustrates how these models complement and reinforce each other rather than conflict. Don't be put off by the terms "coaddict," "coaddiction" or "codependency." Each concept is unpacked in a way that honors partners' pain, validates their experiences of living the crazy roller coaster of betrayal, and invites them into the deepest levels of personal healing. I'm thrilled to have this updated version of a classic."

Marnie C. Ferree, M.A., LMFT, CSAT, director of Bethesda Workshops in Nashville, TN, and author of *No Stones – Women Redeemed from Sexual Addiction* and editor of *Making Advances – A Comprehensive Guide to Treating Female Sex and Love Addicts.*

"Dr Schneider explores the complex web of fear, loneliness, shame, hurt and desperation that bring people together in painful relationships, where sex is mistaken for love, people suffer in silence, explode with anger, and the truth is seldom spoken. Infidelity can include affairs, pornography, flirting in chat rooms, prostitution, sexual internet relationships and most of all deceit, lies and withdrawal of connection. In addition, Dr. Schneider brings a wealth of understanding to the arduous and rewarding process of healing where processing past trauma and neglect, and exploring distorted perceptions and early conditioning can help couples feel safe enough to open the door to honesty and vulnerability. Instead of two separate people trying desperately to fulfill their unspoken emptiness the couple learns to connect with each other through a process of honesty, empathy and understanding.

— **Charlotte Sophia Kasl,** Author of *Women, Sex, and Addiction: A Search for Love and Power, If the Buddha Dated,* and *If the Buddha Married*

"It is long past due for the field of sexual addiction to focus on the here- and-now trauma that partners of sex addicts experience. The shock of discovery, the ongoing struggle to rebuild trust, and dealing with relapse must be addressed as well as any codependency issues. I commend Jennifer Schneider for her sensitive approach to partners who feel betrayed."

— **Dr. Brenda Schaeffer,** Author of *Is It Love or Is It Addiction?*

In *Back from Betrayal*, Dr. Jennifer Schneider presents as clear a picture as there is about what it is like to love and be partnered with a sexual addict (active or recovering). She does so by presenting comprehensive information to help betrayed partners understand both themselves and their sexually addicted significant other – explaining the trauma that is experienced by all parties, along with the resultant emotional roller-coaster. Best of all, Dr. Schneider describes, from both a professional and personal perspective, the process of finding help and recovering from the havoc created by this devastating disorder. Using this volume, betrayed spouses of sex addicts will learn that they are powerless over their partner's behaviors, and that their self-esteem needn't depend on that other person (or anyone else). As a result, *Back from Betrayal* is incredibly empowering, and destined to enrich the lives and relationships of countless men and women who've been negatively impacted by another person's sexual addiction or anyone suffering from the outcome of profound relationship betrayal.

—**Robert Weiss LCSW, CSAT** Author, speaker, clinician & expert on the relationship of human sexuality to digital technology

"Dr. Schneider's newly revised *Back from Betrayal* is a solidly researched self-help book that offers much-needed current resources, useful updated information, state-of-the-art tools, easy-to-understand language to clients, laypeople and clinicians, and especially provides detailed guidance and therefore hopefulness to the reader. I enthusiastically recommend this updated classic be part of every clinician's bibliotherapy library for effective client therapy and treatment for individuals impacted by the shock, pain and confusion of infidelity.

— **Anna Valenti-Anderson**, LCSW, LISAC, CSAT-S, CMAT, in private practice in the Phoenix area and co-author of *Making Advances: A Comprehensive Guide for Treating Female Sex and Love Addicts*.

"The disclosure of a mate's sex addiction and infidelity, cyber or otherwise, is heartbreaking for the partner and sends shock waves through the relationship. Drawing from her research, her expertise in the field of sex addiction treatment and her own soul-searching journey, Jennifer Schneider provides life-giving insights and practical direction for partners and recovering couples who are looking for answers."

—**Connie Lofgreen, MSW, CSA,** author of *The Storm of Sex Addiction: Rescue and Recovery.*

"*Back from Betrayal* is an excellent resource for partners of sex addicts and others who are dealing with sexual betrayal, whether they are young or old, gay or straight, male or female. Dr. Schneider covers all of the basic information the reader will need to understand their situation on an interpersonal, physical, psychological and spiritual level. The reader will get specific guidelines for finding the best sources of help and support in order to recover as well as an in depth look at what makes sex addicts tick. The added sections on pornography and cybersex are particularly relevant for present day readers."

—**Linda Hatch, PhD,** Author of *Living With a Sex Addict*, and *Relationships in Recovery: A Guide for Sex Addicts who are Starting Over*

"*Back from Betrayal* was and still is the BEST book about betrayal for sex addiction partners who have lived through an unbelievable trauma. Years ago, when I had to face infidelity issues in my own marriage, this book put me on the right track to work on myself and to realize everything coming up for me was not just the present trauma. I felt that Jennifer really understood and had empathy for what had happened to my shattered world. It is an absolute must read for anyone including a sex addict to read for their journey through healing."

—**Charlie Risien LCDC AAC CSAT** Counselor in San Antonio, Texas

"Dr. Schneider's *Back from Betrayal* offers hope to readers who are dealing with the spiritual assault of sex addiction or codependency. The reader will find practical suggestions for positive change substantiated by research and many relatable case studies. *Back from Betrayal* is an important read which humanizes an important psychological issue."

—**Katherine Norgard, Ph.D., TEP**, Psychologist, Trainer, Educator, Practitioner in Psychodrama

"Soren Kierkegaard once said that 'life is meant to be lived forward but can only be understood backward'. Schneider's work is a field-tested look that sifts through the carnage of past serial relational betrayal and offers practical tools of guidance designed to help those partners who have suffered to live forward with healing and hope.

—**Ken Wells MDiv, MA, LPC, CSAT, LSAC,** Psychological Counseling Services, Scottsdale, Arizona

Back From Betrayal

RECOVERING FROM THE TRAUMA OF INFIDELITY

FOURTH EDITION

Jennifer P. Schneider M.D.

Recovery Resources Press

The following publishers have generously given permission to use extended quotations from copyrighted works: From *The New Celibacy*, by Gabrielle Brown. Copyright 1980, published by Ballantine Books, Reprinted by permission of McGraw-Hill Book Co. From *Diagnosing and Treating Codependence*, by T L. Cermak, M.D. Copyright 1986, published by Johnson Institute Publications. Reprinted by permission of the publisher. From *Love Must be Tough*, by James C. Dobson. Copyright 1983, published by Word Books. Reprinted by permission of the publisher. From *The Feminine Mystique*, by Betty Friedan. Copyright 1983 by Betty Friedan. Reprinted by permission of W. W. Norton & Co, Inc. From *The Second Stage*, by Betty Friedan. Copyright 1981, published by Summit Books. Reprinted by permission of Simon & Schuster. From *The Art of Loving*, by Erich Fromm. Copyright 1956, published by Harper & Row. From *How to Break your Addiction to a Person*, by Howard Halpern. Copyright 1981, published by Bantam Books. Reprinted by permission of McGraw-Hill Book Co. From *We: Understanding the Psychology of Romantic Love*, by Robert Johnson. Copyright 1984, published by Harper & Row. Reprinted by permission of the publisher. From *Stranger on the Square*, by Arthur Koestler and Cynthia Koestler. Copyright 1984, published by Random House, Inc. Reprinted by permission of the publisher. From *The Booze Battle*, by Ruth Maxwell. Copyright 1976, published by Ballantine Books. Reprinted by permission of Henry Holt & Co. From "Avoiding the Scarlet Letter," by Louis McBurney, M.D. Published in *Leadership Magazine*, 1985. Reprinted by permission of the author. From *The Total Woman*, by Marabel Morgan. Copyright 1973 by Marabel Morgan. Published by Fleming H. Revell Co. Reprinted by permission of the publisher. From *Co-dependence: Misunderstood /Mistreated*, by Anne Wilson Schaef. Copyright 1986, published by Winston Press. Reprinted by permission of Harper & Row. From "Co-dependency: A paradoxical dependency" by Robert Subby, in *Co-dependency: An Emerging Issue*. Copyright 1984, published by Health Communications, Inc. Reprint courtesy Robert Subby. From *A Loss for Words*, by Lou Ann Walker. Copyright 1986, published by Harper & Row. Reprinted by permission of the publisher. From "Sexaholic: Addict of Infidelity," by Bob Womack, in the *Arizona Daily Star* 5 May 1985. Reprinted by permission of the Arizona Daily Star.

FIRST HAZELDEN EDITION PUBLISHED IN 1988.
SECOND EDITION PUBLISHED IN 2001
THIRD EDITION PUBLISHED IN 2005
FOURTH EDITION PUBLISHED IN 2015

ISBN: 150779813X
ISBN 13: 9781507798133
Library of Congress Control Number: 2015901779
CreateSpace Independent Publishing Platform
North Charleston, South Carolina

Contents

Acknowledgments· xv
Introduction: Looking Back· xvii

Part One: The Problem
Chapter 1:   Living with Sex Addiction · · · · · · · · · · · · · · · 3
Chapter 2:   Characteristics of the Traumatized Partner · · · · · · · 29
Chapter 3:   The Family Connection· · · · · · · · · · · · · · · · · 57
Chapter 4:   Understanding the Sex Addict· · · · · · · · · · · · · · 87
Chapter 5:   The Roller Coaster Ride of Living
             with Sex Addiction · · · · · · · · · · · · · · · · · 123

Part Two: The Road to Recovery
Chapter 6:   The Elements of Recovery · · · · · · · · · · · · · · · 193
Chapter 7:   Getting Professional Help · · · · · · · · · · · · · · · 231
Chapter 8:   Recovery as a Couple · · · · · · · · · · · · · · · · · 257
Chapter 9:   Recovery as a Single Person · · · · · · · · · · · · · · 309
Chapter 10: Final Thoughts · 327

Appendix A: Definition of Terms Used in this Book · · · · · · · · · 333
Appendix B: Resources· 337
Appendix C: Suggested Reading · · · · · · · · · · · · · · · · · · · 343
Footnotes · 361
Index · 373
About the Author · 381

Other Books by Jennifer P. Schneider

Always Turned On: Sexual Addiction in the Digital Age, by Robert Weiss and Jennifer Schneider. Gentle Path Press, 2015.

Closer Together, Further Apart: The Effect of the Internet and Technology on Parenting, Work, and Relationships, by Robert Weiss and Jennifer Schneider. Gentle Path Press, 2014.

Understand Yourself, Understand your Partner: The Essential Enneagram Guide to a Better Relationship, by Jennifer P. Schneider and Ron Corn, 2013.

Disclosing Secrets: An Addict's Guide for When, to Whom, and How Much to reveal, by M. Deborah Corley and Jennifer P. Schneider, 2012.

Surviving Disclosure: A Partner's Guide for Healing from the Betrayal of Intimate Trust, by Jennifer P. Schneider and Deborah M. Corley, 2012.

Living with Chronic Pain, Second Edition New York, Hatherleigh Press,2009.

Untangling the Web: Sex, Porn, and Fantasy in the Internet age, by Robert Weiss and Jennifer P. Schneider. Gentle Path Press, 2006.

Sex, Lies, and Forgiveness: Couples Speak on Healing from Sex Addiction by Jennifer P. Schneider and Burt Schneider.   Third Edition, Recovery Resources Press, 2004

Disclosing Secrets: What, to Whom, and How Much to Reveal. by M. Deborah Corley and Jennifer P. Schneider. Gentle Path Press, 2002.

Cybersex Exposed: Simple Fantasy or Obsession? by Jennifer P. Schneider and Robert Weiss. Hazelden Education and Publishing, 2001.

The Wounded Healer: Addiction-Sensitive Approach to the Sexually Exploitative Professional by Richard Irons and Jennifer P. Schneider, Jason Aaronson Publishers, 1999.

The Myth of the Jewish Race, by Raphael Patai and Jennifer P. Wing, Scribner's, 1976.

Acknowledgments

I specifically want to thank Debra Kaplan LPC, CSAT-S for her input in the rewriting of the current edition of this book. She spent many hours thoroughly reviewing the manuscript and made many helpful suggestions and additions. I am so grateful to her!! I also am grateful to Anna Valenti-Anderson, Sharon O'Hara, Bill Herring, Ken Wells, Linda Hatch, Charlie Risien, Marnie Ferree, and Mavis Humes Baird for their comments and suggestions.

Many others assisted me in the preparation of the First Edition. They included: Sheila Tobias, Cynthia Arem, Arnold Arem, and Stuart Gellman; my father, Raphael Patai, and my sister, Daphne Patai. Roxanne Kibben gave me her insights on treatment of codependency. I am particularly grateful to Robin Martin for many helpful discussions, excellent suggestions, and critical perusal of the manuscript at every step. My husband gave me his unfailing support during the writing of the First Edition, reviewed the manuscript, and had many important suggestions. My five children and stepchildren got used to finding me deep in thought at the computer or else involved in endless discussions about sex addiction, coaddiction, and codependency. I appreciate their patience and support.

Because I have promised to preserve their anonymity, I cannot publicly thank the men and women whose stories appear here, but I have expressed my gratitude to them individually.

Finally, I want to thank the editor of the first edition, Kerry Finn, for her encouragement, enthusiasm, and belief in the book.

Introduction: Looking Back

In 1983 I was a happy woman. I was a successful physician and was in a relatively new marriage with a man I loved very much. My husband and I had spent the preceding year learning how to make a success of our stepfamily, and we were doing well. We had just bought a new house that could accommodate his three children and my two, and our hard work with our new family was beginning to pay off.

Then something happened that turned my life upside down: My husband, in great distress, and driven by mounting guilt, told me he had been having an affair for some months. Despite the pain we were both feeling and his guilt over hurting me, he wasn't sure it would not happen again. He realized he was addicted to the excitement of the chase and conquest.

I thought back to our stormy courtship, to the several times he had backed out of a commitment, saying we both "needed to meet other people" (which I knew meant that *he* wanted to meet other women). I knew he had not been faithful during his first marriage, but I had naively assumed that monogamy would not be a problem for him this time. Now he was telling me he had so little control over his actions that he couldn't promise fidelity in the future, no matter how much he wished he could. I felt devastated; our marriage seemed headed for divorce.

Several weeks later, he read a letter to "Dear Abby" in the newspaper. A woman stated that although she loved her husband and did not want to destroy her marriage, she kept getting involved in meaningless affairs. She didn't know how to stop. Abby referred her to a self-help recovery program for people whose lives are out of control because of their compulsive sexual behavior. My husband joined the same self-help program and suggested that I also attend a program based on the Twelve Steps of Alcoholics Anonymous. During medical school I had attended a couple of Alcoholics Anonymous (A.A., a self-help group for alcoholics) and Al-Anon meetings (for families of alcoholics), but I felt they had no relevance to my own life. My husband recognized the similarities between alcoholism and other addictions and advised me to attend Al-Anon, the only program for families of addicts available at that time in our city. I went to my first meeting only in order to help my husband, but it turned out to be very helpful for me as well. Eventually I recognized I was codependent (in my case, someone who looks to others for validation of one's self-worth) and coaddicted (in my case, a person who is in an addictive relationship with an addict). (NOTE: The terms codependency and coaddiction have been given conflicting definitions by the many trailblazing authors in this field who have struggled to give shape to the multiple manifestations of trauma in family members of addicts.)

I also came to realize that it was no accident I had chosen to marry the man I did – that all of my previous important relationships had also been with men who were emotionally unavailable in one way or another. As a child in the Middle East, after my parents divorced and my father left the country, my mother abandoned me at age 5, after which my younger sister and I lived with strangers for several years. When my father remarried and brought us to live with him in the U.S. and subsequently got divorced, I became the parentified child, the good responsible girl running the household and taking care of my sister while my father focused on his work. My dysfunctional childhood experiences were typical of future partners of sex addicts, and even my choice of a medical career was logical in view of the caretaker role I had when I was growing up.

In Al-Anon I found that I subscribed to a set of irrational beliefs typical of many partners of sex addicts: I was fearful of abandonment, I felt my real worth came from validation by another person, and I thought I could control my husband's behavior: if I were more attractive, or kept a neater house, or were more understanding and unselfish, he would be satisfied to stay home.

Through attendance at a self-help program for spouses of sex addicts (See Appendix B for Resources), I came to understand that I was powerless over my husband's behavior, and that my self-esteem did not have to depend on him or anyone else. I became able to set limits on what was or was not acceptable for me in our relationship. Because he was committed to his recovery, was active in a Twelve-Step program, and was now open and honest with me, I remained in the marriage. Even though we married "for the wrong reasons," as he told me, we stayed together for many years for the right reasons – out of choice, not addiction, because our lives were enriched by each other.

In the beginning:

When I attended medical school in the 1970s, medical school curricula included consideration of psychosocial problems. A Human Behavior and Development course provided lectures on suicide, sexuality, and alcoholism. For those of us who were interested, the school arranged visits to Alcoholics Anonymous meetings. Having had no exposure to chemical dependency among my own family or friends, I would otherwise never have attended such meetings and would have graduated, as did most of my classmates, with no knowledge of the valuable resource for recovery that A.A.'s Twelve-Step program provides.

My professor gave me the name of a recovering alcoholic to contact. I phoned her, and a few evenings later I was taken by an attractive, articulate woman to a large meeting hall where a clergyman and a physician told of their struggles with alcoholism and their subsequent recovery. As I looked around the room, I noticed not only chain-smoking crusty old men (who fit my preconception of the hard-core alcoholic), but also well-dressed men and women and, surprisingly, quite a few young people. Their faces projected hope and a sense of belonging. The Twelve Steps of the A.A. program had clearly made a big difference in their lives.

This was an unknown part of society to me, and I decided to learn more. My next step was to find out what life was like for the spouses of alcoholics. My guide suggested I attend an Al-Anon meeting. I did and found it very different from the inspirational A.A. meeting I had observed the week before. At the Al-Anon meeting, a dozen women listened to a crying newcomer describe how her life was totally out of control because of her husband's drinking. "I know how you feel, because I was once there too," confided a member. Several of the women described similar situations they had been through and how their program helped them deal with each problem. By the end of the meeting, the newcomer felt much better and left the meeting with some hope. I still knew nothing about the program, but I could see that these women were helping each other. I made a mental note that if ever, in my practice, I were to encounter a patient who was living with alcoholism, I would tell her about Al-Anon. In my naiveté, I did not expect this to happen very often.

By the time I began private practice, I was in my new marriage. My husband, then a graduate student in counseling, would bring home books and articles about psychotherapy. I read them with interest, and I began attending workshops with him on individual, family, and sex counseling. He spent some months working at a chemical dependency treatment unit for adolescents, which led to my increased awareness of the pervasiveness of alcohol and other drug addictions. This awareness was reinforced by lectures and work-shops on addiction I attended with him. I frequently heard A.A. and

Al-Anon mentioned at those talks, and remembered the meetings I had attended as a medical student.

I began to question patients more extensively about their use of alcohol and other drugs. Not surprisingly, I soon learned that many of my patients, especially those I had been treating for high blood pressure, insomnia, fatigue, abnormal liver function blood tests, and vague gastrointestinal symptoms, had excessive use of alcohol as their underlying disease. I learned how to recognize the clinical and biochemical signs of early alcohol dependency and began referring patients to alcohol recovery programs.

As a female internist, I was often sought out by women who wanted the sympathetic ear of another woman. As I began talking with them, I was struck by how often they were dealing with very difficult situations: spouses who drank excessively, who were rarely at home because their jobs were all-consuming, who were demanding and jealous, or who were engaged in sexual affairs. Some women held full-time, demanding jobs and then came home to housework, meal preparation, and child care, as well as providing a sounding board for their spouses' problems and complaints. They had grown up so firmly entrenched in caretaker roles that they didn't feel they had the right to ask their spouses to share in the work. Moreover, they felt unable to let go of any of the responsibilities they had assumed.

These women had not come to see me because of their relationship problems; rather, they were in my office because of headaches, backaches, insomnia, fatigue, or stomach pains. In the past, I had approached each symptom individually, ordering various tests and prescribing appropriate medications. At times the particular symptom would improve, but the patient would be back a few weeks later with a different complaint. Often, nothing really seemed to help. Eventually, I recognized that the physical symptoms were manifestations of the depression, anger, resentment, and helplessness they were feeling about their circumstances at home. There were caretakers in the family, trying their best to make things better, trying to change their husbands' drinking, overworking, gambling, or other destructive behaviors. They were stuck and didn't know how to improve the situation. They were so committed to a relationship that they couldn't imagine getting out. They stuffed their feelings – often literally. In fact, when I started asking obese women about their home lives, I discovered they were frequently in alcoholic or otherwise unhealthy relationships or had grown up in dysfunctional families.

The women I saw seemed to share a common affliction that was at the source of their varied symptoms. In the mid-1980s this affliction gained widespread exposure thanks to the 1985 bestseller by Robin Norwood, *Women who Love Too Much: When you Keep Wishing and Hoping He'll Change*. A year later three other books addressed the same problem. These were Melody Beattie's bestseller *Codependent No More*, Anne Wilson Schaef's *Codependence: Misunderstood/Mistreated*, and the more clinically oriented *Diagnosing and Treating Codependence* by Dr. Timmen Cermak.

Only when codependency suddenly became personal for me did I realize I was suffering from the same problem. My experience made me much more attuned to my patients' problems, and more able to intervene effectively by referring them to appropriate counseling and to self-help programs.

Back then in my own recovery group and in my office, I became aware of the deep shame we feel when our spouses have cheated on us. Even now, in response to infidelity many of us believe that our mate's behavior is a reflection of our own inadequacy. We blame ourselves, convinced that if we were sexier or more supportive they would not have strayed. We are deeply ashamed to reveal what is happening in our marriage. It took me personally a long time to feel comfortable admitting to others my husband's affairs and stop worrying what others would think of me. Now I recognize that my husband's infidelity reflected only on him.

Yet there is justification for our reluctance to admit our spouses' infidelity. Many people do automatically blame the partner. This was evident on a television program I saw years ago. Phil Donahue interviewed Dr. Patrick Carnes, author of *Out of the Shadows* [the groundbreaking first book about sex addiction], and a married couple who were in treatment because the husband was a compulsive masturbator. The audience reaction was particularly hostile. Several women seemed threatened, asking the wife if she didn't agree that had she been more sexually available to her husband he would not have had to repeatedly resort to pornography and masturbation. (This is the same line of reasoning frequently used to blame a woman for her husband's affairs.) Unfortunately, these words are still repeated today by well-meaning pastors, doctors, and family members, who advise partners to just be more sexual and enjoy porn along with the spouse. There was little understanding that the man's behavior was caused by an addiction, not by his wife. This man had learned to medicate his emotional pain with the escape and relief he got from compulsive masturbation, just as other people alleviate their emotional pain by drinking alcohol or using illegal drugs to excess. **In neither case is the wife to blame, and in neither case can she control her husband's behavior.**

The most important element of maintaining addictive behavior is secrecy. To be able to talk about a problem openly is the first step toward resolving it. To become healthy, you need to understand you are not responsible for your spouse's affairs or cybersex activities and that he or she has a disease which causes them to behave in hurtful ways. Many people can now reveal that their spouse has an alcohol addiction without feeling they are responsible for the drinking or that they are unworthy.

Back in 1987, by being open about my own family problems, I risked being accused of sensationalism. In that era some readers might have asked why I didn't simply write this book as a professional, without owning up to my personal involvement. My answer was that I was following the tradition of counselors in the chemical dependency field. Now, of course, open any brochure for a chemical dependency treatment program and you will find that most staff members list their own recovery from alcohol or other drug abuse as part of their credentials. Likewise, those who counsel family members admit their experiences in addicted families. In the addiction field it is considered an asset to have experienced and grappled with the problem. When a therapist can say, "I know what you're going through – I've been there myself," he or she can cut through the isolation that is part of addictive behavior. This powerful therapeutic tool enables the client to feel that the counselor can really understand.

This, of course, is very different from the traditional approach of the psychiatrist or psychologist, whose role is to listen to the client, supply insights where they are deemed helpful, and make suggestions for better ways of coping. Therapists are very careful to provide a minimum of personal information, even about their marital and family status. They want to project to the client the image of a healthy person, one who has no significant emotional problems.

Therapists have not always been able to openly admit their own addiction history. Eighty years ago, when the Alcoholics Anonymous movement first began, alcoholism was considered as shameful as sex addiction is today. Very few people were willing to speak openly about their own alcoholism or their involvement in an alcoholic family. It took many years for chemical dependency to be considered a disease and for the medical and psychotherapeutic community to acknowledge the validity of the A.A. approach as a road to recovery. When the first edition of *Alcoholics Anonymous: The Story of How More Than One Hundred Men Have Recovered from Alcoholism*[1] appeared in 1939, a review of the book in the *Journal of the American Medical Association*[2] described it as "a curious combination of organizing propaganda and religious exhortation" and concluded, "The one valid thing in the book is the recognition of the seriousness of addiction to alcohol. Other than this, the book has no scientific merit or interest." However, this book, which introduced the Twelve Steps and described the recovery program that has been successful for so many years, is still the basic text for members of A.A. and is the model for all other self-help recovery programs based on A.A.

The march of time – Increasing opportunities for infidelity:

Rereading *Back from Betrayal* after many years, I am struck by how much has changed. In 1987, when I wrote the first edition of this book, hardly anyone had heard of sex addiction. The concept that multiple extramarital affairs, a socially acceptable behavior in many cultures including our own, could be a manifestation of an addictive or compulsive disorder, was a hard sell. After the book was published, I gave talks to professional audiences of sex therapists, psychiatrists, and addiction clinicians, most of whom were dubious that too much of a good thing could be anything but good, or that a *behavior* could be as addictive as a drug. I learned to develop a thick skin and not to take personally the attacks that sometimes followed my presentations.

For example, in November 1989 I spoke at the 32nd Annual Meeting of the Society for the Scientific Study of Sex ("Quad S"), held in Toronto, Canada. This society's members are sex therapists. In a session called "New Perspectives in Sex Therapy," I gave a presentation titled "Sexual Problems in Couples who are Rebuilding Their Relationship after Multiple Extramarital Affairs." The talk which immediately followed mine, given by Marty Klein, a well-known member of the society, was called "Why There's no Such Thing as Sexual Addiction – and Why it Matters." The timing of his presentation, immediately after mine, and its content, were clearly designed to undermine any change which my talk might have made in the way sex therapists would view future clients who had multiple affairs.

Since then, of course, much has changed. In the late 1990s the American people watched their President self-destruct politically by engaging in extramarital affairs with a long series of women. Phrases like "compulsive sexual behavior" and "sex addict" became the stuff of daily media comments for many months, and the consequences for the First Couple were played out in full view. The public witnessed Bill Clinton's gradual and incomplete television disclosures and his subsequent impeachment trial, as well as the recurrent struggles of Hillary Clinton to believe his denials, her demoralization after the truth was fully exposed, and the choices she eventually made – to separate her life from his and become a U.S. senator, then Secretary of State, and in 2015 a possible candidate for President. Currently only the rare member of "Quad S" is still unwilling to recognize that infidelity can be a manifestation of an addictive disorder.

The other change that increased the public's awareness of sex addiction has been the arrival in the 1990s, of a new technology that resulted in vastly increased opportunities for the expression of addictive sexual problems. This, of course, was the commercial application of the internet. Back in 1987, computers were large machines found primarily at corporations, institutions of learning, and the government, and the idea of computers communicating with each other would have seemed like science fiction to most people, had they even imagined it. The World Wide Web had not yet come into existence. In the following years, use of personal computers and the Internet exploded. By 2000, about half the homes in the United States had computers, and most of them had access to the Internet. About one in four Internet users, or 21 million Americans, visited one of the more than 60,000 sex sites on the Web at least once a month in 2000. By then, sex on the internet had become a multibillion dollar industry.

Whereas most men and women who accessed internet sex were "recreational users," some became hooked on it, giving up time with partner and family, risking job loss, and at times getting arrested because of their online sexual activities. A large group of people became "cybersex widows" and "widowers," having lost their partner to the computer. Support group meetings of partners of sex addicts became filled with stories of relationships falling apart because of one partner's cybersex involvement. Even when the infidelity did not involve physical contact with another person, the consequences could be equally devastating for the relationship. A whole new dimension was added to the concept of sexual betrayal.

This new phenomenon led therapist Robert Weiss and me to write a book, *Cybersex Exposed: Simple Fantasy or Obsession?*, published in 2001. By then, compulsive online sexual activities had become a typical part of the acting-out behaviors of sex addicts who had multiple affairs. As a larger percent of the population acquired home computers, the number of cybersex addicts increased, and by 2005 Rob and I published an updated version of our book, titled *Untangling the Web: Sex, Porn, and Fantasy Obsession in the Internet Age*. Little did Rob and I realize that within a few years emerging technology would again change the face of sex addiction.

In the past few years, the rapid proliferation of mobile electronic devices has broadened the opportunities for sex addicts to experience their "drug of choice." As Robert Weiss and I described in our latest cybersex book, *Always Turned On: Sex Addiction in the Digital Age* (2015), social media such as Facebook, Twitter, Instagram, and Snapchat have changed the way people interact, as have smartphones, texting/sexting, dating/hookup apps, ubiquitous GPS technology, selfies, video chat, and wearable technology. No longer do online sexual activities take place only while stationary at a desktop computer at home or on the job. Today, people carry or wear their technology in the form of smartphones, iPads or other tablets, or laptops. These mobile devices are *Always Turned On* and readily available, 24/7. As has been true for more than a decade, pornography can be accessed online, and now at any time and any place because the devices contain GPS apps which make possible instant real-life meetings with potential sex partners. Additionally, unlike the older desktop computers, the mobile devices do not save a record of the user's activities, making it harder for others to reconstruct the person's internet history.

Twenty years ago, the letters I received from desperate partners described discovery of a spouse or mate's real-life affairs. Ten years ago-the emails were from partners asking for help after they discovered a mate's collection of pornography on their home computer, or came across the mate's sexual exchanges with strangers, or walked in on him masturbating to porn or while "chatting" online with someone. Then, as now, partners were able to view on desktop computers the internet "history" of websites that had been accessed, enabling them to keep tabs on the mate's online activities. But now that cyber-sex activities can be conducted on mobile devices without leaving an overt digital footprint, it is becoming much more difficult for partners to verify or calm their suspicions – all while infidelity is reaping advances in technology for sex addicts to have ever-increasingly furtive opportunities to "act out."

At the time I wrote the first edition of this book, the sex addiction field was where the alcoholism field was in the early days of A.A. – misunderstood, shameful, and secret. But in early 2015, when I Googled "sex addiction," I got 29,900,000 hits! Clearly times have changed. This is largely due to the interconnectedness of the world. It is much harder to keep secrets. When a President of the United States, Governors, and Congressmen had multiple affairs, when a married Congressman texted sexual images to other women, information about these behaviors was widely disseminated. Careers and marriages were threatened, speculation about *why* such leaders would take these risks were discussed in the media, and information about sex addiction was found everywhere. Help has become more widely available, and more easily accessible. A Google search for "sex addiction treatment," yielded 15,200,000 hits. A request for "treatment of partners of sex addicts" yielded 155,000 hits. The internet may have enabled a sex addiction explosion, but the internet has also made it possible to find treatment with little more than one search. When you or your spouse are ready to get help and make some changes, you will find it.

The march of time – Codependence versus trauma, or Throwing the codependent baby out with the bath water:

Another change in the 21ˢᵗ century is a shift in the way trained therapists interpret the feelings and behaviors of partners of sex addicts as they respond to the compulsive sexual activities of their significant other and their cover-ups. As you'll read in later chapters, we have learned that dishonesty, whether by withholding information or actively lying, is as destructive to the relationship as is the infidelity itself. People who suspect that their partner is involved in secret sexual activities outside the relationship frequently respond with information-gathering, traditionally disparaged as "snooping," "spying," or "detective work." This behavior was traditionally considered unhealthy and a symptom of a mental health problem.

In 1988 when I wrote the original edition of this book, I focused on the role of the partner's childhood and/or youthful experiences in creating an adult with vulnerabilities; these contribute to their being attracted to an addict, to needing the mate in order to feel whole, to becoming people-pleasers, to a willingness to accept a spouse's behaviors that a well-adjusted person would not accept, and also a belief that if they know enough about their mate's activities they could control the situation. This constellation of traits has been termed *codependence*. These individuals became, in essence, addicted to the addict (this is termed *coaddiction*). At that time, I strongly suggested that the betrayed partner seek counseling in order to improve their own mental health so that they would be able to empower themselves and make healthy choices regarding their relationship.

In recent years therapists working with partners of sex addicts recognized that many of them were demonstrating behaviors suggestive of post-traumatic stress disorder (PTSD), and concluded that the partner had been traumatized by the mate's compulsive sexual behaviors with their accompanying secrecy and lying. Much like soldiers who returned from–active duty and found themselves reacting in alarm to a loud noise, the partners would over-react to any behavior of the addict's that reminded them of his or her previous acting out. The new perspective of these sex addiction therapists is that partners' snooping is their way of trying to create safety in order to feel safe, not a sign of codependence or coaddiction. They were newly traumatized people trying to survive in shocking circumstances. What they needed from the therapist was validation and support, not being labeled as having an undesirable personality trait.

All this makes a lot of sense to me. But in their desire to use this new approach in counseling, some therapists disposed of the older model altogether. They went from one extreme to the other. They seemed to suggest that partners of sex addicts were healthy until they accidentally ended up with a sex addict whose behavior traumatized them, which is why they then developed psychological problems. To me, this is like throwing the baby out with the bathwater. Many spouses or partners of sex addicts came from very dysfunctional families. Some may have been physically, sexually or emotionally abused in childhood and therefore are vulnerable to being newly traumatized because the previous, unresolved traumatic experiences are brought to the fore along with the current betrayal and infidelity. It is also common for partners to recreate their patterns of unresolved trauma from childhood by unwittingly choosing romantic partners who unconsciously play out those dysfunctional dynamics.

Research among soldiers returning from war has shown that soldiers who had experienced early trauma, such as childhood abuse or neglect, were at greater risk of developing PTSD in wartime. The earlier experiences had sensitized them to developing PTSD in the aftermath of traumatizing experiences which occurred years later. In their behavioral health treatment, these soldiers needed to deal with both sets of traumatic experiences – the more recent ones in war, and the earlier ones in childhood.

I believe that the same is true today for partners of sex addicts. In Deborah Corley's and my 2012 online anonymous survey of partners' reactions to their mate's disclosure of sex addiction relapse, over half (57.8%) of the 92 partners surveyed reported being a victim or survivor of significant trauma or neglect in the past, i.e. *before* the current betrayal by their mate.[3] Examples of the earlier trauma included "severe childhood physical and sexual abuse," "father was an alcoholic," "molestation from a boy in high school," "rape,", "abandonment was huge in my childhood," and "sexually molested as a child." These early experiences significantly impacted their reaction to the betrayal by the sex addict that they later experienced.

When asked in the 2012 study whether the term "co-addict" or "codependent" described them, 41.3% of partners said yes, 18.5% said somewhat, and 40.2% said no. At the same time, when asked whether the term "victim of interpersonal relationship trauma" described them, 77% of partners said yes, 15% said somewhat, and 8% said no. One third of the group (31%) said that both terms applied to them, 30% related only to being victims, and the remainder had a combination of responses. In other words, a large proportion of partners saw in themselves a mixture of features of both categories.

So – what is the best approach to therapy for betrayed partners? Initially it is important for the therapist to validate the partner's experience and empathize with her or him. The therapist's first step is to forge a bond with the client and acknowledge the trauma. These elements are essential at the beginning of treatment, but this is only the start of a longer process. Many partners of sex addicts also need to work through their earlier experiences, to understand and overcome the unhealthy coping strategies they may have developed early in life and which now prevent them from feeling in control of their lives and able to make good choices for themselves.

Partners need a combination of treatment approaches – both for the relational trauma of the betrayal they experienced (expressed as minor or major symptoms of PTSD), and for consequences of their childhood or earlier adult trauma (or both). These symptoms have been termed coaddiction or codependency.

These two diagnoses have overlapping treatment approaches including individual and group psychotherapy, but in addition, each has specific elements that have proven effective. For trauma work, this can include EMDR (Eye Movement Desensitization and Reprocessing) and SE ®(Somatic Experiencing). For codependency/coaddiction, this includes participation in Twelve-Step peer-led support groups. Partners of sex addicts can benefit from a combination of approaches. We will primarily refer to those in relationship with a sex addict as "partners," although at times we will use the term "coaddict" or "codependent" when it seems pertinent. If this seems confusing at times, refer to Appendix A for a definition of terms used in this book. I often refer to the sex addict as the "mate." Also, although I frequently use the term "married" for brevity rather than "involved in a relationship with," I am addressing both unmarried and married partners.

All the nonattributed quotations in this book come from personal interviews with sex addicts who acknowledged infidelity (in real life and/or online) and with partners who were involved with sex addicts. The names have been changed, but their words and stories are real.

In addition to the formal interviews, my conclusions are based on conversations with many men and woman in self-help groups for sex addicts and partners as well as on writings and lectures by experts in the field. In the more than 25 years since the first edition of this book was published, sex addiction has become an active subject of scholarly research and writing. The findings and conclusions of this book have been amply supported by additional research. You can read more about the subject in the books, articles, and websites listed in Appendix C, "Suggested Reading."

One last point: When you read statistics based on self-reporting (questionnaires, interviews) in an area where there is so much unconscious as well as conscious denial, remember that under-reporting is a real risk. For example, people often suppress memories of childhood sexual abuse, and may not remember this until after several months of counseling. Thus, if 20 percent of a sample of compulsively sexual men answer "yes" to a survey question about any incest or molestation experience, this does not mean that only 20 percent of the men were in fact abused. All it tells us is that at the time of the survey, 20 percent of the men *remember* being abused, or are willing to divulge it; the actual figure may be much higher. An integral part of addiction, trauma, and codependency is the suppression of feelings, and this is often accomplished by "forgetting" troublesome experiences. Much of one's childhood is often buried in the unconscious mind. This important fact must be remembered before drawing any conclusion about factors that explain the development of addiction and codependency in any particular person.

The march of time – Male partners of sex addicts:

In 1987, having personally lived through the pain of my husband's affairs and my own recovery from the trauma of the betrayal I experienced as well as my own codependency related to childhood abandonment, my thinking was focused on helping other female partners. But the past decade has brought about an increasing recognition of the magnitude of sex addiction problems in women. Back in the 1930s alcoholism was considered to be a man's problem; in the 2000s, we know that there are almost as many women as men alcoholics. Because out-of-control drinking was more shameful for women, they were more reluctant to come forth and ask for help – that is until Betty Ford cleared the way for other women to come out from behind closed doors and admit, "I, too, am an alcoholic."

The same thing has been happening for women sex addicts: With time, more are admitting their problem and getting help. The first (and ground-breaking) book about female sex addiction, *Women, Sex, and Addiction*, written by Charlotte Kasl, appeared only in 1989. Courageous professionals such as Marnie Ferree have gone public with their own sex addiction history and recovery and have written books about it (see her book *No Stones: Women Redeemed from Sexual Addiction*, first published in 2002 and most recently in 2010). In 2012 Ferree edited a book, *Making Advances: A Comprehensive Guide for Treating Female Sex and Love Addicts*. Women who have multiple sex partners have traditionally been stigmatized with names such as "slut" or "whore." The increasing recognition that they have an addictive disorder and can benefit from treatment has encouraged more women to ask for help. Currently, women constitute about one-third of the membership of Sex and Love Addicts Anonymous, a Twelve-Step program, and it is likely that in fact, sex addiction in women is probably as common as in men.

Most of these women have male spouses or significant others. Being the husband of a promiscuous woman has traditionally been more stigmatizing than being the wife or partner of a sexually acting-out male. It has been more difficult, therefore, for the male partner to seek support and help in dealing with his mate's infidelity. And let's not forget that among gay couples there are many men who've been betrayed and lied to by their mate; they too need recognition of their pain and support. In his 2013 book, *Cruise Control: Understanding Sex Addiction in Gay Men (Second Edition)*, Rob Weiss devotes a chapter to helping betrayed men. In earlier editions of *Back from Betrayal* I included a chapter for male partners, but in the current book I have tried to integrate the experience of male partners throughout the book. Finally, I want to stress that this book is not written exclusively for married people. Many single people will recognize themselves in these pages. The important factor is not the wedding ring, but the nature of the relationship and the expectations the partners have of each other.

The march of time - New information about psychotherapy

Since *Back from Betrayal* was first published, much more has been learned about the needs of sex addicts and their partners in counseling.

I became very interested in ethical issues relevant to counseling sex addicts and couples, especially issues related to disclosing secrets. Sex addicts have secrets. When, to whom, and how much should they reveal these secrets? What should they tell their children? If they confide their sexual behaviors to the therapist, can the counselor ethically do couples counseling while holding on to the addict's secret? What do partners need to know about their mate's acting out? And what are they better off not knowing? Is it possible to rebuild trust? Relapse is a frequent event in addiction recovery; in the face of relapse, how do partners decide whether to stay or leave? In the past decade Dr. Deborah Corley and I did research about disclosure, and in 2002 Dr. Corley and I wrote a book about our findings, *Disclosing Secrets: When, to Whom, and How Much to Reveal.* With additional research findings, in 2012 we updated our book and published a pair of guide books: *Disclosing Secrets: An Addict's Guide for When, to Whom, and How Much to Reveal* and *Surviving Disclosure: A Partner's Guide for Healing the Betrayal of Intimate Trust.* A section in the new edition of *Back From Betrayal* describes our findings.

Over the years I have continued to be confronted by challenges. These included the end of my marriage. I am very grateful for my long-term Twelve-Step recovery, which has enabled me to enjoy life as a single person and to make healthy choices for myself. As for this book, some readers may contend that a person who is addicted to real-life or online affairs or pornography is not in the same category as one who is addicted to alcohol. They may argue that pursuing new sexual partners is a voluntary activity, and that calling it an addiction or compulsion may serve only to absolve oneself of responsibility for one's actions. I would ask such readers to keep an open mind. It is not my intent to provide anyone with an excuse for hurtful behaviors, nor to urge the spouse to go along with it on the basis that the person has an illness. On the contrary, a major emphasis in this book is to show partners how to stop enabling behaviors that protect the addict from experiencing the unpleasant consequences of his or her acts, thereby encouraging the behavior to continue.

My goals:

It is my hope that this book will reach the many men and women who are suffering silently and alone as their spouses or mates repeatedly connect with others online or in real life, who are too ashamed to talk with anyone except perhaps their closest friend about what is happening, and who feel that somehow their mate's infidelity is their fault and an indication of their inadequacy.

This new edition has several goals for you:

- to familiarize you with the nature of sex addiction and the currently available menu of compulsive sexual behaviors
- to validate the trauma you have likely experienced as a result of your mate's on-line or real-life infidelity and lies
- to review your own past history to recognize what your own vulnerabilities may be and how codependency/coaddiction may be influencing your feelings and limiting your choices
- to recognize the impact of a mate's sexual addiction on the couple relationship
- to learn how to get help and what the elements of recovery for the spouse or partner consist of
- to familiarize you with the Twelve-Step program of recovery, which can be helpful for you and also will provide you with knowledge of the language and process that can help your sexually addicted spouse or significant other
- to provide suggestions for your own recovery, whether you are still together with your mate or moving on as a single person.
- to help you understand what you need to do in order to make healthy choices for yourself.

Part One:
The Problem

CHAPTER ONE

Living with Sex Addiction

What is life like when you are married to or in a committed relationship with a sex addict? Each relationship is different, of course, but here are the stories of several such partners who appear to be stuck:

Beth's Story

There were what Beth calls signs she should have spotted when they were dating, but it wasn't until four years after they were married that Beth discovered she had an unfaithful husband.

She had noticed that Barry was spending less and less time at home. One day she asked a neighbor if he had seen Barry. Yes, he responded, he had seen Barry loading a woman friend's bicycle into the back of his car and driving off with her.

Beth drove over to the woman's house and spotted her husband's car parked there. She drove home, telephoned the woman and asked to speak to Barry. She recalls,

I told him I thought it would be real swell if he got home right away and he did. He told me his friendship with the woman was real important to him and it had nothing to do with us. Then he told me he was going to Mexico with her, which he did.

A dozen years later, separated but still married to Barry, Beth says she was devastated at the news of his trip, yet was able to rationalize it this way:

I told myself he had never made a decision on his own and this was a decision he had made. So it was okay. I just waited at home for him. I wasn't sure he was ever coming back.

But Barry returned and his fling seemed to have been just that – an isolated incident frozen in Beth's memory but fading into the past. He went into business and became a workaholic. She devoted herself to the tasks of a homemaker.

They had two children, and Beth was pregnant with their third child about four years ago when Barry left one evening for a baseball game and didn't come home until the next morning.

I called the police and the hospitals – I thought something had happened to him. Then I thought maybe he had gone back to work after the game and fallen asleep at the office. I put the kids in the car at 3 A.M. and drove over there, but he wasn't there.

She did that, she thinks, because she had to have reality "slap" her in the face. The reality became even sharper that morning at six when Barry called her and asked if he could come home.

Beth had been slapped into the realization that she was married to a cheater. Or, as she prefers to call it, a sexaholic. She remembers a feeling of terror:

This time it was not just me – I would be left with two small children – more than I thought I could handle. And I was pregnant, and I was feeling fat and ugly. I felt my responsibilities were overwhelming.

She began trying to "catch" her husband and confront him with evidence of his infidelity. She stooped to actions she concedes were not only degrading, but useless: smelling his clothing, going through his car.

"Your clothes smell like perfume," she would ay. Or "How can a normal person come home at four in the morning and just have taken a shower?"

Each time, however, Barry had an excuse. And he would add, in an accusatory tone, "Look how suspicious you've become!"

Each time he would flip things around to where I felt like I was a bad person, a bitchy wife. How could I be making his life so miserable?

He would call her about 5 P.M. and say he had a few more things to do at the office and would be home about six-thirty. One day Beth decided to find out just how busy he was, so she drove over to his office and parked so she could see his door. It wasn't long before a young woman drove up and ran into Barry's office.

I was furious. I went home and called him. I asked the kids, "Wanna talk to Daddy?" and I put them on the phone. I couldn't think of what else to do.

Once Beth followed Barry after he left home for work. He stopped at one girlfriend's house on the way to work and had a lunch date with another. When he came home, he and Beth had an argument, and he left at 11 P.M., returning at 2 A.M. freshly showered.

Why did Beth spy on him? What good did it do? No more good than something she had witnessed her mother doing in a vain way to control Beth's alcoholic father by marking the levels on his liquor bottles.

Beth and Barry began seeing a counselor once a week, after, she says, Barry convinced her she was crazy. He quit going, Beth said, after the counselor understood what the real problem was.

One day the counselor asked me, "Do you realize this person you're married to is compulsively sexual?" I didn't know what that meant. I felt it must be something I'm doing – maybe he sees other women because they have jobs, because they're prettier than I am, because they're more intelligent than me.

A year later, still feeling responsible for their problems, still spying on Barry, and arguing almost constantly with him, Beth decided to leave. He wasn't pleased at the news, but she took the kids and left town.

When she returned three weeks later, Barry greeted her warmly with a cake that said, "Welcome Home." Beth was still angry, so she and her husband went into their bedroom to talk. Exhausted from her trip, she lay down on her bed. Her pillow reeked of perfume. "It was like aaaarrrruuuuggghh," says Beth, emitting a strangled exclamation.

Shortly afterward, Barry moved out. Since then, they have had numerous short-term reconciliations, but the only time he moved back in was the next Christmas. A day or two later he stayed out late, returning at 3 A.M. freshly showered.

Barry told Beth how bad he felt about himself, about the pressure he was under. She thought she must have been pretty rotten to accuse him of sleeping around. As for herself, she insists,

I really feel strong about myself. I feel it's okay that I don't know what will happen. I think there's a fairly good chance we'll reconcile[1]

Beth's passivity in the face of her husband's multiple affairs may be difficult for some readers to understand. Her fear of losing her husband, her attempts to spy on him, her willingness to take the blame for her husband's behavior, and her wishful thinking that things were likely to improve despite all the evidence of his ongoing affairs, are typical of many partners of sex addicts – they are not only victims of current relational trauma but also most likely grew up in a dysfunctional family with emotionally unavailable parents, resulting in early development of codependency.

Carmen's Story

Here is Carmen's account: Her husband, unlike Beth's, had just two affairs, but eventually identified himself as a sex addict.

Some people have told me, "So your husband had a couple of affairs! So do the majority of married men at some time. What makes his situation different? Why does he consider himself an addict?"

I'll tell you why. The essential problem was not that he had two affairs, but rather that his preoccupation with connecting with women interfered with all other aspects of his life. Wherever he went his roving eye would pick out a potential connection – usually someone whose appearance or body language suggested vulnerability or lack of self-confidence. He would then begin planning how to meet her and would fantasize what the meeting might lead to. His original purpose for attending the meeting or the class would be forgotten. He would arrange to have coffee or lunch with her. Even if she didn't accept, the emotional high he got from the experience of pursuing her made our home life dull by comparison. He would return home and walk around with a long face, finally confessing to me his unhappiness with the lack of excitement in our life. At times he would pick an argument with me so as to justify (in his mind) connecting with someone who would be more understanding or less demanding. Of course, I didn't understand this at the time; I just knew he seemed terribly unhappy for no particular reason. I tried my hardest to make him happy, but nothing worked.

We would get into a vicious circle: I'd feel rejected by his statements of boredom with our life and I'd respond by shutting down communication with him. He would then feel justified in concentrating on his latest fantasy. Eventually we would make up and things would be okay for a while. But just when our life seemed to be going very well, he'd come home and tell me how unhappy he was. I felt I was on a roller coaster. I could never predict what state of mind I'd find him in when I got home from work. And since my sense of well-being depended on him, my moods also kept swinging widely.

I kept expecting something bad to happen. Several times he stayed out late and wouldn't tell me why. He said he was helping someone and had promised secrecy. When he finally told me about an affair he'd been involved in for months – and a briefer one a year earlier – I realized that I had suspected it all along.

Feeling as if you're living on a roller coaster is a common way that many partners describe their life with a sex addict. They experience the mate's mood swings, try to understand and empathize and explain the spouse's behaviors, and often find themselves stuck in the addict's cycles, blaming themselves and trying to fix the situation.

Marlena's Story

Marlena is a 38-year old married mother of two boys, ages 10 and 13. She works as a computer programmer, designing web sites. Throughout her marriage, her husband Morgan has been interested in viewing pornography. Years ago, when Morgan began accessing porn on the internet, Marlena went along with this in an attempt to spice up their sex life. But Morgan quickly became hooked, spending up to 25 hours per week searching for and collecting erotic pictures of his specific tastes in women, observing sexual acts, and masturbating to them. He began spending time in sexually oriented chat rooms. With the advent of built-in video cameras on computers (Webcams) that enable online one-on-on real-time sex, Marlena became certain that Morgan was participating in this activity when she was out of the house. Their sexual relationship suffered. Marlena explains:

At first we explored internet sex together, but after a while Morgan did it in private. I'd approach him for sex and be turned down. I'd go to bed alone and he would do his thing. Morgan has not touched me sexually in over a year. He hasn't even hugged or kissed me in months now. In the beginning I tried everything, from erotic clothing to wigs and role playing. We had a delicious sex life, but one thing was missing – real intimacy. I tried to discuss this with him on several occasions, but he refused. When I tried to explain to him how hurt and rejected I was feeling, he denied he was doing anything wrong. He said he wasn't having "real" sex with anyone, and it was no different from the pornographic magazines he used to look at. I've lost him to the Web.

He says that girls there don't demand anything of him and they accept him for what he is.

He used to spend endless amounts of time on the computer, sometimes until the wee hours of the morning. Several times, when it was his turn to walk the children to catch the bus to school, he forgot to take them because he was on the computer looking at girls. When my younger son was 7, he cut himself with a knife while slicing an apple and needed stitches. Morgan was supposed to be watching the boy in the kitchen, but instead he was on the computer.

Having him look elsewhere for sexual stimulation has been very painful for me. I've developed depression and panic attacks, and am now on Paxil [an antidepressant] and Klonopin [an anti-anxiety drug].

My counselor says that women who stay in those relationships end up coping either with alcohol or drugs. I'm trying to accept that this is not my fault.

We live in the same house, but don't talk unless necessary. We have separated twice, and each time he came back promising to stop. All that happened was that he became more secretive in his activities. I know more about the computer than he does, and I feel compelled to check his computer history for signs of activity. Recently there's been less, and I suspect the reason is that he's now using his smartphone or tablet when away from home to view porn or for sexting. For all I know, he's using some hookup app to meet women in real life. I can't be sure since there's no history on these mobile devices. I'm just hoping he'll see the light and stop, but I'm losing faith. I believe this will only get worse before it gets any better, if it ever does.

Matt's Story

Matt, a 34-year old married social worker and father of two children, considers himself a "cybersex widower." His wife of 12 years, Linda, spends many hours on the internet, exchanging e-mails with a man with whom she has had sex both online and in person. Matt learned that her lover, a professor, once lost his job for making sexual advances to female graduate students. Other information about this man led Matt to conclude that his wife's lover is sexually addicted. Matt researched cybersex addiction – the compulsive use of the internet for sexual gratification including arranging for real-life sexual encounters– and tried to explain to Linda that this man is not good for her:

Linda won't listen to me when I tell her that 90% of male cybersex addicts have severe pornography problems; she thinks he's so perfect and wonderful. Most of the journal articles describe cyber-widow feelings, but being the husband, it's much the same. We've had no sex for six months, and she's given me every excuse in the book. When we did have sex, I wondered who my wife was making love to (it wasn't me!). She locks herself in the computer room every night and has stacks of e-mail that she downloads and hides. She has ongoing paranoia that I hacked into her e-mail. She totally stopped sharing in household chores. She kept driving off in her car for large blocks of time with no explanation, or she'd say, "I'll be back in 10 minutes" and return hours later. She comes home late at night from her part-time job. She takes diet pills even though she has a perfect figure. She won't discuss anything with me, and refuses to admit that she did anything wrong, although she acknowledges that she's having an affair with this man. I'll probably be filing for divorce soon.

Matt tolerated intolerable behaviors and reported being understanding rather than overtly angry. He related feelings of hopelessness, rejection, and inadequacy, consistent with depression. When many other men would have long since abandoned the marriage, Matt stayed. Matt even went to a church counselor and tried to understand and have compassion for Linda, but eventually he came to feel that divorce was the only option. A judge awarded Matt custody of the couple's two children.

Millions of people in the U.S. share the distress of the partners whose stories you just read. About half of all men have at least one affair during their marriage, according to Dr. Alfred Kinsey's classic study, done in the 1940s, of sexual behavior in American men.[2] This was confirmed in 1981 by Shere Hite, whose survey found that 72 percent of men married two years or more had extramarital sex.[3] Certainly most of these men were not addicts. Rather, the fact that affairs are so prevalent indicates that the needs of many people are not being met within the marriage.

Traditionally, marriage was viewed as primarily an economic arrangement, designed to insure financial security and a stable environment for the children. In cultures as diverse as China, India, and the Jewish ghettos of Europe, arranged marriages were accepted because they fulfilled the purpose of marriage as a practical, functional arrangement. In these cultures, marriages were not expected to fulfill the partners' emotional needs, nor their longing for romantic love. Only in modern Western society have we made romantic love the basis of marriage and the cultural ideal of "true love."

"Romantic Love" – and Sex and Love Addiction

What is "romantic love"? According to Robert A. Johnson:

Romantic love doesn't just mean loving someone; it means being "in love." This is a very specific psychological phenomenon. When we are "in love," we believe we have found the ultimate meaning of life, revealed in another human being. We feel we are finally completed, that we have found the missing parts of ourselves. Life suddenly seems to have a wholeness, a superhuman intensity that lifts us high above the ordinary plane of existence. For us, these are the sure signs of "true love." The psychological package includes an unconscious demand that our lover or spouse always provides us with this feeling of ecstasy and intensity.[4]

The tradition of romantic love endows the lover with power and responsibility to make the life of the beloved whole, meaningful, happy, intense, and ecstatic.

What this list actually describes is not real love, but rather *limerence*. This term, coined by Dorothy Tennov in 1979, describes a state of mind in which one person has obsessive, compulsive, and intrusive thoughts, feelings, and behaviors regarding another person.[5] There's an overwhelming drive to have the other person reciprocate the lover's feelings. According to Tennov it is the state of being completely carried away by unreasoned passion or love, even to the point of addictive-type behavior. Limerence is a powerful, intense attraction to someone, but unfortunately its power diminishes as the relationship progresses. If you're wondering why this is so, here is one explanation:

A pamphlet entitled, *So Your Happily Ever After Isn't* contrasts the myth of living "happily ever after" with the reality of being "comfortable" in a marriage. It lists the criteria for romance. To feel limerence, which definitely includes a romantic "high" with another person,

- You have to feel somewhat insecure with him, not totally sure he cares.
- You have to not know him well; he must be a little strange, unpredictable.
- There must be barriers to your encounters, such as physical distance between you or the need for secrecy.
- There must be limits on the time you can spend together.[6]

Strangeness, insecurity, barriers, and limits are more the precursors to fantasy than the components of a stable relationship. As *So Your Happily Ever After Isn't* tells us, when you get to know the other person well enough to see him as a real person and learn about his faults, the thrill of romance is likely to diminish:

The truth about all highs is that they gradually fade. You gradually get to know the guy and he becomes predictable. Or you get to feeling overly secure. . . The barriers fall. The limits are exceeded. The tingle fades, and there you are wondering where your "happy" went, and if you really want the tingle, the tension, the "high," then you have to go looking for another Prince. And another one after him, and another one after him. There's nothing wrong with wanting highs. The only problem with it is that if you only get sexual romantic highs and that's *all* you want, you're probably going to spend a lonely and disastrous old age. Princes get few and far between when you're forty. . . . Remember: some women only think they're "happy" when they're "in love." Which means that some women are really fouled up with the Wretched Habit of Romance.[7]

There are many people whose life is dedicated to replicating the intensity of limerence. In practical terms, this means that when the initial euphoria diminishes, they look for the next exciting relationship. This, of course is a description of a sex and love addict.

But even for healthy couples, as they get to know each other better, the mystery dissolves and the idealization of the loved one yields to reality. Tennov quotes a long-term couple who reported, "We were very much in love when we married; today we love each other very much." In a long-term marriage, the intensity and ecstasy once felt are not likely to survive. What does characterize a successful long-term relationship is *intimacy*.

Intimacy – What Is It, and Is It Possible with Someone You've Never Met?

In our 2014 book, *Closer Together, Further Apart: The Effect of Technology and the Internet on Parenting, Work, and Relationships*, Robert Weiss and I attempted to explain what is intimacy. We wrote,

Healthy, intimate, trusting relationships require the following:

- **Respect:** shown by taking an active interest in others, having empathy for their challenges, and championing their successes.
- **Support:** given by lending a helping hand when needed, providing advice when asked, and by genuine acts of kindness and acknowledgement.
- **Quality time:** exhibited by communicating and interacting, learning about each other, and playing together in ways that lead to a lasting connection.
- **Validation**: given by valuing who another person is, by recognizing what he or she brings to the table, and by championing all that is special and unique about that person.
- **Affection:** displayed through physical acts such as hugging, kissing, and embracing, and also by simpler acts such as placing a hand on someone's shoulder as a display of understanding or solidarity.
- **Trust:** earned over time via reliability, consistency, honesty, and commitment.[8]

Note that intimacy is not the same as intensity. Intimacy requires more effort and more commitment than does intensity. In at least a few of these areas summarized above, digital exchanges come up short. I asked several psychotherapists to weigh in on the possibility of intimacy without actually meeting. Therapist Gail Lyle elaborated on the difficulty of demonstrating honesty, caring, respect, and responsibility in virtual relationships:

Yes, I believe that people can have intimacy via Internet or even through old-fashioned letter writing such as was the case in passionate World War II relationships.

However, in non-real time relationships it is easy to hide the shadow side of self and project what we want ourselves to be to the other person. One can wait till after the dark mood passes before going online. The online time is considered precious and one can be highly motivated to put important negative issues on the back burner for a latter discussion that never comes to pass. It is easy to hide the flaws and so one presents one's self in an idealized manner. It is difficult to be consciously aware of what one selfishly hides to present this idealized self. So, these online relationships are often shallow in allowing opportunities for the participants to experience "knowing" to the full extent such as can be done in the multidimensional world of real-time. And participants in these relationships are robbed of the opportunity to share in the security to the fullest of unconditionally loving the other person and knowing that the other person loves with full knowledge of the flaws.

How does one share respect and responsibility through the click of a power button and a camera lens in a world where only two people exist? Real-time offers ample opportunities for intimacy to develop through respect and responsibility. And what about caring? It is limited when one turns off the power to go to bed with a stomach virus. The next day, when the power is on, the caring partner asks, "How are you feeling?" and states, "I wish I could have been there to help." Compare this to the partner who missed a ball game to stay with you through the sickness and held a wet towel to your head as you threw up in the toilet, knowing all the while that the virus was highly contagious. How powerful was the touch of the partner's hand on yours in reassuming you that you were not alone!? Real-time caring is based on commitment, and it grows upon itself. Real-time caring speaks more loudly to our hearts than the commitment of just being there when the power is turned on.

So going back to the earlier comparison, yes, there may be some internet relationships that are more intimate than long-term marriages.

Nonetheless, internet relationships have inherent limitations that make for a weak foundation for a transfer to a long term committed real-time relationships. It's like comparing apples to oranges. While within the world of satellite transmissions, intimacy may exist in some form, this intimacy may not be enough to hold a relationship that exists within real-time. In real-time, a lot more is required to experience knowing, respect, responsibility, and caring.[9]

Lyle makes an excellent point regarding what actually constitutes caring. Is asking how you feel the same as caring? In reality, it does not really demand that the other be present and "show up" in the relationship. Real-time caring involves a greater commitment.

Other therapists provided their perspective:

I can practice those principles to a lesser extent via electronic media than in person but they are real. But the crucial element of touch is missing, essential to me in deepening personal intimacy especially with romantic/sexual partnerships–a whole added aspect.[10]

I think of relationship intimacy as the deep emotional bond between committed partners when each can share personal feelings, hopes, disappointments, and dreams and trust that the other will be interested and present. I think that online relationships have a pseudo-intimacy that is mistaken for real intimacy. Real intimacy requires vulnerability, willingness to take some risks of being oneself with another and, therefore, possibly be rejected. Online relationships lack the range of communication possible in the real world, such as non-verbals and getting to experience the other person in a variety of settings, that are required to really know someone. In fact it is this restriction of information that is conducive to posing online.[11]

The verdict now seems to suggest that true intimacy is unlikely though not wholly impossible between two people who have met only online. I learn so much about someone else by being in his or her presence, by talking on the phone, and by simply spending time with him or her. There is something communicated energetically, almost telepathically I find, by being around someone. Online, in emails or instant-messages or social network postings, one can reveal just so much about oneself and learn just so much about others. There are limits. Indeed, the idea that "I knew so much about him/her just from our emails" shows me how much two people, craving connection, can deploy fantasy in place of the sometimes uncomfortable and rarely quick process of learning, revealing, and knowing the other on successively deeper levels. In other words, the question posed says more to me about cultural misunderstandings of what intimacy is than about the tricky nature of intimacy itself.[12]

Relationship intimacy involves the giving and receiving of commitment, passion, and friendship. These three components would allow me to share my deepest and most secret parts with another, trusting that they will still care for me in spite of it, and me risking my fear of abandonment while sharing my deep shame. I don't believe someone can have true intimacy with someone they have never met.[13]

In several respects, online relationships substitute fantasy for reality. If you review Johnson's four elements of romantic love earlier in this chapter, you can see why a person can experience these feelings for someone in the absence of a real-life connection. And this is one reason why sex or romance addicts find the internet so powerfully appealing. Intensity, however, is not the same as intimacy. The very elements that create the *intensity* of romantic love – the uncertainty, the distance, the barriers, and the time limitations, dissolve as the couple get to know each other better. Yet many couples stay together happily for many years.

What Keeps Some People Happily Married for Many Years?

According to Francine Klagsbrun, author of *Married People: Staying Together in the Age of Divorce,*[14] the key to keeping a relationship going is commitment. Commitment is giving up something of ourselves to help our partner grow. It may be willingness to give up our protective shell and leave ourselves vulnerable to hurt.

Most people will not allow themselves to be vulnerable unless they are accepted by the other person. According to Klagsbrun, acceptance is a prerequisite for intimacy, and from acceptance grows trust. Acceptance and trust are both most likely to occur when the marriage is monogamous. She explains,[15]

> The reason marriage provides the greatest possibilities for intimacy is because marriage is predicated on the idea of exclusivity. And one of the differences between marriage and other friendships is the importance of exclusivity.

Based on the couples she interviewed, Klagsbrun complied a list of characteristics of successful long-term marriages:

- An ability to change and to tolerate change
- A willingness to live with the things one can't change
- An assumption of permanence in the relationship
- Trust between the partners
- A balance of depending on one another
- A balance of power
- Enjoyment of each other
- A shared history that is cherished.

Notice that what is absent is any mention of romantic love or of lasting ecstasy and intensity.

Nonetheless, according to sociologist Morton Hunt, nearly all American husbands and wives at some point in their marriage find themselves wishing for an affair and imagining it in their minds.[16] The intensity of falling in love is not easily forgotten, and it is natural to want to experience it again. Unlike the greylag goose and several other animal species, people are not naturally monogamous.

Monogamy is a social institution which developed primarily for economic reasons. The moral condemnation of extramarital involvements is a legacy of the Judeo-Christian tradition and is far from universal. On the contrary, in a study cited by Hunt,[17] only 16 percent of 185 societies studied by anthropologists insisted on lifelong monogamy, and 39 percent actually approved of extramarital liaisons of specified types, Because men wanted to be sure that their sons were their biological offspring, and because women were often considered the property of their men, women in most societies were denied sexual freedom.

In the United States at the beginning of the 21ˢᵗ century, although lip service is paid to the desirability of monogamy, infidelity is widely tolerated. For many people, an affair is a way of having one's cake and eating it too. It is a way both to participate in a stable, long-term marriage (or partnership) with its economic and social benefits, and at the same time to enjoy the excitement of romantic love and re-experience the ecstasy of a new sexual involvement. For those who perceive stability in a relationship as boring, an affair is a way of escaping the boredom and adding a measure of variety and excitement. An affair is generally rationalized as a way of fulfilling needs not being met in the primary relationship.

Not all affairs are the same. An extramarital liaison can consist of an all-consuming passion that goes on for years, a visit to a prostitute, a casual sexual encounter with someone whose last name is not known and who will never be seen again, or a real-time online sexual relationship enhanced by exchanging real-time videos of each other. Even imagined affairs can be harmful or beneficial. Hunt says,

> Occasional fits of fantasized infidelity usually indicate nothing more than the normal human desire for variety, which they partly satisfy; continual obsessive fantasies of infidelity are more likely to indicate severe frustration and marital discontent, which they cannot alleviate but which they may prepare the daydreamer to relieve by means of actual extramarital relationships.[18]

In other words, for some dissatisfied people, fantasizing about affairs is the first step to a real affair, and whole process occupies such a large part of a person's inner world that little is left for the marital or primary relationship. This is what happens to the man or woman who is addicted to real-life or online infidelity or pornography.

Consequences of Infidelity

Even when there is no question of addiction, infidelity is harmful. A major element is the dishonesty that is usually necessary. Affairs are usually carried out in secrecy – at least they're kept secret from the spouse. A 1986 survey of female readers of *New Woman* magazine revealed that whereas 41 percent of the married (or otherwise involved) women had participated in one or more affairs, only 19 percent of the readers knew for certain that their husbands or lovers had cheated on them.[19] In view of the results of the surveys conducted by Kinsey and Hunt, what the *New Woman* survey tells us is that many people are successfully concealing their infidelity from their spouses. Most people who have extramarital affairs or engage in cybersex (online sexual activities) apparently still believe that their actions would be unacceptable or threatening to their spouse.

The dishonesty that is involved in most affairs leads to guilt. The greater the emotional investment in the extramarital relationship, whether real-life or online, the more the married lover is likely to feel guilty. Even if he or she believes his spouse does not suspect, he knows he is lying to her, and his self-esteem is likely to suffer.

Decreased attention to the couple relationship is another likely consequence of infidelity. In the cheater's mind, the marriage relationship appears dull in comparison to the excitement and novelty of the affair, and the partner can't hold a candle to his new, exciting lover. The cheater's energies are focused outside the marriage, and problems within the marriage are likely to be avoided rather than dealt with. Time and energy that might be spent with the spouse and children are devoted instead to the affair.

In addition to these costs, there are other potential consequences:

- The possibility of contracting a sexually transmittable disease
- The risk of losing one's job if an affair with a co-worker comes to light, or if the workplace computer is used for online sexual activities
- Potential physical retaliation by an irate spouse
- The emotional and financial trauma of divorce
- The possibility of an unwanted pregnancy

Many men interviewed in Morton Hunt's survey of extramarital behavior felt that their affair did not affect their marriage adversely; some, in fact, said their sexual relationship with their wives had improved as a result of the affair. But this may be little more than a rationalization of a failure to acknowledge the harm done. The author of the survey concludes: "Many supposedly unharmed or even benefited marriages suffer unseen emotional decay as a result of the external intimacy, and later collapse with a suddenness that takes the partner by surprise."[20] Many people who believed their affairs were harmless forms of recreation that added variety and zest to their lives have found themselves in a major marital crisis when they were discovered.

While extramarital sex is very common in the United States, it is even more prevalent in other societies where there is a greater acceptance of a "division of labor" between wife and mistress. Because cultural norms differ, this book primarily addresses those who live in the United States; however, extramarital sex is problematic in many other countries, where an increasing number of people have identified themselves as sex addicts and have formed self-help recovery groups based on the Twelve Steps of Alcoholics Anonymous. For example, in 2015, Sexaholics Anonymous groups existed in 44 countries, including Canada, Mexico, Brazil, Spain, United Kingdom, Belgium, Netherlands, Russia, Poland, Israel, Iran, Australia, and Japan, among others.[21]

Sex Addiction

Many married persons in the United States have been occasionally unfaithful, whether in real-life on online. Some use pornography compulsively, or frequent massage parlors. For some, this caused no problem; this book is not about them. It is not about men and women for whom some sexual activity is an expression of a desire for variety. Rather, this book is for the person whose mate has a *pattern* of such behaviors, Instead of dealing with the marriage problems, this man (or woman) will escape from one relationship into another or distract themselves with online pornography. When not involved in an affair, they may be preoccupied with imagining it or planning for it. The excitement of the chase is to them what a drink is to the alcoholic. It is useful in terms of diagnosis and approach to treatment to regard them as addicted to sex. I use the terms addiction and compulsion interchangeably in this book, although some researchers split hairs over the meaning of addictive versus compulsive sexual behaviors.

How likely is a person who has an affair to be an addict? Patrick Carnes, Ph.D., author of *Out of the Shadows: Understanding Sexual Addiction*, believes that about 6 percent of the American population is sexually addicted.[22] In a survey, reported in 1953, of married women who had affairs, Kinsey found that 41 percent had only one affair, 40 percent acknowledged two to five affairs, and 19 percent reported more than five.[23] Twenty years later, in 1972, a different survey of married women gave very similar results – 40, 44, and 16 percent respectively.[24] If these figures can be used as a rough estimate of married men who have affairs (in general, more men than women have affairs), and if we consider it likely that many of the men who have had more than five affairs during their marriage are engaging in affairs compulsively, then we may guess than perhaps 10 percent of married men who have affairs are sexually addicted. Another substantial proportion use sex addictively at some time in their lives; at other stages, they will refocus their energies on their work, becoming workaholics and away from compulsive sexual activities.

In recent years, sex addiction is increasingly being acted out on computers and on mobile devices (smartphones and tablets), and many people who were not previously sexually compulsive have gotten hooked on cybersex. This may serve as an end in itself, or can be the gateway to connecting with sexual partners in real life. The result of the new technology is an increased likelihood of infidelity.

If you are wondering whether your mate might be a sex addict, here is a brief questionnaire (PATHOS) recently created by Dr. Patrick Carnes that screens for sex addiction: [25]

- Preoccupied: Do you often find yourself preoccupied with sexual thoughts?
- Ashamed: Do you hide some of your sexual behavior from others?
- Treatment: Have you ever sought therapy for sexual behavior you did not like:
- Hurt others: Has anyone been hurt emotionally because of your sexual behavior?
- Out of control: Do you feel controlled by your sexual desire?
- Sad: When you have sex, so you feel depressed afterwards?

If you recognize that your spouse is likely a sex addict, then you need to understand that stopping the behaviors will require that your spouse accept that he or she has a problem and seeks help. You cannot control your spouse's actions, but you can seek help and support for yourself.

A friend asked me. "You make a good case for an affair being more exciting than monogamy. But how can you decide whether it is immaturity or compulsion that makes someone seek affairs?" The answer lies in the person's ability or inability to control his or her actions: loss of control is the primary characteristic of compulsive behavior. Should the sex addict's partner find out about an affair, he (or she) will probably admit only to that particular relationship, and may promise not to do it again. But, if the person is actually struggling with compulsive sexual behavior or sex addiction and a onetime infidelity has gone beyond just being an extramarital dalliance, then sooner or later, despite his best intentions, the addict will once again find himself with another sexual partner or back on the computer. He may make promises to himself—not to have an affair with someone in the same city, not to have an affair with another employee at his office, or with a student at the college where he teaches, or with one of his parishioners if he is a minister. He may decide to cut down his computer sex activities to only one or two hours a week. He is like the alcoholic who tries to limit himself to drinking only beer, or to drinking only after 5 P.M. or only on weekends.

As their disease progresses, alcoholics will break their own rules, and so will persons who use affairs or cybersex compulsively. These individuals have a disease very similar to alcoholism. Like the alcoholics, they have lost control over a problematic behavior. The specifics differ – instead of numbing their low self-esteem and pain with alcohol, addicts forget it temporarily through the "high" of the chase and conquest. The addiction model has been very useful in understanding this behavior. Because the concept of chemical addiction is more familiar to most readers than is the idea of an addictive behavior, I frequently refer to alcoholism throughout this book to make a point about sex addiction.

It's important, however, for the reader to understand that recovery from sex addiction is more like recovery from compulsive overeating than from alcoholism. Most recovering alcoholics find they must abstain from alcohol altogether to remain sober. Compulsive overeaters do not have the option of avoiding food; they must learn how to eat "normally" or in a more healthy way. Similarly, the goal of recovery from sex addiction is not to avoid sex; rather, it is to learn how to be a sexual person in a healthier way. Nonetheless, the analogy with alcoholism is useful in understanding the behavior of the sex addict and his or her spouse.

The sex addict's focus is not the sex act itself so much as it is all that precedes it: The feeling that accompanies the initial contact with a potential new sexual partner; winning her or him over with one's sensitivity, openness, and attention; and then, in some cases, getting the sex partner into bed.

The spouse of the sex addict is in a no-win position. No matter how attractive or sexually available the spouse is, she or he cannot provide the addict with the one thing they seek – a new person to conquer. Partners are doomed to failure in their attempts to keep the addict at home.

Look again at Beth's, Carmen's, Vincent's and Marlena's stories.

Do any of them sound familiar?

Does your spouse or significant other have a pattern of online and/or real–life sexual infidelity, or do you suspect that they do?

Do you tell yourself that if they really loved you they would change?

Do you believe, despite all evidence to the contrary, that things will somehow improve?

Do you blame yourself for having not tried hard enough to please him (or her)?

Do you make excuses for their behavior?

Do you believe that if you could only get their current affair partner out of their life then all your problems would be over?

If you've answered "yes" to several of these questions, you might be dealing with the complex issues related to compulsive sexual behavior or sex addiction. Only the addict can act to get the help he or she needs for healthier coping with stressors. As a partner of a sex addict, you have to remember that you didn't cause the problem, nor can you control or cure it. But you can get help yourself in order to create healthy boundaries and self-care in the midst of your partner's addiction.

If You are a Woman whose Husband is Sexual with Other Men

Some heterosexual male sex addicts act out compulsively only with other men, whereas others have a palette of potential sexual partners that includes both men and women. Other married men are in fact gay or bisexual and seek out male sexual partners. These interactions may range from emotion-laden affairs to casual sex in pornographic bookstores or parks, as well as online sex. Sometimes, the wife who learns of these activities is devastated. Other women will dismiss them with the consoling thought that "at least it's not another woman." To the husband, these relationships may be equivalent to an affair with another woman or a visit to a female prostitute, but the wife's denial system will not permit her to recognize this. The husband may encourage his wife in her denial, saying, "You're the only *woman* in my life," or "You're the only one who really counts."

The feelings of wives I interviewed whose husbands had sex with other men were very similar to the feelings of women whose husbands had sex with other women. The recovery process for the partner is also the same. There is one difference, and that is society's attitude toward the "wronged" woman. Because society is generally more tolerant of a man who has an affair with a woman than a man, there is more support for the wife in the latter situation. The man is perceived to be engaging in unacceptable behavior, and the wife is encouraged to leave him. On the other hand, there is less support for the wife who chooses to stay married to a man who engages in same-sex activities than for one who has heterosexual sex. The woman whose husband has been involved with other men may feel more ashamed and isolated, or she may feel less threatened by another man than another woman.

The woman whose husband is having sex with other men needs first of all to understand the meaning for her husband of these activities. I recommend you start by reading the book *Is My Husband Gay, Straight, or Bi? A Guide for Women Concerned about their Men*, by Joe

Kort. Another very helpful book is *Cruise Control: Understanding Sex Addiction in Gay Men* by Robert Weiss. Some men are sexually attracted to other men *although* they identify as being heterosexual. Other men's gender orientation is gay or bisexual, and their sexual attraction to men is fundamental to who they are. Heterosexual men who are sexually attracted to men are probably more common than men who are actually gay or bisexual. It is very important for both the husband and partner to understand this distinction, because it portends a very different potential outcome for their relationship. The husband may need to go to a knowledgeable therapist who can help him sort out his feelings. Whereas it may be possible for heterosexual men to work through their issues and rebuild a good relationship with their wives, the solution for the man with a strong homosexual identity may be to leave the marriage and live as an openly gay man. The gay male sex addict may appropriately choose to work on recovery from his sex addiction with the goal of eventually finding a monogamous homosexual relationship.

If You Are a Male Partner of a Sex Addict

The prevalence of sex addiction in men is believed to be about 6% of U.S. men. Marnie Ferree, director of a program for sex addiction, reports that about one-third of those who attend her program are female. And when it comes to the increasing use of computers to access sexual content, recent statistics show that about 1 in 3 visitors to pornographic websites are women.[26] This may be an underestimate of the prevalence of sex addiction in women, since sex addiction is more shaming for women and they are less likely to come forward. In the past this was true for alcoholism as well. The history of Alcoholics Anonymous is instructive: At its founding in 1939, A.A. was a fellowship for men, and alcoholism was considered a disease of men. Since then, alcoholism has been increasingly recognized in women, who now represent almost half of the membership of A.A. It is likely that the prevalence of women who admit to sex addiction will eventually approach that of men. Currently many women struggle with their own sex addiction, and most of these women have male spouses or significant others. This means that many men are left trying to cope with their wives' addiction. By focusing this book more on female partners of sex addicts, I am not minimizing the very real pain of the male partner

There are some different issues for male than for female partners. Men who have affairs generally get approval from their peers; their wives don't get much sympathy. The wife is often blamed, and a conspiracy of silence exists among men to protect the promiscuous husband. Consequently, the wife feels shame and isolation, in addition to guilt at her wish for monogamy in the face of society's tacit approval of men's infidelity. In contrast, a woman who has multiple affairs gets no approval from society – her husband is regarded as the innocent victim, and his wife is condemned. However, he has a special pain, the pain of fearing that he is "not really a man." More than this pain, he is probably obsessed with the specifics of his sexual technique and where he failed. Because of society's support, he may feel less isolated than a woman. Moreover, he does not "need" to feel as much guilt, since people agree that his wife is the one to blame. Unfortunately, he is likely to be encouraged to leave her, and to get less support than do betrayed wives for trying to work things out in the marriage.

CHAPTER TWO

Characteristics of the Traumatized Partner

Many partners believe that life without their spouse would be intolerable. Consider the case of Irene:

When I had my first baby my husband enlisted in the Army. Then when my son was four years old Jack had an affair. For the next eight years I knew he was seeing other women because of the lipstick and makeup on his clothes. I was afraid to say anything, and he would always deny anything was going on. When my daughter was born, Jack re-enlisted in the Army and was gone for a year. My little girl was sick for much of that time, but Jack wasn't around to help. Now he has a new girlfriend, and if he would just stop seeing her I know everything would be so much better. He's told me he can't guarantee he will be faithful next week or even tomorrow. He said he's a sex addict, but I told him, "Oh, baloney, that's just an excuse men use." When he isn't running around, he's a wonderful husband, so supportive of me. I can't give up on him – he's been my whole life.

As I explained in the Introduction, in recent years there has been a shift in the way therapists view partners of sex addicts. Traditionally the term *coaddict* was used not only as a name for any spouse or partner of a sex addict, but also to imply that these people had behaviors preceding the current relationship related to childhood trauma (behaviors termed *code-pendency)* resulting in impaired thinking in certain areas, which, when they found themselves in relationship with a sex addict, translated to a set of behaviors that may not be in the partner's best interest[1]. Appropriate psychotherapy for them required looking into their own past experiences, helping them to improve their self-esteem and to increase their self-empowerment so as to make better choices. It was recognized that partners often came from families with addiction and that the parents were often emotionally unavailable.

More recently, a new generation of therapists believed that this perspective was "blaming the victim," imbuing them with names that were considered pejorative, whereas in fact they were healthy people who were simply victims of trauma visited upon them by having inadvertently married a sex addict who betrayed them. From this perspective, the major role of the counselor is to validate and support the betrayed partner rather than focus on their early-life experience. Supported by knowledgeable sex addiction therapists, I believe that the optimal approach to counseling betrayed partners now is to validate and support the partner in her/his pain subsequent to the discovery of the betrayal. At an appropriate time and if necessary in the therapeutic process following the initial support, therapists then help the partner explore previously unresolved neglect or traumatic experiences. By so doing, the partner begins the work of healing from the trauma of infidelity (which is, in and of itself, a difficult and long enough process) without the complications of the underlying and unresolved trauma from previous experiences. The current therapeutic (and perhaps optimal) approach aims to improve a partner's emotional well-being while increasing self-esteem and authentic self-empowerment in the relationship.

I don't believe that the terms *coaddict* and *codependent* are demeaning and punishing. Millions of people have been in relationship with an unfaithful spouse, and the personality and background of these people are diverse. Some become more traumatized and others less traumatized by the infidelity. Some had horrendous childhoods, others had loving parents and a happy childhood. Those who came from dysfunctional homes are likely to have greater difficulty in dealing with the spouse's betrayal and to experience greater relationship trauma than those with the healthier childhood years. The beliefs and behaviors of betrayed partners fall on a spectrum, and you may be close to either end or at the middle

Those partners who identify as coaddicts have a belief system very similar to that of the sex addict. This is not surprising, since such a partner is herself (or himself) essentially an addict – to the relationship. In addition, some partners develop other addictions to help them cope with the unmanageability of their life. These include problems with food, compulsive housekeeping, workaholism, dependency on alcohol or other drugs, or over-involvement with the children.

The spouse of an alcoholic may drink to keep her husband company – and eventually find herself addicted to alcohol. Such a sequence was beautifully portrayed in the classic film, *Days of Wine and Roses*. Similarly, the partner of a sex addict who takes part in his sexual adventures may come to enjoy them and may herself become sexually compulsive. At the least, partners often cross their own value lines, eroding their sense of self. The primary addiction of these partners, however, is to their mates. If the couple gets into a recovery program, the partner will usually find the relationship addiction more difficult to give up than the alcohol or sex. This is because the partner's alcoholic drinking or the compulsive sexual activity has as its main goal to hold on to the mate; the drinking or the sex itself is not the partner's preferred addiction.

What, then, is addiction? It is a "pathological relationship with a mood-altering substance or experience."[2] The experience to which the partner is addicted is the relationship with the sex addict. The partner is preoccupied with the addict; he is the center of her conversations with her friends. She fantasizes about him when she is alone. She plays out, in her imagination, scenarios of conversations they might have. She thinks of possible good and bad outcomes of actions she is considering taking, and of ways she can influence his behavior. At times she is so focused on her inner thoughts that she fails to notice what is happening around her. Jeannie, a 37-year old dress shop owner, says,

Last month I had my first car accident. As I was driving the kids home, I started thinking about the extra motel charges on Paul's MasterCard. The longer I thought about it, the angrier I got – not just at the idea that he was so obviously again involved with another woman, but also that he thought I was so dumb that I wouldn't even notice that it was right there on the credit card bill. I was considering how best to confront him – and then suddenly I heard a loud crunch and felt a jolt! I had simply not noticed that the car in front of me had stopped, and I piled right into it at 30 miles per hour. Thank heavens the kids and I were wearing seat belts! We were all bruised, but nothing worse. The kids started crying and I felt terribly guilty. Our car was nearly totaled, and our insurance rates are going up. I told Paul I'd been distracted by the kids and had turned around to look at them; he believed me. He was really very understanding. I decided to say nothing about his credit card.

Partners may also be addicted to the excitement of the relationship. The guesswork, the obsession, and the constant turmoil keep them very involved and prevent them from having to deal with their own uncomfortable feelings. They are usually unaware that they need turmoil in their life. On the contrary, their fondest wish is for a loving, caring, consistent mate who is always emotionally available. They frequently believe that it was an unfortunate quirk of fate that put them in a marriage with someone who keeps them guessing.

If there was a high level of tension in the partner's family of origin, he or she most likely has become "comfortable with the uncomfortable" or has learned to "accept the unacceptable."

They have no real sense of what it's like to live without drama, conflict, or chaos. By the time they reach adulthood, the intensity of the feelings evoked by their reactions to the mate *are* in a sense their feelings; they have never experienced a significant relationship that does not include extreme highs and lows. They confuse the biochemical reactions from stress, shock, or fear with emotions. They perceive the stress in their primary relationship as love or sexual attraction. A relationship lacking such drama or stress is felt as boring and lacking in love; for the partner, the ups and downs are familiar, similar to what was often experienced while growing up in a dysfunctional family.

When partners leave their family of origin and marry, external events look different and they don't connect them to their past. Nonetheless, in order to feel really alive, they may need to have a certain level of stress in their relationship. They may tend to confuse the intensity of their physical reactions with love. If things get too calm, they may provoke an incident or create a crisis in order to get a dose of the natural high that stress creates. This can be one reason for returning to the spouse after a separation or getting involved in another, similar relationship. For the partner, to feel intensely is to be vital and directed; not to feel intensely is to be bored or even depressed.

Here is what I wrote about myself 25 years ago; at the time my husband, after a series of affairs, was in a recovery program:

When I left home in the morning, I never knew how things would be when I got back in the evening. I always tried to phone Brad during the day to get some idea of how he was feeling. If he sounded angry, I tried to figure out how I might have caused it and what I might do to improve things. I tried to relate his moods to what was happening with us, but usually there seemed to be no connection. My moods depended on his moods, and I would find myself swinging from a real high to a real low without understanding why. Life was never boring – we had a very intense relationship. Our sexual relationship was very intense too.

For such a couple to develop a healthy relationship, they *both* need help. "Otherwise," as Robin Norwood pointed out in her classic book *Women Who Love Too much*, "should her man begin to seriously address his own problems in a healthier way, she suddenly may find herself yearning for someone more exciting, more stimulating, someone who enables her to avoid facing her own feelings and problems."[3]

Life with a mate who is addicted to sex can be particularly exciting because unlike alcoholism, which can be a solitary pursuit requiring no social skills, the man who is successful at attracting women has learned how to seduce a woman and how to appear caring and tender. At times, he will turn these charms on his wife. Beverly, a 35-year old mother of three who is now divorced, says:

Our relationship was always exciting. He would bring me flowers unexpectedly, with a romantic card. He told me once that when he had been with another woman, he would come home very late so I wouldn't be mad anymore, but rather worried and glad to see him.

In our early years together, I never dreamed that a compulsively sexual man could be sensitive, tender, and loving, and at the same time be lying, cruel, and unfeeling. A Jekyll and Hyde. Sometimes he used to tell his girlfriends he couldn't see them because he had the kids for a day – and they would call me to see if he really had the kids or if I did. I understood why they called – they couldn't believe that such a "nice guy" could lie through that sincere smile.

Several of the partners I interviewed alluded to the intensity and excitement of their relationships. Clarissa and her husband, a sex addict, are also recovering alcoholics. Clarissa remembers, "Our relationship was always very intense. There were no peaceful moments. We drank together and we had intense sex. As Patrick Carnes has pointed out, partners mistake *intensity* for *intimacy*.[4]

The chaos and drama in the life of the sexually addicted couple can prevent them from dealing with their bad feelings, irrational beliefs, and the general unmanageability of their lives. The tension creates the illusion of excitement.

Partners often have a set of deep-rooted beliefs about themselves, their relationships, and about sex. These beliefs are interrelated, and each supports the others. (These irrational beliefs developed many years before being in relationship with a sex addict, so they are not limited to individuals who are partnered with addicts). They believe that they are unworthy, that no one would love them for themselves, that they can control other people's behavior, and that sex is the most important sign of love. (A similar set of beliefs is discussed by Carnes.[5]) We will explore these beliefs and their consequences for the partner.

"I am not a worthwhile person."

Many partners believe they are unworthy and therefore don't deserve to be happy. They believe that deep inside, they are deeply flawed. One partner states:

I believed there was something missing in my emotional and spiritual makeup. What would be considered the essence of my personality or person-hood, the core of my character, simply wasn't there. I wasn't a whole person. My shame stemmed from my belief that I was wrong as a human being, with no possibility of being fixed. My fear was being discovered and dumped, and my defense was to construct a chameleon-like personality adaptable to all situations and people. My irrational thinking allowed me to believe that my personality, which people responded to and that men were attracted to, was fake, not a real part of me. I could neither see nor appreciate the special and extensive talent, skills, and abilities I had and used in order to interact with a variety of situations and a variety of people.

Partners fear they may be seen as bad or unacceptable by others. They feel different from other people, which to them is equivalent to bad. They feel a wide gulf between the outside they present to others and the inadequate person they believe they really are. Not wanting to let others learn about the real person inside, these individuals will cover up feelings and won't let people get too close. They will not allow themselves to feel vulnerable. They believe that if people knew what they really like, others would not want to be with them. They commonly feel a sense of isolation and loneliness. Jason, a quiet, soft-spoken schoolteacher who is the father of a little boy, explains,

I was the typical oldest child, the good child, mommy's helper, a perfectionist, very quiet and shy and good. I was in honors classes at school, but I didn't have many friends. In junior high we moved to a different community, and after that I never got into any circle of friends. I remember feeling very lonely and isolated and turning to books, going for long walks with my dog, not dating, just being off by myself because I lived so far out of town. But now I see that my younger siblings grew up in the same house yet had all kinds of friends over all the time. So it was me, not where we lived. I've always felt like I didn't quite fit in.

Some partners remain isolated as they grow up, but other lonely young women often learn to exchange sex for attention, and become quite sexual at an early age.

Jean Harris, former headmistress of a prominent girls' school, spent many years in prison for the 1980 shooting death of her long-time lover, Dr. Herman Tarnower, a well-known author of *The Scarsdale Diet*. Dr. Tarnower was an acknowledged womanizer who repeatedly cheated on Harris. Mrs. Harris did not have women friends, and felt uncomfortable around women, suspecting they knew something she didn't.

Partners who feel worthless believe they have to acquire worth from the outside, from other people. Psychologists call this *external referencing*. The individual needs outside approval even to exist. She believes, I am nothing without a man, and may attempt suicide if her relationship ends. She doesn't trust her feelings and reactions, and does not value her own opinions. Skilled at seeing things from the other person's perspective, these partners tend to discount their own. They may suppress their feelings so that much of the time they don't feel anything. They may constantly apologize, even when it isn't their fault, ready to take blame for what goes wrong in the family.

Alice, a biologist married to a man who had several affairs, recalls,

When Alan first asked me out, I was overjoyed. He was by far the most handsome man I had ever dated. A few weeks later we visited a girlfriend of mine in Washington, D.C. She pulled me off into a corner and murmured, "Wow! Where did you ever find such a gorgeous guy?" That was the ultimate in validation for me. If a gorgeous guy like Alan was interested in me, that meant I must be a really worthwhile person. Somehow that meant more to me than the fact that I had a Ph.D. and was making a success of my life! It was as though none of that really mattered.

Alice's feelings are typical of the person who measures his or her worth by what other people think. Ellen is a self-confident, assertive, 40-year old administrator who is now in a Twelve-Step recovery program for partners of sex addicts. She recalls how she used to be:

I didn't know who I was without a male to tell me. I was always trying to be cute so that a man would take care of me. I didn't believe that I, a woman, could function without a man.

Jean Harris also measured herself by what others thought. What was important was to live up to other people's expectations of her. Harris did not believe she deserved much in her relationship with the well-known Tarnower. Because he was a bachelor, she felt she was in a no-win situation. Believing she was only one of many women in his life, she could not permit herself to think he needed her. Harris kept apologizing for her lover's insensitivity and for the poor way he treated her. Her low self-esteem led her to believe she didn't deserve any better. When Tarnower made it clear that he was losing interest in her, she decided to pay him a final visit and then kill herself with a gun. In the struggle for the weapon, Tarnower was killed and Harris was convicted of his murder. Her book, *A Stranger in Two Worlds*,[6] written from prison, reaffirms her love for him.

Clarissa and Charlie were an alcoholic couple who began having problems in their marriage after becoming sober. They separated over the issue of his affairs. Clarissa says:

After he moved out I felt like nobody. I felt empty. I couldn't even get the kids to school. We just stayed home and I cried. I started going to A.A. (Alcoholics Anonymous) meetings every day because I didn't know what else to do. I stopped eating and lost weight.

For Clarissa, life was hardly worth living without Charlie. Eventually they reconciled, but he was unable to remain faithful and they separated again. Clarissa went through another depression, and though it wasn't as bad as the first one, she says, "I lost myself again." She and Charlie are still on an emotional roller coaster.

Faith, a 32-year old mother of a small child, is married to a wealthy businessman who does not bother to hide his affairs. He is so preoccupied with his outside involvements that he has very little emotional energy left for his wife. Faith has learned to cover up her feelings and is proud of her ability to control her emotions. She tolerates behavior from her husband that would make other women furious. "Henry has told me he really admires me for knowing when to make a fuss and when not to." She rarely makes a fuss.

Another aspect of the need to look outward for validation of their existence is to lack boundaries. To have a boundary means to have a sense of being separate, of having separate feelings and a separate reality from others. Partners who don't know how they feel because they haven't yet talked with their spouse today do not have healthy boundaries; they don't know where they begin and another person ends. Physical abuse constitutes invasion of one's boundaries, and so does emotional abuse. These partners are so dependent on another that they lack a sense of self.

Codependents are very needy people. Having "been there" so long for so many people, they desperately want someone else to be here for them – they need someone to rescue them from loneliness and isolation. This other person is expected to make up for all that's missing inside, to calm their hunger and thirst, to meet all their other needs. The trouble is that they are so needy they're willing to settle for nearly anyone. And once that person is in their life, they may even convince themselves they cannot live without him or her.

"No one would love me for myself"

The consequence of partners' second belief, that no one would love them for themselves, is that they must *earn* the mate's love. They confuse being needed with being loved. If the mate accepts their caretaking they think it means he or she loves them– even if the mate does not act kind or caring or loving. They believe that if someone is in a relationship with them, it's because he or she wants something from them – that there's always a price to pay.

These partners believe that people cannot be depended on or trusted. They are drawn to a man or woman who is needy, who they believe needs fixing, and they make themselves indispensable to this person. Believing that the more she can do for him, the less likely he is to leave her, the partner assumes increasing responsibility for the mate's life.

Faith, 33, lives with her wealthy husband and small daughter in a luxurious house on a well-cared-for estate by the seashore. Her husband has not made love with her for several years, ever since the birth of their child. She knows he has affairs, and that this pattern began long before her daughter was born. Faith is grateful that she has the house and that she and Henry are friends, but she sorely misses the intimacy their marriage lacks. Why, then, does she stay in the relationship? "He needs me and he's afraid of losing me." Faith does not believe she is entitled to happiness and is willing to settle for being needed rather than loved.

Gillian, a 44-year old lawyer, met her husband in college when he was dating someone else seriously. He was very good-looking, but what really appealed to her was that "he had a lot of problems and he needed to be taken care of." Her husband went to medical school while she stayed home and took care of him and the children. He had several affairs, but she didn't confront him. Instead, she felt guilty for complaining to him about his frequent absences; her complaining made her think of herself as a bitch.

Gillian not only pretended she didn't know about Gerald's affairs, she also was so out of touch with her feelings that she didn't even feel concerned about his deception or his inattentiveness to her – until the day she went to his office with her ten-year-old daughter to surprise him for lunch and found him having sex with his nurse. She recalls, "I didn't really feel anything until I caught him in his office." Then she experienced "incredible pain and a need to find out why it happened." Now divorced, she is in S-Anon, a Twelve-Step recovery program for partners of sex addicts, still trying to understand her life.

Partners who have codependent traits are terrified of abandonment, and will do anything to keep the relationship going. For the sake of the marriage they ignore their own feelings and needs. They excuse the mate's behaviors even though they may feel deeply hurt. They avoid conflict and smooth things over. They fear arousing the mate's anger or showing their own. An argument awakens their fear of abandonment, so they avoid discord. In all likelihood this dynamic began in earlier childhood with a parent who was overly critical or absent. In either case, a critical parent often threatens rejection, which is experienced by the child as abandonment. Neglect in a parent-child dynamic will, in effect, produce the same feelings of abandonment since the parent wasn't there for the child whether physically and or emotionally.

This unresolved trauma of childhood neglect or abandonment will feed the addictive cycle in the adult relationship or marriage. Until the underlying childhood trauma is processed, it is likely the partner will stay to consciously or unconsciously re-create this fear of abandonment

These partners need frequent reassurance that they are loved, to the point that the mate may end up feeling smothered. Layers of anger and resentment over repeated hurts, real and imaginary, are buried inside these partners with no healthy outlet. They will deny experiencing these feelings rather than risk showing them.

To prevent conflict, partners use denial, the pretense that a problem does not exist. The denial may be unconscious, as when they seem not to know what's happening around them; or it may be conscious, as when as when they are aware of the mate's activities but find excuses to rationalize the behavior or their own failure to take action to change the situation.

For example, they may ignore evidence of an affair and minimize the problem rather than confront their mate. They will pretend to friends and family that the marriage is fine at a time when things are falling apart. They continue to believe that if they only hang on long enough, the mate will change for the better. Unfortunately, one consequence of denial is *enabling*; that is, at a time when a marital crisis may be the only way to get a person to look realistically at his or her destructive behavior, the partner's failure to take action in the face of an unacceptable situation enables the addict to continue the same behavior. George's wife, experiencing guilt over having had sex with several other men, went to see a therapist. George took the position that it was no big deal:

I accept the therapist's explanation that she had a compulsion for relation-ships more than sex. I think that if my wife had been really interested in sex, she'd have had more than five partners in seven years.

Peter felt uncomfortable when his wife began going to Twelve-Step meetings for her sex and love addiction. His response was,

I think she got depressed over a relationship that ended long ago, and her addiction was just a way of handling the feelings of the depression. I think she's cured. I don't think she needs to continue going to meetings.

Peggy Vaughn, who wrote a book with her husband about how they dealt with his multiple affairs,[7] recalled that once when he came home from a trip she found a long blond hair in his suitcase. Because she was a brunette, her first impulse was to cry and scream. She knew on one level what was going on, but had to find a way to deny it. She finally recalled that the wife of one of the men her husband worked with went on the trip, and she had a blond wig. Peggy tried to tell herself that the hair she found came from the wig, ignoring a lot of obvious clues in trying to reassure herself.

Helene, a 38-year old recovering alcoholic who is now divorced from her husband, says, "He had repeated affairs, but it was okay, because had a tremendous sex drive and I just wanted to be left alone." Years later she is still excusing his behavior.

Clarissa tolerated her husband's affairs for a long time for fear of losing him.

We had always worked together at home. I knew what Charlie did every moment of the day. He was always home at night. So when he started not coming home nights, I knew he was having affairs. I let it go on. We never even talked about it. I would fix him sandwiches when he got home and say nothing.

Eventually Clarissa was unable to keep up the pretense, and they separated temporarily. Charlie is still very much in Clarissa's life, and she admits she is still afraid of his anger and of not pleasing him.

Irene, whose husband told her he is addicted to affairs, took an active role in getting rid of Veronica, Jack's latest girlfriend. She called up Jack's sister and told her about the affair. Jack's sister then phoned Veronica and "really told her off." Jack's sister also phoned Veronica's husband and told him what was going on. The affair was soon over, and Irene is convinced that things are much better now. "We're working together again. He's smiling and laughing again. He's so relieved that Veronica is out of our lives."

Irene believes that eliminating Veronica from Jack's life has solved her problem. Despite Jack's long history of cheating and his admission to her that he can't promise fidelity even as long as next week, she continues to deny that there is an ongoing problem. Eliminating the "other woman" is still unrealistically seen by many partners as a viable solution to an affair. In my city of Tucson early in 2005, a woman walked into her husband's office and shot another woman dead. A police investigation revealed, not surprisingly, that the husband was having an affair with the now-dead woman. The killer with the distorted thinking will not get to have her husband to herself for many years – she is spending them in prison – and her children have lost their mother.

Beverly, who was married for many years to a man who eventually recognized he was a sex addict, says:

When we went into counseling, I was so afraid to say anything that might anger him – and therefore risk losing him to one of his girlfriends – that we spent three months talking about everything except his affairs. Until he finally yelled at me in utter frustration after a therapy session, "When are we going to talk about the affairs, the sex?" I realized it had been too scary for me.

Currently in a Twelve-Step recovery program for families of sex addicts, Beverly understands how the fear of her husband's anger kept her from acting in her own behalf.

"I can control other people's behavior."

Partners often believe they can successfully manipulate those around them to accomplish their goals. To illustrate the concept of control, let's consider the mother who, in order to get her 15-year old son to school on time in the morning, wakes him up, nags him to get dressed, and keeps reminding him that he is running late. Every day the two go through the same ritualistic tug-of-war – the mother nagging and prodding, the son procrastinating. Ask the mother why she doesn't just let her son get himself off to school, an she will answer, "If I didn't get involved he would never get to school on time." She is unable to let go and to let her son experience the natural consequences of his behavior. The way out for her is to remove herself from the situation. Her son might oversleep and arrive late at school. If this were to happen more than once he might get detention after school or some other unpleasant discipline. It is likely that he would then modify his behavior and learn to get himself to school on time.

By her continued involvement with her son's morning routine, the mother's controlling behavior only succeeds in enabling her son to continue oversleeping and depending on her to get him off to school. In other words, rather than encouraging change, trying to control another's behavior perpetuates the status quo. It prevents him from experiencing the consequences of his actions and thereby learning a new behavior.

To argue that one person cannot control the ongoing behavior of another is not to deny that one person can influence another. Television or internet advertisements can influence us to buy a certain product or vote for a certain candidate. Letters to politicians may influence their views on given issues. It is often possible to get other people to behave as we like them to – all we have to do is set up the consequences so that the outcome we want is a lot more attractive to the other person than any other outcome.

For example, you may be able to get your daughter to clean up her room by promising her five dollars if she cleans it up, a spanking if she doesn't. If your daughter than cleans up her room, you may delude yourself into believing it was because you asked her to; the reality, however, is that she decided it was in her best interest to do so. The fallacy of control is in not realizing that people act in particular ways because they have decided it is in their best interest, not because you told them to.

Partners' erroneous belief that they *can* control other people's behavior is actually a defense against feelings of helplessness and powerlessness. In childhood they often felt helpless to influence events around them. This led to great insecurity. In adulthood they try to control and manipulate their environment in order to avoid feeling helpless. Unfortunately, the ability to control another person's actions implies great responsibility. They believe they are responsible for the success or failure of their relationships. As Robin Norwood points out, "Help is the sunny side of control."[8] Partners will "help" their mate and their friends to do things they should do for themselves, just like the mother who "helps" get her son off to school on time.

The partner's controlling behavior enables the addict to continue in his or her addiction, as is described dramatically by Ruth Maxwell in her book, *The Booze Battle*. Although she writes about alcoholism, the same can be said for the sex addict and his or her spouse. The alcoholic's wife covers up for her husband because she does not want him to suffer the consequences of his drinking (such as getting fired). She reasons this would be so upsetting to him that he would then have further justification to drink. She picks up the pieces after her husband in order to reduce his need to drink. As he drowns his pain in alcohol, she surrounds him with a blanket of comfortable unreality.

Instead of making it increasingly difficult for her husband to recognize his behavior and seek help, she makes his drinking increasingly easy for him to tolerate.

While the wife is busy making changes in her husband's environment to reduce his reasons for drinking, she in fact eliminates his incentive to make the one change that is needed: treatment for his addiction.

Keeping silent about one's feelings is another enabling behavior; this keeps the sex addict from feeling uncomfortable about how his or her sexual acting out may be hurting the spouse. Partners keep silent for fear of a confrontation, or because they don't believe they deserve to have their needs met, or because they fear driving their mate further away with their negative comments. They are always waiting for the "right time" to talk to the mate. The right time is not when he or she is angry or preoccupied – this is too scary. But when the mate is in a good mood, partners want him to feel good about their relationship rather than spoil it with complaints and demands.

Because they believe erroneously that their words and actions have a significant impact on the mate's sexual behavior with other people, many partners don't want to risk saying or doing the wrong thing. Unaware that their mate's affairs were caused not by the partner's inadequacies but rather by their own addiction, partners cover up their doubts and pain and attempts to present their best side to him or her. The partners thereby deny their mate needed feedback that might make him or her realize sooner that the marriage is in trouble. Consequently, the addict is able to persist in the infidelity, believing that the spouse doesn't suspect and that "what she doesn't know won't hurt her."

For spouses of sex addicts, attempts to control the mate center on his or her sexual behavior. If the spouse suspects that the mate is interested in a particular person, she may turn down a party invitation if she knows the other person will be there. Partners don't even consider whether they would enjoy going to the party; it is more important to keep the mate from seeing the other person. Or, a businesswoman may give up a travel opportunity that might be professionally advantageous to her because she doesn't want to leave her husband alone. She forgets that she can't *always* prevent her husband from seeing the other woman.

A housewife who suspects her husband of playing around calls him at work twice a day to be sure he's there. Her husband, meanwhile, feels increasingly tied down. He loses credibility with his staff because it's clear his wife doesn't trust him. His resentment against his wife provides him with the excuse he seeks to spend more time with the understanding young lady he met on the elevator.

I interviewed men who admitted they needed excuses to justify their cheating and to assuage their guilt feelings. At times they deliberately engaged the spouse in an argument to create emotional distance between them. In this way, these people could justify seeking emotional closeness elsewhere. But frequently the spouse, by her own actions, gives her husband the excuse he's looking for. If she calls him at work, looks through his belongings, smells his clothing, and in other ways put herself in the role of a controlling mother, the husband may feel like a little boy who has the right to rebel. Thus, the wife's attempts to control her husband's behavior merely succeed in encouraging his addictive acting out.

A common way for partners to attempt to control the mate is through their sexual behavior. They will dress seductively, buy sexy nightgowns or flimsy underwear, learn new sexual techniques, or threaten or hint at having sex with others in order to make the mate jealous. They may even engage in sexual activities that they consider immoral to please him and to keep him at home. Partners may try to manipulate the environment in every possible way to control their mate. They usually fail, as Beverly relates:

I wanted so badly to make him happy, but every time I did something to please him he was more critical, so I tried harder. When I found out about his affairs, I offered to have any kind of sexual relations he wanted, and the requests got more and more uncomfortable for me. I yelled at my kids, I cried, I begged, I bullied – nothing worked.

A terrible consequence of partners' belief that they can control their mate's behavior is that if their attempts to change him or her do not succeed, they feel they have personally failed. They blame themselves, feel guilty, and determine to try even harder. Their self-esteem (which may be low to begin with) descends further. One man who was beginning to understand his relationship addiction, asked, "Why, when I've had no success at controlling my husband's behavior, do I feel compelled to keep trying?" The answer is, because the alternative is to admit that he *cannot* control his spouse's behavior – and this is too frightening a realization for many people.

"Sex is the most important sign of love."

Partners who believe that sex is the most important sign of love confuse having sex with being loved. If a man is sexual with her, she takes it as evidence that he loves her. Jessica, a 45-year old intensive care nurse, recalls:

There were many times when I was unsure of how Bill felt about me. He would act distant, or seem preoccupied, or we'd have a disagreement. At those times I felt that if I could just get him to go to bed with me, then everything would be all right. The physical intimacy was reassurance to me that he still loved me. My fear that he would leave me was temporarily stilled after we'd make love.

It is normal to feel anger, rejection, pain, and abandonment if your mate, to whom you're committed, has sex with someone else. But because many partners believe that sex is the most important sign of love, their response is magnified, and they feel a terrifying personal rejection as though their world is falling apart. Their fear of abandonment looms large and their self-worth plummets. They may feel that their life is at an end. Helen, a counselor who is now divorced from her sex addict husband, explained:

Because my "man" was the vehicle with which I gained acceptance in society and personal validation of being capable, lovable, and needed, his hookups endangered my very existence as a functioning part of the human race. Therefore I tried to look and behave with him in such a way that he could see that, indeed, I was worth "keeping." The other side of this precariously balanced, irrational belief system was that in keeping him I would maintain my place of value with the "others." The fear which provided motivation to continue this balancing act was that both my man and society would discover I was a fake – that they had been misguided – and they would dump me.

Gerard, a 33-year-old gay man, reported having sex only once every few months with his committed partner, who kept rejecting Gerard's sexual advances. The partner was heavily involved in cybersex activities on the computer. According to Gerard,

Although I know that I am bright and attractive, emotionally I feel ugly, worthless, and unwanted by him or anybody else. The issue is not the difference between him having online sex or actual physical contact, it is that someone else is receiving his attention and I am not. I would not care at all if he masturbated online with a host of others, as long as I was an active part of his sex life.

Many partners also believe that sex is the price paid for love. They use sex to get their mate to love them more. Fearful of refusing sex even if they're not in the mood, they believe if they are always available the mate will be less likely to stray. New lovemaking positions or techniques may become part of their repertoire. If they are not sexually satisfied they are likely to pretend they are, in an attempt to make the mate feel good.

In sex addicts' ongoing quest for novelty, they sometimes attempt to enlist their partner's participation. The partner may find herself involved in sexual activities that are against her values. She may take part in humiliating or degrading sexual behaviors in order to control and please the mate, believing that such participation will keep him interested in her. She will usually guard such activities as shameful secrets that she is reluctant to reveal.

One 22-year old woman, a mother of two infants, sat in silence through several meetings of a Twelve-Step self-help group. Dressed in a leather skirt and vest, draped in beads and long earrings, and sporting a short, punk-style haircut, she seemed out of place among the older, more conservatively dressed women. Only after hearing several other stories did she explain why she was there: Her marriage was in crisis because she no longer was willing to accede to her husband's wishes. What he wanted her to do, and what she had been doing for several months, was to go out alone at night to a nearby convenience store, pick up a stranger, bring him home, and have sex with him while her husband watched. Her husband had also been having extramarital affairs, and she had believed that participating in her husband's voyeuristic activities would keep him at home. But now she was too scared to continue.

Another woman in the same group admitted,

My husband was always telling me I was very narrow-minded for insisting on monogamy. He said I was preventing him from expressing his full sexuality, that sex with other people would have nothing to do with our relationship. He kept pressuring me but I wouldn't change my mind. I told him I was willing to do anything he wanted me to sexually, but I couldn't deal with his affairs.

Then he suggested, if I was so threatened by the idea of him making love with another woman, how about if I choose the woman, someone I knew and liked, and that the three of us have sex together. He was really turned on by the idea of two women working on him at the same time. I was very anxious to please him, and felt guilty at how unhappy I was making him. So I said I'd consider the threesome idea. He and I actually talked about various "candidates" among my single girlfriends. Looking back on it, I must have been crazy! Just as I was about to sound out one of my friends, my husband told me it wasn't such a great idea after all. I found out later that the real reason was that by then he was involved in another affair.

Because both sex addicts and many partners have sexual issues as well as irrational beliefs about the role of sexuality in their lives, their behaviors may be similar. The sexual history of the partner can at times sound exactly like the history of the sex addict. For example, Marisa, a sophisticated 28-year old dress designer recounting her past described how she spent many evenings in bars hoping to meet a man. She had many sexual partners, some never to be seen again after one night, others present for weeks or months. When she married, she became involved in increasingly violent sexual activities with her husband, and also – at her husband's request – participated in group sex and in sex with other men while her husband watched. She was uncomfortable doing this, but she wanted to please her husband. When the marriage finally fell apart, she returned to the bar scene and to one-night stands.

Was Marisa a sex addict? There is often an overlap between the sexual behavior of addicts and partners. Partners may become complicit in the attempts to keep the addict happy although they do not want to do this. They might rationalize that this is okay. Some women ultimately identify themselves as both addicts and coaddicts. I believe the answer can usually be found by examining the *goal* of the behavior. Further discussion with Marisa revealed that she believed sex was the way to obtain love. What she hoped to find in the bars was not just a sex partner, but rather someone to love her and nurture her. When she did finally marry, she engaged in unorthodox sexual activities to please her husband, even though she was frightened by some activities and uncomfortable with others. And when the marriage ended, she returned to the only way she knew how to "catch" a man – the bar scene. Whereas the addict's goal is sexual gratification – and for women addicts, power over men –Marisa's use of sex to obtain love and satisfy another person's needs identified her as a coaddict rather than an addict.

In summary, whether partnered or not, individuals who can be described as codependent have several basic irrational beliefs:

- I am not a worthwhile person
- No one would love me for myself,
- I have the power to control people, and
- Sex is the most important sign of love

Married to a sex addict, they are in a vicious circle in which their beliefs support the mate in his or her addictive behavior, and the mate's behavior validates partners' erroneous beliefs. Their efforts to get the mate to change inevitably fail, and they respond by trying harder. The more out of control their life becomes, the harder they try to control and fix things. As they continue to fail in their efforts, their self-esteem slides ever downward and they become more resentful and angry. Fearful of expressing anger because they fear it will drive the mate further away, they turn their anger inward and may become depressed. Feeling helpless and powerless, partners may cope by overeating, drinking excessively, or becoming addicted to Valium or other sedatives. Some partners respond by becoming compulsive housekeepers, or by taking on so many workplace or volunteer responsibilities that they don't have time to think. Others focus all their attention on the children. Still others bury themselves in work, becoming the valued administrator who does the work of three people and never takes a vacation.

Partners may take on the role of martyr. They will entertain (or bore) friends endlessly with tales of the mate's outrageous behavior. To every suggestion their friends make, they will reply, "Yes, but. . ." When friends say, "Your husband doesn't deserve such a good, understanding wife," they feel vindicated. When a neighbor asks, "How can you put up with the rat?" they feel rewarded. Meanwhile they continue in the vicious circle of enabling.

Finally, the partner's anger, resentment, and depression may be expressed in physical symptoms. This is the woman who visits her doctor because of fatigue, lack of energy, insomnia, headaches, back-ache, vague abdominal discomfort, or weight gain "although I hardly eat anything." Unwilling to admit what is going on at home – and frequently so out of touch with her feelings that she truly doesn't know what she feels – she prefers to seek help by talking about her physical symptoms. Physical illness is a more acceptable way to get attention – from the doctor and from the family.

It is important to note here that therapists who are not skilled in the nuances of sex addiction treatment or clergy who offer guidance to the partner might minimize the significance of a partner's lament concerning the addict's use of pornography or requests for more sex. These well-meaning professionals might also suggest that the partner become more sexual which only further worsens the depression and physical and emotional exhaustion.

Old Patterns Made New

Partners' core beliefs are usually firmly in place by young adulthood, and thus likely to influence their choice of mates. Diane, the 35-year old schoolteacher, is married to a man who spent many hours surfing pornographic websites and had anonymous sexual encounters with men. A big problem in their marriage has been that Diane's husband, Dick, is afraid to talk about his feelings. Communication between them has been consistently poor. Before her marriage, Diane had one other serious relationship.

I was unofficially engaged to Harold in high school, and I went to bed with him a couple of times, feeling really guilty. At the end of my senior year he broke it off, saying it wasn't fair to me. I don't know what he meant by that – he wouldn't go into it. He didn't express emotions at all. He was a real defensive kind of guy, and it was hard to get anything out of him.

This boyfriend sounds very much like Dick, the man Diane later married.

Jessica, the 45-year old intensive care nurse, recalls,

When I first found out about my husband's affairs, I felt like an innocent victim. I couldn't believe he'd done this to me; I was furious at him. I felt hurt, rejected, and betrayed. I was sure I'd never forgive him. I thought he was sick and I was just fine. But when I got into a Twelve- Step recovery program, I realized I too was sick. I did a First Step, which is when you write down your own relationship history. It was an eye-opener. My first sexual relationship was with an exciting, very attractive man. When I took him home to meet my parents, they acted very strange. I could see they thought he wasn't a good match for me, but they wouldn't tell me why. After we made love twice, he admitted to me that he was gay, and told me he really preferred his boyfriends. I was crushed. I was 21 at the time, and for the next 20 years every important man in my life was emotionally unavailable to me for one reason or another. My husband just happened to be the last one.

In the early weeks or months after learning of your mate's betrayal, it is normal to feel like a victim. You *are* a victim – a victim of relationship trauma. You have been betrayed and deceived by the person you thought loved you and had your best interest at heart, and this is traumatic for anyone. You need support and validation for the pain you are feeling. But, this is only the beginning of your recovery. Although it is tempting to cast all the blame on your straying spouse, it is likely that your own pre-existing vulnerabilities have played a part in your feelings, beliefs, and decisions regarding your current situation and your future, and even in your choice of partner.

Before you read the next chapter, I would urge you to write down a history of your important relationships, from childhood to the present time. Were they satisfactory? Were your parents nurturing or emotionally unavailable? Not having one's needs met in childhood is a type of abuse which often results in a person seeking in later relationships what one didn't have earlier. Neglect in childhood may be experienced as traumatic. Understanding what emotional or physical neglect or emotional abandonment is will help you better understand how your adult relationships may mirror your childhood experiences. If need be, consult with a trained therapist who understands how to work with these issues referred to as family-of-origin work and complex post-traumatic stress (trauma that involves early breaches in attachment). You may be surprised to find a pattern, as Jessica did, of emotional unavailability in your adult relationships which were repeated from your earlier years.

CHAPTER THREE

The Family Connection

I grew up in a normal family. My mother was 33 when she had me; my father was 39. He was a very loving husband and father. My parents had a good, closely knit relationship. My father was in the liquor business, but my mom and dad had only one drink a day. My father never ran around, and neither did my mother. I was an only child, and both of them doted on me. They were good parents. My mom never worked and was always home for me. So there was no dysfunction in my family.

I was very independent outside the home, but at home I was very dependent on my mother. She picked out my clothing. I felt I could never please her; very few people ever pleased her. She was one of those people who couldn't be pleased, and I always came up short. When I met Lawrence, I just transferred my dependence from my mother onto Lawrence, who was willing to accept it. He would pick out my clothes, tell me what to wear, what jobs to take, and how I should run my life.

–Laura

Laura is the 45-year old wife of a computer programmer and mother of four children. Slender and athletic, she exercises daily and eats only nutritious foods. For years her husband had multiple affairs with both men and women, online and in real life. In addition, Lawrence wanted sex with Laura several times a day, every day. Afraid of abandonment, she never refused him sex and pretended ignorance about his affairs. Now both are in recovery programs for sex addicts and for partners. Laura believes that her childhood was normal, and that her emotional problems resulted only from her unhealthy relationship with her husband.

Mary Ellen, a 40-year-old social worker divorced from a repeatedly unfaithful husband who is a recovering alcoholic and sex addict, also believes she had a normal childhood.

My childhood was happy. I lived on a farm and had many responsibilities. My family was very busy and traveled a lot. My mother became nearly totally deaf when I was ten. From then on, she became insecure, and I did too. I felt I couldn't talk to her, that she didn't want to know what I had to say, particularly when she wouldn't put on her hearing aid or wear her glasses to read lips. So I began to have a negative self-image, as did my brother.

My mother would never allow my father to be with us without her. She was very demanding of his time. As children we never felt we knew him. It was like being raised in a single-parent family. My mother was so insecure that she needed my father all the time. We did things together as a family, but there was never a chance to talk with either of them separately. I was the one with the broad shoulders in the family, so my mother used me as her confidante. She really had no friends – she was extremely jealous of women. She was not a forgiving person, and she was very rigid – everything had to be done a certain way. I was brought up with a lot of "shoulds" and "oughts."

My mother drank. It was only one martini before dinner, but she was out of it. There was no way we could have discussions at dinner; it was a monologue. I remember realizing that feelings were not appropriate, that crying and being emotional were not appropriate. Tears were punished. I stuffed everything by overeating and over-exercising. My mother was an impeccable dresser. If I was ten pounds overweight, she made me feel I weighed 300. If I came in wearing something that was dowdy, she sent me back to change. She didn't want to be seen with me because I was such a country rube.

My father enabled her; he worshiped her. We had a dominant mother who was unreachable by anybody. She commanded – we called her the queen. We never lived up to her expectations.

Mary Ellen had anything but a "normal" childhood, but it took her months of counseling and Twelve-Step recovery work before she clearly recognized this.

Childhood Roots

In the last chapter we saw that many partners share a common belief system that keeps them in a vicious circle in their relationship with a mate who has affairs. How did they acquire those beliefs? Research in the alcoholism field has yielded important information on the family background of many people who later become alcoholics or partners of addicts. Although the specifics differ, the families seem to have certain characteristics in common. These have been studied most fully in alcoholic families, but it is now recognized that other kinds of families also fit the pattern. The most common types of families that produce emotionally troubled children are:

- Families where there is alcoholism, drug dependence, or other addiction.
- Families where there is chronic mental or physical illness.
- Physically, sexually, or psychologically abusive families.

These families, which have been termed dysfunctional families, can raise children who show codependent behavior; this behavior can lead to both addiction and coaddiction (addictive relationship with an addict). Both addicts and partners may start out as codependents, although they may have different ways to cope with painful experiences.

An early description of codependency came from Bill W., the co-founder of Alcoholics Anonymous, who after many years of sobriety continued to have bouts of depression. Bill wrote in a letter more than 50 years ago:

Suddenly I realized what the matter was. My basic flaw had always been dependence – almost absolute dependence – on people or circumstances to supply me with prestige, security, and the like. Failing to get these things according to my perfectionist dreams and specifications, I had fought for them. And when defeat came, so did my depression. . . . My dependency meant demand – a demand for the possession and control of the people and the conditions surrounding me.[1]

Bill recognized that beneath his alcoholism lay personality traits that have been termed codependency. Robert Subby defines this as:

An emotional, psychological, and behavioral condition that develops as a result of an individual's prolonged exposure to, and practice of, a set of oppressive rules – rules which prevent the open expression of feeling as well as the direct discussion of personal and interpersonal problems.[2]

In other words, it is the rigid family rules which product codependency. Subby also states:

Codependency is a condition which precedes the (addictive) experience. In essence, it is the practice of oppressive rules within the family which support compulsive-obsessive behavior patterns such as alcoholism, overeating, overworking, and perfectionism.[3]

The most fundamental characteristic of codependency is looking outward for one's self-worth. In a dysfunctional family the child may not be allowed to develop. Imagine a young boy who lives by rules dictating which feelings are okay and which feelings aren't. As a result, he changes only in ways he believes will please the adults, whereas he suppresses his individuality. The child loses touch with his feelings because he is not allowed to express them. When he grows up suppressing his private self and perfecting his public persona, eventually there is no private self, just a reaction to others. By the time he reaches adulthood, he doesn't know what his own thoughts or feelings are.

Codependents constantly worry about what others think. Their main goal in life is to try to figure out what other people want, and then give it to them. Their self-esteem comes from their success as people-pleasers. Meanwhile, they persuade themselves that they have no needs of their own. To assure success at pleasing, they become extremely sensitive to the momentary mood of their parents and other important adults. In their home, they may "walk on eggshells" so as not to make a mistake. This characteristic behavior is called hypervigilance, which is an extreme sensitivity to signs of approval or disapproval from others that continues into adulthood. The slightest evidence of disapproval from another person is enough to make them steer a different course.

The Dysfunctional Family

The young child in the dysfunctional family can develop a core feeling of shame. How does this happen? Young children are egocentric by nature – they feel that the world revolves around them and that they are the cause of both positive and negative events that happen. Thus, if a parent does not treat a child with love, she believes it is because she is not lovable. If she is not lovable, it must be because she is an unworthy person. She not only feels guilty about specific things she may have done or not done, but she also develops a deep feeling of shame about her very existence. If adults are overly critical of her (as is common in shaming or dysfunctional family systems) the child learns to feel shame as a core sense of self because she can never measure up to their expectations. Her feeling of shame is validated and reinforced as a shameful being. Since she is naturally egocentric, the child then blames herself for the bad things that happen around her. She feels responsible for the worsening situation at home, and feels guilty over her inability to make things better. Although feeling responsible causes her guilt and shame, it allows her to believe that she has some control of her environment. This is safer than feeling that things are out of her control.

If we hypothesize that the dysfunctional family can be the origin of codependency, then how do we explain the many addicts and partners who say their childhood was normal? Did Mary Ellen and Laura have normal childhoods, as they believe? What is "normal"? Is it the same thing as "average"? Is it the same as "healthy"? One approach to answering these questions is to describe the features of a dysfunctional family, and then to see if these key elements were present in the childhoods of some partners.

The oppressive family rules that often lead to codependency have been summarized by Claudia Black as "don't talk, don't feel, don't trust."[4] This means, don't talk to anyone about what is happening at home and about your feelings; don't express your feelings because feelings are painful and they make other people uncomfortable, and don't trust anyone but yourself. The child who comes to believe these rules feels isolated, unworthy, and even emotionally numb. Subby's book describes the following rules:

"Don't feel, don't talk about your problems."

A common rule in dysfunctional families is that it's not okay to express feelings or talk about problems. Mom and Dad often do not discuss the real problems. The children are often urged not to tell their teachers or the neighbors there is anything wrong at home. Sexually abused children may be threatened with dire consequences if they admit to anyone what is happening.

Helene, the 38-year old recovering alcoholic whose former husband had several affairs, was the daughter of alcoholic parents. "When

I was ten years old, my father began molesting me. He started touching me right in front of my mother. I didn't feel comfortable with this, but my mother's silence told me I should be silent too." She submitted to the abuse, which later included years of sexual penetration.

What are the consequences of a rule against discussing problems? Robert Subby states:

> Since we aren't supposed to talk about problems, then there is something horribly wrong with us that is not wrong with most people. If we admit to having a problem, then we fear that we will also be judged by others as weak and unhealthy. Ultimately, this results in a deep sense of shame about a very real part of everyday life, i.e., that we all have problems.[5]

When she was a child, Alice, the 42-year old biologist, frequently heard her father say, "Children should be seen and not heard." No one in the family was interested in the children's feelings. Alice's father was a self-made man who thought that talking about feelings was a waste of time; only actions counted. Alice's little brother was told, "Big boys don't cry," and he learned not to.

The result of not expressing feelings is that, eventually, the child learns to deny having feelings. She no longer knows what she feels; everything is blocked out. Helene relates,

When I was 21 my father visited me at college. He invited me to stay with him at his motel. I knew what was going to happen, but I went anyway. I remember going into the room and kissing my father but I don't remember anything else until after the weekend was over. I know we had sex but I don't remember it. Later, when I got married, my husband and I never talked about feelings. After I was divorced from my husband, a sex addict, I had a lot of men in my life. We had sex, but I didn't love them. I had no feelings.

Gillian, the 44-year-old lawyer who divorced her husband because of his affairs, characterized her family as "very loving and perfect. My father never showed his anger. If it got too bad he would just leave."

Mary, too, learned not to show her feelings. She did not confront her husband about his betrayal, and in fact "didn't feel anything until I caught him in his office in *flagrante delicto* [while the crime is blazing]."

Cynthia Koestler gained notoriety when she killed herself at age 55 in a double suicide with her terminally ill, 77-year old husband Arthur, a well-known writer and acknowledged philanderer. Her suicide note said, "I cannot live without him." In her autobiography, Cynthia said she learned to control her feelings early in her life.

> I was always rather proud of the way I could keep my feelings under control. During my school days we had been taken to see a film called "Mrs. Miniver" and while the whole school sobbed during the performance, I had not shed a tear.[6]

There are many times when it's inappropriate to cry, but a pattern of suppressing emotions can be an unhealthy precursor to psychological and emotional problems, such as chronic depression.

"Be strong, be perfect, make us proud, don't be selfish."

Another rule common in dysfunctional families is "be strong, be perfect, make us proud, don't be selfish." This rule consists of unrealistic expectations. Children who live with this rule find they can never measure up. They grow up feeling they can never please their parents, no matter how hard they try. Despite their accomplishments, they feel like failures inside.

When Alice brought home a 95 percent grade on a math test, her workaholic father took a look at it and asked, "What happened to the other five percent?" Alice and her brother eventually got Ph.D.

degrees and prestigious jobs, but Alice still fights feeling she should always be doing more. She also tends to have unrealistic expectations of other people.

In Marilyn's family of origin, nothing she accomplished was ever good enough for her parents. No matter how hard she tried, she always failed to please them. Eventually she gave up trying. After graduating Phi Beta Kappa from a prestigious college, she drifted from job to job, finding ways to sabotage any possible success. For a while she experimented with mood-altering drugs. Her marriage to an abusive alcoholic lasted fifteen years; she divorced him after he had a series of affairs. Now 43 and active in Al-Anon, Marilyn has just finished a master's degree in counseling and finally has a job she enjoys.

Children who experience unrealistic expectations in their families often take either the path Alice chose (and become very successful workaholics), or they may give up early, as Marilyn did. In both situations they tend to feel guilty and inadequate.

A common unrealistic expectation is the "don't be selfish" rule. This rule teaches that it is selfish to attend to one's own needs. As Subby writes,

> If we believe that our own needs are wrong, we will never be able to get those needs met. What often happens in codependency is that we try to feel good about ourselves by taking care of others, and eventually our self-esteem becomes dependent on caretaking. Without someone to take care of, the codependent is left with no purpose or worth. The more we take care of someone, the more we fail to take care of our own needs. In time we start to feel resentful toward those whom we care for because they fail to recognize what we are dong for them. The result of these angry feelings is that we experience even more shame, and so even more caretaking. As the pain builds in each of us, we begin to blame and point out the failings of others.[7]

Since everyone has needs, the "don't be selfish" rule is guaranteed to produce shame and guilt.

Another consequence of this rule is that many codependents find it difficult to have fun. In a dysfunctional family, there are always jobs to be done that are more important than having fun. The child learns that he doesn't deserve to enjoy himself. In adulthood, he has difficulty relaxing and playing.

"Do as I say, not as I do."

A third important rule in dysfunctional families is "do as I say, not as I do." When Jack, Irene's womanizing husband, was a boy, he used to accompany his father on the rodeo circuit during the summer. He recalls,

I witnessed a lot, and I was expected to keep my mouth shut. I didn't understand some of what was going on. I just knew that you don't tell your mother these things you see, the drinking, the women, and about being left alone in a motel room while your father and his buddies were out drinking and womanizing.

Jack's father used to talk to him about honesty, responsibility, and commitment, but Jack learned from what his father did, not what he said – he learned to lie, cheat, and manipulate. He also learned not to trust people. Jack's father told him to treat his mother with respect, but reality was very different:

I witnessed beatings just like you'd see if two men were in a fistfight. I recall one night when he actually dragged my mother across the yard by her hair.

From his father's actions, Jack learned to pay lip service to one code of behavior while actually engaging in another. He learned he could not trust what people said; what they felt on the inside was very different from what they presented to others. Jack held responsible jobs, jug-gled a wife and girlfriends, but inside he felt like a worthless person.

"Don't rock the boat."

A fourth rule the child learns is not to rock the boat, to maintain the status quo at all costs. This rule teaches a child enabling, that is, protecting the addict from experiencing the consequences of his behavior. The child watches as Mother stands at the window for hours waiting for Dad to come home, crying as she wonders whom he's with. The next day, life goes on as though nothing happened. The child sees that Mother does not confront Dad, and he learns that it's more important to keep peace at home than to risk an unpredict-able reaction by bringing issues up.

According to Robin Norwood, author of *Women Who Love Too Much*, a key element in every dysfunctional family is keeping secrets. In the case of a family where the mother is chronically ill, the oldest daughter often assumes many of the responsibilities of the mother. She cares for her mother and is praised for her role. Her feelings, however, are mixed. At times she feels it's too much for her, she can't handle it, she's tired of feeling that she's holding up the world. She feels resentful and angry at her mother because of the burden the illness has laid on the child's shoulders. But it's not acceptable to express those feelings – after all, it isn't the mother's fault that she is ill. So the daughter not only covers up her feelings, which are natural under the circumstances, but comes to believe that she is a selfish, bad person for even having those feelings. If I were a better person, she thinks, I wouldn't feel angry and resentful of Mother. She feels guilty, ashamed, and unworthy. When she gets praise for her devotion, she tells herself, "If they only knew what I am really like inside, they wouldn't praise me and wouldn't like me." To atone for her sins, she tries even harder. She is firmly caught up in the cycle of codependency.

The dysfunctional element in this home is not the mother's illness but the child's reinforced belief that she cannot express her feelings. The rule here is that Mother's illness takes precedence over the child's needs, and the child is accused of being selfish if she expresses those needs. In the dysfunctional family, children are not considered to have needs of their own.

An excellent television docudrama on "The Hallmark Hall of Fame" told the story of the oldest hearing daughter of deaf parents. As is true of most such families, from early childhood on the daughter served as her parents' interpreter, their ear to the word. A poignant scene found her, at age eight or so, talking with an undertaker, making funeral arrangements for her brother who had just been killed by a fall from a balcony. Rather than react to her brother's death as a little girl would, she immediately had to assume the role of an adult and negotiate the financial arrangements for the funeral. Her parents expected her to always be the responsible one, and she was. They did not acknowledge the feelings of a child her age and essentially did not permit her to be a child.

In her adulthood she had difficulty establishing intimate relationships. It was only when she was finally able to accept and work through her resentment and anger over her lost childhood, and learned how to have fun, that she became more emotionally healthy.

The dysfunctional elements in the daughter's home were her parents' unrealistic expectations of her and the family rules that prevented her from talking about her feelings. The family rules told her she was being selfish if she wanted to attend to her own needs or have some fun. The rules denied that the problems of a little girl could have as much validity as those of her deaf parents.

The emotional consequences of living in a home with deafness were described by Lou Ann Walker in her book *A Loss for Words*, an account of her experience growing up as a hearing child of deaf parents. Her parents were loving and caring, yet she grew up feeling guilty, ashamed, isolated, and wanting to please others. How did this happen? Walker states:

I acted as interpreter and guide for my parents the entire time I was growing up. I was an adult before I was a child. I was quiet and obedient around people because I didn't know what was expected of me. Outside our house speaking and hearing seemed to be valued more than anything. And that's what we had nothing of at home. I was the child who did all my parents' business transactions, nearly from the time I was a toddler. I was usually the one to relay to Mom and Dad that a friend had died when we received a call. I was the one who had to call up other friends or relatives to give them the bad news. A child doesn't know that his childhood is sad; it's just his life.[8]

Lou Ann learned to cover up her feelings and to behave like a responsible adult instead of the little girl she was. She also learned early to feel guilty:

In a family where there is deafness, guilt is a constant undercurrent, tainting relationships, sometimes even shattering that family. My own grandparents constantly exhorted me to be good, themselves feeling guilty for not doing more for their children, hoping somehow I would make up for things.[9]

Lou Ann's pervasive feeling of guilt came about because she had come to believe that her feelings were wrong. For example, she was tempted by an offer her uncle and aunt made to spend some time with them, to live in a normal family. She let herself fantasize about life with them:

What an ache, what a longing, what a maze! At that very moment I was deeply ashamed of myself. I loved my parents fiercely. I would jump to their defense at any time. And yet I had these horrible, treacherous desires. And after the two weeks, when I got back home, I was terrified Mom and Dad would figure out the secret.[10]

Because there was a significant gap between Lou Ann's inner suppressed feelings and what she believed she should express, she felt more worthless and more guilty.

> My greatest fear had always been: The more you get to know me, the less there is to know. I was a black void. On the outside I was bright and shining and cheerful. Inside I was hollow. I was a caretaker and I felt deep down inside I could never do enough for others because I could never make my mother and my father whole. On the outside I was trying to remain the good girl my aunts and uncles had warned me to be. The difference between the façade and the interior kept growing. I felt guilty. And never once had I ever been able to indulge myself in feeling bad. 'You shouldn't feel sorry for yourself. Think of your mother and father. It wasn't their fault,' I'd been told. In a bizarre psychological turn of events, I couldn't even feel sorry for myself without feeling the guilt. I had no right to feel bad, to feel lonely or out of touch or anything else. I had been boxed in on every side and that was what was struggling to get out. Just the right to feel.[11]

Lou Ann subsequently spoke with her sister about their childhood. For the first time they shared their feelings of guilt and inadequacy. "Both of us began to cry. She and I had been so close all the time we were growing up. We'd talked about everything – except this."[12]

Despite the closeness and love in the family, Lou Ann learned that only certain feelings were acceptable, and that she was responsible for other people's happiness. She grew up with a pervasive feeling of shame and guilt. Only an emotional crisis years later forced her to face her feelings, share them with others, and begin healing.

Lou Ann Walker's experience is also relevant to the concept of *emotional incest*. In her book, *The Emotional Incest Syndrome*, Patricia Love writes,[13]

> This is a style of parenting in which parents turn to their children, not to their partners, for emotional support. . . Being a parent's primary source of support is a heavy burden for young children. Forced to suppress their own needs, they struggle to satisfy the needs of the adults. Because of this role reversal, they are rarely given adequate protection, guidance, or discipline, and they are exposed to experiences well beyond their years. In adolescence and adulthood, they are likely to be plagued by one or more of the following difficulties: depression, chronic low-level anxiety, problems with self-esteem and love relationships, overly loose or rigid personal boundaries. . .

Love's book focuses primarily on families in which a parent uses a child to satisfy the parent's unmet emotional needs. However, similar damage to the child can result when the parent's physical needs drive the parentification of the child. In a healthy family, according to Love, parents listen to the child's woes but don't depend upon the child to listen to theirs. They take care of the child's needs but they don't allow the child to feel responsible for their needs (p.107). This, unfortunately, was the opposite of the situation in Lou Ann Walker's childhood home.

What is a Normal Family?

In this chapter we have seen examples of homes characterized as normal and as loving, but in fact dysfunctional enough to produce codependency in the children. What, then, is a normal family? First, let's define normal as healthy along a continuum, rather than as a statistical average. I would say that a healthy family is one in which it is acceptable to discuss problems and to express feelings, in which parents' expectations of the children are realistic, in which the values the parents teach the children are actually lived by the adults, and in which unacceptable behaviors are confronted and dealt with rather than covered up.

Furthermore, a healthy family nurtures the children and values them for who they are so they grow up believing they are worthwhile people, regardless of what college or trade school they attend or what career they choose.

A normal family is not the same as the stereotypical traditional American family, with two parents, two children, a dog and a cat – a family in which Mom spends all day at home while Dad goes to the office. A normal family can be a single-parent family, or one with two same-sex parents, or one in which both parents work (currently the norm), or one in which there is physical disability.

Now let's look again at Mary Ellen and Laura, the two women quoted at the beginning of this chapter, who believed they had healthy childhoods but somehow ended up married to sex addicts. Laura's mother had unrealistic expectations: Not only was she very controlling, but she seemed to want to make Laura into an extension of herself. Not surprisingly, Laura could never please her critical mother, no matter how hard she tried. Giving up any attempt at autonomy, she let her mother make all the decisions for her; in that way, Laura could avoid taking responsibility for the consequences of those decisions. Later, Laura transferred her dependence to her husband. Today, at age 45 and in a recovery program for spouses of sex addicts, she is learning that she doesn't have to please her mother. Despite her stable childhood home, she lived with unrealistic expectations and rules against expressing feelings.

Like Laura, Mary Ellen also grew up in a stable home. But her mother's reaction to becoming deaf when Mary Ellen was ten created significant dysfunctional elements in the family. Mary Ellen was no longer permitted to have a one-on-one relationship with her father. She was cast in an adult role as her mother's confidante. At the same time, she was not permitted to express her feelings or discuss problems. She was not able to live up to her mother's expectations.

Research on adult children of alcoholics has shown a tendency of these children to minimize the problems of their childhood. "It wasn't really that bad," they say. "There were a lot of good things in my family. It's true that my father yelled and hit me when he was drunk, but when he was sober he was wonderful to me. He was always trying to make it up to me. It's true he forgot his promises to take me to the ball game, but when he sobered up he was really sorry about it."

From my interviews of partners of men who have affairs, I found a similar tendency on the part of some women to remember only the good in their childhood. But just as with Laura and Mary Ellen, when one asks for details of their family of origin, it becomes evident that enough of the unhealthy family rules were present to explain the person's codependency.

The belief that it wasn't that bad is an aspect of the codependent's lack of knowledge of what is healthy and what is normal family interaction. A codependent learns to have high tolerance for inappropriate behavior because she lacks confidence in her judgment. And, she is likely to accept someone else's word that a given behavior is acceptable even if she suspects it is not. When her mate tells her it is her possessiveness and insecurity that makes her want monogamy in their relationship, she believes him and tries to change her views for him. If he asks her to sleep with another man while he watches, and assures her that many people do it, she tries to suppress her discomfort and assumes that her husband knows best. She tolerates inappropriate behavior from herself and her mate because she's not really sure what is appropriate.

When a woman tolerates years of emotional abuse, alcoholism, or other active addiction in her mate, yet seems unable to do anything about her situation, the appropriate question to ask is, "Why?" Often the answer lies in the dysfunctional family in which she was raised.

Many single women are managing alone, with or without children. A first-marriage, two-parent family is no longer the norm in the United States. According to the 2013 American Community Survey, only 48.7% of households included a married couple,[14] and, according to a 2013 Pew Survey, approximately 40 percent of marriages were second or third marriages.[15] In 2013, 13 percent of families were headed by single women. A year earlier, women accounted for 47% of all workers, and in 53% of households comprising a married couple, both were working.[16]

Of note here, many women would like to leave a bad marriage, but economic considerations keep them bound in unsatisfactory relationships. A person with no wage-earning skills and small children often has no immediate options besides staying in the marriage. Financial and emotional dependency cannot be changed overnight, and no one should be blamed for not leaving a bad marriage until they are ready. Nevertheless, it is often true that relationship addiction, rather than lack of funds, is the primary reason that keeps many people in an unhappy or even abusive marriage with an addict.

Family Background of Partners

One often hears the question, "Is it a matter of chance that one person marries an alcoholic, another a workaholic, and another a sex addict? Or is it something in the person's childhood?" The answer is far from clear, especially since the mate frequently has several coexisting addictions, such as alcoholism and sex addiction. Many sex addicts were sexually abused in childhood; so were many people who married sex addicts – but many were not. It is impossible to find a common denominator in their childhoods.,

Nonetheless, factors in one's family of origin and early experiences do influence the nature of one's compulsive behavior. One way or another, many partners eventually learn that sex is the best way to get love. Some learned this by being sexually molested; others, hungry for love in junior and senior high school, found that giving sex guaranteed many boyfriends. Some children grew up in families where infidelity was happening, although they may not have realized it at the time Although they may have learned about them only in adulthood, the infidelity influenced their childhood home environment.

Andrea, a schoolteacher who is very active in her church, grew up with a workaholic, emotionally distant father, and a domineering, controlling mother. After a stormy relationship, her parents divorced at the time she graduated from high school. Andrea does not remember receiving much physical affection from her parents; she does remember trying hard to get her parents' approval. Andrea doesn't recall any family problems when she was growing up. "I either wasn't aware of problems, or I didn't want to know about them." Nonetheless, when she told her father about the problems she and her husband, Arthur, were having with his sex addiction, she learned some surprising facts about her childhood years.

I've recently found out from my dad that he was involved with other women in the course of his marriage. One of them was my mom's best friend, and they did some things like spouse-swapping. He didn't tell me anything about my mom's activities, only that he thought that since Arthur and I were having some problems in our marriage, it might be helpful for us to know that he'd had some problems in that arena too. But the implication I got was that maybe my mom had done a lot of that too, playing around with other men. . . . I wonder if they weren't both having sex with a lot of other people and I had some indication of it on some level, that something was wrong which I didn't want to look at too closely, and maybe that's why I don't remember much about my childhood.

One woman who clearly remembers an intensely sexual atmosphere in her childhood is Nancy, a 40-year old mother of five. Nancy and her husband, Monte, had a stormy marriage marked by several separations and reconciliations because of his affairs.

My father never physically molested me, but he was verbally sexual with me. He would make dirty jokes about my body. At times I'd be in the bathroom putting on makeup and he'd come in and urinate and walk around naked. I was disgusted by him. I had one aunt who was very pretty and very well endowed, and at one party I saw him feeling her. I can still remember the disgust I felt. I felt very sorry for my mother, and angry with her at the same time. My father used to keep Playboy magazines in the house, so I grew up looking at pornography, reading all the books he had.

I think my father also had affairs. One day when I was in the house and my father was outside washing the car, the phone rang. It was a woman on the phone and she wanted my dad. I asked, "Who's this?" She answered, "It's Baby." So I went out the back door and I called, "Dad, there's a woman on the phone and she says her name is Baby." My dad turned white and proceeded to have a heart attack. I can still remember him walking into the house, clutching his chest, and then the ambulance coming. I thought it was my fault, and I went around for years feeling guilty of having caused his heart attack.

I felt so lonely all of my life, so I tried to find companionship by having boyfriends. As early as fifth grade I was going steady with boys, and by the following year I was kissing and petting because it gave me a feeling that they cared about me. If someone wasn't being sexual with me, they didn't care about me. All through high school I had boyfriend after boyfriend.

Not surprisingly, Nancy married a man to whom sex was very important.

Alice, the 42-year old biologist whose parents were divorced when she was very young, was brought up by her father.

I always thought of my father as a very sexual person. He has been married five times, and each wife was in her 20's or 30's when they got married. His current wife is only a few years older than me. When I was in high school he was between marriages. He used to tell my brother and me he would be gone until morning because he had a business meeting. We knew darn well that he was going to spend the night with a girlfriend, so we'd laugh and say, "Enjoy your business meeting!" He was a very formal person who rarely hugged or kissed us, and he used to be very embarrassed by our laughter.

Alice married a man who was also very sexual, and whose affairs caused major problems in their marriage.

Several partners I interviewed were molested sexually in child-hood. Patty, a petite 25-year old married to a much older dentist, was repeatedly molested by two teenage neighbors when she was six or seven years old. They would lie on top of her and rub against her. She didn't understand what was happening, but had a sense that it was wrong and that she shouldn't tell anyone about it.

Another woman was fondled sexually by a male babysitter. Still other partners had been victims of incest. Rita, whose husband formerly had affairs, had sexual relations with two of her three brothers. She grew up in a chaotic household with an alcoholic father whose behavior varied unpredictably from being loving to being physically abusive. Rita's husband was also the child of an alcoholic.

Helene, a recovering alcoholic who is divorced from a man addicted to both alcohol and sex, was an incestuous relationship with her alcoholic father for many years, beginning at age ten. She learned to stuff her feelings and to exchange sex for love in her relationships.

Several women, hoping to obtain love, engaged in sex early in life and became pregnant. Marcy, the wife of a cheater, dated her husband against her parents' wishes and married him at age 18 after getting pregnant. Sarah, a certified public accountant who is now divorced from a sex addict, grew up in a stable but rigid home. A model student in school, she became pregnant at age fourteen. After giving the baby up for adoption, she returned to school and to an active sex life.

This brief survey of partners does not definitively answer the question of why they married sex addicts rather than other types of addicts, but it does suggest there were certain risk factors in their early years. There was often a heightened awareness of sexuality in the family of origin. Early sexual experience, either with peers or through sexual abuse, was another frequent finding. One way or another, these women came to believe that sex was the most important sign of love. More research needs to be done to understand how this belief originated. What seems clear, however, is that partners who can also be described as coaddicts learn in their formative years to be "comfortable with the uncomfortable"; for those married to sex addicts, this includes the sexual arena.

Family Roles in the Dysfunctional Family

Now that we have explored the rules and circumstances in the family of origin that can predispose one to codependency and coaddiction, let's turn to the roles that children play in the dysfunctional family. These roles, in alcoholic families, were first delineated by Sharon Wegscheider-Cruse.[17] It is now recognized that similar roles can be played in all types of dysfunctional families. The roles described by Wegscheider-Cruse are the Hero, Scapegoat, Lost Child, and Mascot. The child does not consciously choose these roles; rather, she finds an available niche in the family panorama and is supported by the family her position. This is because each role contributes to the stability of the dysfunctional family in some manner.

These roles are not fixed nor mutually exclusive. For example, when circumstances change, such as when an older child leaves home, the roles may change. Moreover, a child may display elements of more than one role at a time. Nonetheless, it is valuable to look at these patterns because each role tends to be carried over into adulthood where it can cause problems.

The Family Hero

The role typically assumed by the oldest child is the Family Hero, also termed the Responsible child by Claudia Black.[18] The Hero is the child who feeds and dresses her younger siblings when the parents are too involved with other things. If her father throws a few dishes around in a fit of anger, she will clean up in order to help her mother. When her mother is so depressed about her father's behavior that she lies in bed all day immobilized, the Hero will take over the household responsibilities. Her goal is to maintain the status quo and prevent things from getting worse. Deep down she believes if she does a good enough job, things will improve and her parents will be as happy as they used to be. By helping out as successfully as she does, she unwittingly enables her parents' compulsive behavior —she helps prevent them from experiencing the consequences of their own dysfunction. Beverly, the attractive socialite and divorced mother of three small children, grew up in an alcoholic family:

My father always came home at six, but his drinking progressed to the point where he could barely make it in the back door. As he was falling asleep at night in his room he would rant about those "goddam women," meaning his wife and daughters. I tried to be his son, to help him repair things around the house. I tried to be pretty and good to please him and to make him stop drinking, but he didn't. My efforts were just not good enough.

No matter how hard they try, Heroes inevitably fail. They feel guilty and inadequate over their inability to make things right in the family. Their usual response is to try harder, and this becomes their usual behavioral style. They become overachievers. They gain their self-worth from their accomplishments, and judge themselves by their achievements. They may develop a compulsive drive to achieve.

Often admired at school, Heroes may excel at scholastic activities or at sports. Their parents support and promote their single-minded pursuit of excellence. They set high goals for themselves and often expect too much of others as well. In adulthood, they are usually good at whatever task they undertake. The Hero's career choice is likely to be a helping profession – teacher, counselor, physician, nurse, or minister. No matter what career they choose, they are likely to take it very seriously and do well at it.

The Hero's primary emotions are guilt and inadequacy. As Wegscheider-Cruse tells it, "The Hero goes through life always feeling that no matter how good he is, he must be a little better before he has a right to take satisfaction in his achievements."

The Scapegoat

The second child in a dysfunctional family often assumes the role of Scapegoat or the Acting Out Child. Because there is already one Hero in the family, the next child seeks attention through negative behavior, which becomes his usual behavioral style. He covers his underlying hurt with anger. This is the child who is most likely to become addicted to alcohol and other drugs, to become pregnant, to drop out of school, or to get in trouble with the law. Because he or she is the identified problem child in the family, his or her presence makes the rest of the family members seem healthy by comparison. When whole families come into treatment, it is often because of the acting out of a Scapegoat child.

Although approximately 20 percent of adult children of alcoholics identify with this role in their childhoods, it's likely that a higher proportion of children play out on this role. Scapegoats are under-represented in the community and in treatment programs because many have eliminated themselves in their youth – by committing suicide, or by dying of a drug overdose, car accident, in street violence, or by having committed a crime and ending up in jail. A Scapegoat may change roles and become a Hero when an older sibling leaves home and her position becomes vacant. If the Scapegoat survives to adulthood, she is likely to carry her "it's not fair" attitude with her. Having learned in childhood that chemicals kill pain and provide pleasure, and that family life centers around the addict, she has an increased risk of becoming chemically dependent. Although she comes across to the world as a rebel, her primary emotion is hurt.

The Lost Child

Another family role is that of the Lost Child or the Adjuster (according to Black). Usually a younger sibling, this child has found the best way to avoid trouble is to adopt a behavioral style of invisibility. He lives in a fantasy world, playing elaborate games with his toys, and may become an avid reader, television viewer, or internet surfer. His activities are mostly solitary. The Lost Child gives his parents a sense of relief. "At least we don't have to worry about him," they tell themselves. The Lost Child avoids taking responsibility, and develops no particular opinions on any issues. His primary emotion is loneliness. He does not do well, but may get attention by developing illnesses such as asthma or allergies. The Lost Child feels ignored and forgotten. He may comfort himself with food and become obese.

In adulthood, the Lost Child becomes the student or office worker whose name you just can't seem to remember. Accustomed to living in chaos, he tends to marry a partner who causes uproar. He may become a collector of material goods.

The Mascot

The remaining role is the Mascot. Often the youngest child, he defuses explosive situations in the family by focusing attention on himself through humor. Tension and hyperactivity constitute his behavioral style. As he grows older he may take tranquilizers and other drugs to calm himself down. In school, he is the class clown. In adulthood, he finds that people do not take him seriously. His predominant emotion is fear, which he covers with his clowning behavior.

Although the Responsible Child is the one whose enabling activities are most clearly visible in the family, children in each of the other roles also contribute to the stability of the dysfunctional family system. Thus, the escapades and problems of the Scapegoat can become the focus of concern of the entire family, so that they don't have to confront the addiction and coaddiction of the parents. The Lost Child, by not making waves, tries to minimize the need for change. And the Mascot, with her clowning and hyperactivity, defuses the crises that may be necessary for the parents to realize they need help.

Children who play any of the four roles – Hero, Scapegoat, Lost Child, or Mascot – may simultaneously be enablers: they may feel responsible for the problems in the family and try, with whatever behavior they have adopted, to improve the situation at home. This was confirmed by most of the people I interviewed. They tried their best in childhood to please their parents and to make things better. Accustomed to being caretakers in their families of origin, they were attracted to partners who needed fixing.

Why Learn About Our Childhood?

In a letter to a newspaper column dealing with alcoholism, a reader questioned the preoccupation of adult children of alcoholics with learning about their childhoods. The reader wrote:

> Once again we are blaming Mommy and Daddy for whatever the individual does, and that's just another cop-out. This is similar to blaming poor potty training for a murderer's crime. If our society would force people to take responsibility for themselves this would be a better world.[19]

Al, the recovering alcoholic who writes the column, replied, "Once I was led to understand who I was and why I acted the way I did, I was able to become a socially and personally responsible member of the human race for the first time." An important step in the early stages of recovery is to understand the roots of one's codependency.

If we can review our childhood in order to understand rather than to blame, then we can move forward. By defining the rules that govern our lives and the part they played many years ago, we can begin to change them for rules more appropriate to our present situation. It's also important to understand that our parents did the best they could under the circumstances. Often they were enmeshed in their alcoholism or other addiction or codependency and had very little left for their children.

In early recovery, many people experience a great deal of anger at their parents. One of the tasks of recovery is to forgive them, and a good way to begin doing this is to ask our parents to tell us about their childhood. Addictions typically span several generations, so we are likely to find that our parent grew up in a family in which their needs were not met. Asking for this information can be very difficult for any addict or partner who grew up in a family where secrets were hidden. Talking with your parents about their own experiences may be the beginning of improved communication and a better relationship with them. If your parents are dead and thus unavailable for discussion, or if they are unwilling to talk openly with you about themselves, or insist that everything was fine in your childhood and that there were no problems, you may have a harder time forgiving them. The subject of forgiveness is discussed further in Chapter Six, "The Elements of Recovery."

Bill is a recovering sex addict who felt he was never able to please his father; nothing he did quite measured up. Bill's father, a self-made man, was contemptuous of his son's failure. Bill eventually decided that if he didn't try, no one could blame him for not succeeding. He focused his energies on pursuing women rather than a career, and became very successful at his chosen occupation. His marriage to a career woman permitted him to live in comfort while devoting his energies to womanizing. At age 40, Bill was still preoccupied with winning his father's approval and felt worthless because he could not do so.

When Bill eventually entered a recovery program for sex addiction and learned about the family dynamics that can produce codependency, he found himself feeling very angry with his father. Bill felt he could not share his feelings with his father, a prominent leader of his community who was very sure he was right about everything. During his next visit to his parents, Bill did ask his father about his father's childhood. Bill's father, outwardly self-assured and self-confident, described his own father (that is, Bill's grandfather):

Grandpa had to work hard all his life. He never really had a childhood. He had to support his mother [that is, Bill's great-grandmother] and brothers because his father was too busy running around with other women. My mother [Bill's grandmother] and I were very close; we have the same personality and were always on the same wavelength. Grandpa was very fond of me, but he spent a lifetime putting down Grandma. I was very resentful of him for doing this, and I kept defending her. I said to him, "If she's so terrible, why'd you stay with her?" My father was always hugging and kissing me, but it took me many years to be able to stand up to him.

    I've been very successful, Bill. Everywhere your mother and I have lived, we've always been respected. But in my heart of hearts, I've always felt like an outsider. People say all these nice things about what we've done for the community, but I realize that deep down they think we're outsiders, we're those aggressive, rich carpetbaggers. If you realize that people don't really care, you don't get hurt. I always say, eternal vigilance is the best defense.

Bill learned from this discussion that his great-grandfather had been a sex addict. He also began to see his father in a very different light. Bill's father felt like an outsider who always had to have his defenses up to avoid being hurt. In childhood, Bill's father listened countless times as Bill's grandfather denigrated his wife, the mother with whom Bill's father so strongly identified. Undoubtedly Bill's father had felt he could not measure up to his father. When Bill began to see his father as a human being with weaknesses and a troubled childhood, instead of as an all-powerful judgmental figure, he was able to feel more sympathetic and less angry with him. He realized that his father was the product of his upbringing.

Seeing our parents as real people is an important step toward forgiveness. Understanding our origins does not negate the need to grieve for our lost childhood and to experience anger over our parents' role in our present difficulties. Other steps that are necessary for our recovery include understanding the family patterns, building an emotional support system, allowing our feelings to emerge in order to experience the anger and grief, and, finally taking responsibility for changing our behavior.

When we look back to our childhood and identify the dysfunctional elements, we can use the information as a springboard to change. The goal here is to understand the family roots without blame. Accusing our parents of having caused our present problems will not accomplish anything. Just as our personality and behavior are in large part an outcome of our childhood experiences, so too was our parents' behavior an outcome of their childhood experiences. The vast majority of our parents did the best they could given their limitations. And it is important to revisit your past, not for the purpose of assigning blame or finding fault with your parents, but rather in order to hold the adults in your life accountable (if not responsible) for their decisions. Once we understand that as children we are never responsible for the decisions the adults made, we have a new opportunity to better understand the origins of our codependency and to develop a healthier sense of self.

If we can make some changes, then the next generation – our children – will have an easier and healthier time of it than we did.

CHAPTER FOUR

Understanding the Sex Addict

An allergy to chocolate will provide a simple illustration of the concept of addiction. Suppose you found that whenever you eat chocolate you break out in hives. You would probably then choose to avoid chocolate, no matter how much you like the taste. But suppose instead you eat some chocolate, develop itchy hives all over your body, eat more chocolate, get more hives, tell yourself you're not gong to eat any more chocolate, but soon find yourself consuming a chocolate bar and you break out in hives. You are unable to top eating chocolate despite the painful consequences. You have lost control over your chocolate consumption, and you continue consuming chocolate despite adverse consequences. These are the first two elements of any addiction, and they constitute a *behavior disorder*.

In addition to a behavior disorder, all addictions also include a *thinking disorder*. The addict becomes preoccupied – obsessed – with the addictive drug or behavior, spending a lot of time finding it, using it, and recovering from its effects. The addict also has distorted ideas about the role of the drug or behavior in his life. The American Society of Addiction Medicine defines addiction as follows:

> Addiction is characterized by inability to consistently abstain, impairment in behavioral control, craving, diminished

recognition of significant problems with one's behaviors and interpersonal relationships, and a dysfunctional emotional response. Like other chronic diseases, addiction often involves cycles of relapse and remission. Without treatment or engagement in recovery activities, addiction is progressive and can result in disability or premature death consumption.[1]

The inability to stop using the drug or behavior is the behavior disorder; the inability to recognize the negative consequences is the thought disorder that maintains the behavior problem. Alcoholics deny they have a drinking problem and at the same time rationalize their drinking as the logical consequence of other problems, such as marital discord or the stresses of their jobs.

Addictions are also characterized by *tolerance*, which means you need more of the chemical or the compulsive activity to get the same effect. Using the same dose gives progressively less satisfaction. As time goes by, addicts typically require more and more of their drug of choice in order to feel good. The chocolate addict finds himself craving two chocolate bars instead of one. The sex addict takes increasing risks in order to get the same level of excitement. Addiction is thus progressive, with diminishing returns.

Finally, addiction to certain drugs is associated with a specific *withdrawal syndrome* when the drug is abruptly stopped. Alcoholics who go cold turkey experience the shakes, insomnia, elevated blood pressure and heart rate, and at times seizures and hallucinations. Not all drugs of abuse have recognizable withdrawal symptoms, and withdrawal is not a *requirement* for an addiction to be present. Behavioral addictions are less likely to have specific withdrawal symptoms beyond a general irritability and poor concentration.

Sex addiction was recognized over 40 years ago by Erich Fromm, author of *The Art of Loving*, who wrote,

The deepest need of man is the need to overcome his separateness, to leave the prison of his loneliness. . . . One way of achieving this aim lies in all kinds of *orgiastic states.* These may have the form of an auto-induced trance, sometimes with the help of drugs. . . . Closely related to, and often blended with this orgiastic solution, is the sexual experience. The sexual orgasm can produce a state similar to the one produced by a trance, or to the effects of certain drugs. Rites of communal sexual orgies were a part of many primitive rituals. It seems that after the orgiastic experience, man can go on for a time without suffering too much from his separateness. Slowly the tension of anxiety mounts, and then is reduced again by the repeated performance of the ritual.

As long as these orgiastic states are a matter of common practice in the tribe, they do not produce anxiety or guilt. . . . It is quite different when the same solution is chosen by an individual in a culture which has left behind these common practices. Alcoholism and drug addiction are the forms which an individual chooses in a non-orgiastic culture. In contrast to those participating in the socially patterned solution, such individuals suffer from guilt feelings and remorse. While they try to escape from separateness by taking refuge in alcohol or drugs, they feel all the more separate after the experience is over, and thus are driven to take recourse to it with increasing frequency and intensity.

. . . In many individuals in whom separateness is not relieved in other ways, the search for the sexual orgasm assumes a function which makes it not very different from alcoholism and drug addiction. It becomes a desperate attempt to escape the anxiety endangered by separateness, and it results in an ever-increasing sense of separateness, since the sexual act without love never bridges the gap between two human beings, except momentarily.[2]

In other words, Fromm reasons that alcoholism and other drug addictions in our society are unsuccessful ways of overcoming isolation, and that sexual activity can be used, equally unsuccessfully, to provide exactly the same temporary relief.

This assertion was echoed by Stanton Peele, who wrote in his 1975 book, *Love and Addiction*:

> Interpersonal addiction – love addiction – is just about the most common, yet least recognized form of addiction. [p.5] . . . Addiction is not a chemical reaction. Addiction is an *experience* – one which grows out of an individual's routinized subjective response to something that has special meaning for him – something, anything, that he finds so safe and reassuring that he cannot be without it. [p.6] . . . The addict, heroin or otherwise, is addicted not to a chemical, but to a sensation, a prop, an experience which structures his life. What causes that experience to become an addiction is that it makes it more and more difficult for the person to deal with his real needs, thereby making his sense of well-being depend increasingly on a single, external source of support. [p.23][3]

Other contemporary writers have also liked some forms of sexual behavior to alcoholism and other drug addiction. For example, James C. Dobson, a Christian minister, in his book *Love Must be Tough*, urges women to stop enabling the behavior of unfaithful husbands:

> The lure of infidelity is an *addiction* to [a certain type of] individual. . . . While some people are chemically dependent on alcohol or heroin or cocaine, this kind of infidel is hooked on illicit sex. Psychologically, he needs the thrill of the chase, the clandestine meetings, the forbidden fruit, the flattery, the sexual conquest, the proof of manhood or womanhood, and in some cases, the discovery. And like the drug abuser, he is constantly attempting to reform. He promises with sincerity never again to yield to his habit. But unless his entire social milieu acts to support that commitment, he is likely to forget it.[4]

All of these writers emphasize that the essential feature of addiction is the *experience*, not the particular drug or behavior chosen. The important elements are:

- The compulsive nature of the experience (i.e., the loss of control)
- The continuation despite its negative consequences
- The preoccupation or obsession with the drug or behavior

For the person whose addiction is to extramarital sex, to masturbation to online pornography, or to other sexual activities, the mood-altering experience is not just the sexual act itself. It is a mistake to think of this type of person as being oversexed, or just needing lots of sex. As Troy, a 30-year-old, formerly married, recovering cocaine addict explains:

I was preoccupied with women. They ranked a real close second to drugs. I would go to the cocaine connection before I'd go on a date, but I tried to do them both. I had several one-night stands, but mostly I spent a lot of time in pursuit, not in the actual catch. Occasionally I'd score, but it was mostly the pursuit, it wasn't the scoring, that was fulfilling. It was more the rush and the adrenaline of the pursuit and of living in the fantasy of the pursuit, the possibilities that existed in that. Afterwards there was the guilt of whether Sara, my wife, found out. I always thought it was honorable if I went to great lengths to make sure she didn't find out.

Fantasy is a consistently found element in sex addiction. "When I was feeling bad as a kid,' says Alan, a 45-year old married sex addict. "I could always escape into my room and create the kind of world I wanted. It was a world where I had lots of power, where girls found me exciting and wanted to be with me."

Typically, fantasy and masturbation become interconnected. One man told me:

I remember the first time I came upon a pornographic website. It was like what my A.A. friends told about having their first drink – it made them feel so good they never forgot it. I remember the feeling I got when I looked at those soft, friendly girls. I knew they'd like me and would take care of me. I'd masturbate while thinking about them. After I married, after my wife and I made love she would fall asleep and then I would go to my online pornography and masturbate as I created in my mind the kind of sexual pleasure I wanted.

Alan says,

Fantasy was my first drink. I would see an ad for scanty underwear in a magazine and I would drink in the image. Then, when I was alone and in need of comfort, I would replay in my mind, over and over, the image of that girl in the ad. Masturbation just fueled the flame, and next thing I'd be on the phone calling a girl to set up a lunch date. I would then fantasize about what we might say to each other and how we might end up in bed.

For many sex addicts, as for Alan, fantasy leads to a compulsion to follow through with actual behavior. It is difficult for them to separate fact and fantasy. This was brought home to Alice, Alan's wife, when she told him she'd had a vivid erotic dream involving one of her business associates. Alan's response was, "What will you do next time you see him?" Alice was surprised. "Nothing – it was just a dream!" But for Alan, such a dream would make him believe there was a real connection with the person he had dreamed about, and he would be inclined to follow through with action the next time he encountered that person.

For affair addicts, the fantasizing, the anticipation, the planning, the risk-taking – these elements are at least as important as the sexual act itself. For some, the risk aspect adds real excitement; they call it, "living on the edge." Troy says:

Sure I was worried about catching a disease! If I got herpes or crabs or any kind of disease and brought it home to Sara, then it would be certain I'd be caught. That element of risk just added to the excitement. I like taking risks. I was asked by my therapist, "If there were no more women on this earth for you to pursue, how would you carry on with life?" I answered, "I would do something thrilling like jump out of an airplane or race fast cars." Even today, in my work several stories up at the end of a man-lift, the adrenaline rush of the fear is a real high for me. It's one of the few things I get high on these days, besides sex, which is still a big addiction.

Is Sex Addiction Real??? Sex and the Brain

In 2013 the Fifth Edition of the *Diagnostic and Statistical Manual of Mental Disorders*, the "bible" of psychiatric illness, was published. Despite a large amount of research and experience by clinicians, and despite efforts by professionals in the field, sex addiction was once again not included as a mental disorder. Surprisingly, some professionals outside the field still do not believe that this is "real." For example: As an associate editor of *Sexual Addiction and Compulsivity: The Journal of Treatment and Prevention*, I get to review articles submitted to the journal, along with other reviewers' comments. In early 2015 I was sent a manuscript which presented the evidence that sex addiction is a disease. Despite a reference list in the manuscript of over 60 publications in respected journals, the reviewer had two major criticisms, stating that there is no scientific evidence for sex addiction and there is no unifying definition or diagnostic criteria for sex addiction.

The publications cited in the manuscript included a 2014 study by Valerie Voon and colleagues[5] in which a group of subjects with compulsive sexual behavior (i.e., sex addicts) and another group of "healthy" individuals were shown sexually explicit videos, and also non-sexual videos. In the group of sex addicts (but not in the "healthy" subjects), functional MRI brain scans obtained when viewing pornography activated the same brain regions (dorsal anterior cingulate, ventral striatum and amygdala) as are activated in alcoholics and drug addicts in response to viewing their drug of choice. In other words, brains of individuals who are addicted to a drug or a behavior respond physiologically in the same way.

The reality that all addicts – whether to drugs or behaviors – respond similarly was recognized years ago by the American Society of Alcoholism, which changed its name first to the American Society of Alcoholism and Other Drug Dependencies, and some years later to the American Society of Addiction Medicine (ASAM). ASAM's revised short definition of addiction, published in 2011, said,

> Addiction is a primary, chronic disease of brain reward, motivation, memory and related circuitry. Dysfunction in these circuits leads to characteristic biological, psychological, social and spiritual manifestations. This is reflected in an individual pathologically pursuing reward and/or relief by substance use *and other behaviors.* [italics added][6]

The evidence for the reality of sex addiction includes neurobiological studies as well as the fact that addiction treatment appears to be the most effective treatment for this disorder, as clinicians in the field have recognized. It seems that some professionals resist accepting the concept that compulsive sexual behavior is a type of addiction no matter how compelling the evidence. Those of us who have seen the destructiveness of sex addiction as well as the rehabilitation of our mates via addiction treatment are more informed than some professionals.

Other Compulsive Sexual Behaviors in the Sex Addict

In the twenty-first century, people who are chemically dependent are increasingly likely to be using more than one drug compulsively. Alcoholics are usually also addicted to nicotine and caffeine, and many to marijuana and other drugs as well. Some cocaine addicts also use heroin to calm down after the high of cocaine, a combination known as a "speedball." Sex addicts, too, usually have combination of behaviors in their repertoire. Carnes has found that sex addicts have an average of three compulsive sexual behaviors.[7] Some are abusive of others and are criminal, whereas others are legal. Some of these behaviors are normal, and are considered problems only when they become compulsive and cause negative consequences. For example, nearly everyone fantasizes and masturbates, many view pornography on the internet, and a large proportion of marriages have at one time or another experienced an extramarital affair, not to mention the widespread use of internet pornography. Behaviors that can be sexually compulsive include fantasy, masturbation, pornography, extramarital affairs, telephone sex, prostitution, anonymous sex and one-night stands, voyeurism, exhibitionism, inappropriate touching of other people, inappropriate sexual comments and jokes, fetishism (the need to use objects in order to become sexually aroused), professional sexual exploitation (sexual relationships of professionals with patients, therapy clients, or parishioners), sex with animals, child molesting, and rape. Although some items on this list are frightening, most affair addicts are not involved with victimizing behaviors.

Among affair addicts, certain other compulsive sexual behaviors are common. Fantasizing forms a big part of the mental life of sex addicts who pursue other partners. Fantasy is often combined with masturbation, and many addicts also compulsively masturbate to pornography. These days, internet sex is usually a significant part of the sex addict's repertoire. He or she may not only view pornography online but often has sex partners on the internet as well as in real life. Here is the story of Hank, a 41-year-old systems analyst:

When I was a teenager I started downloading and masturbating to porn and chatting with women I met online. Eventually this advanced to nightly participation in video chats and mutual masturbation via webcam. A few years ago, when I got a smartphone, I took my show on the road, texting my regular online partners and seeking out new ones. Thanks to a couple of hookup apps, I was able to meet several women in my hometown. Suddenly, despite having no previous history of in-the-flesh adultery, I found myself meeting nearby women for casual sex. I sought help only when my wife found out about my behavior and threatened to leave me.

Looking back, I'm amazed by the immense amount of time and energy I put into cybersex. As a teen it interfered with my schoolwork. My homework either didn't get done at all or was done poorly because I was in a rush to get online. As an adult, it created emotional distance, frustration, and impatience in dating relationships and later with my wife and children, and it took up work time and office resources. Plus, waiting until my wife went to sleep and then staying on the computer until two or three in the morning left me, more often than not, tired, exhausted, depressed, and physically unwell. Our marital sex life became practically nonexistent, and I watched my wife blame herself, thinking she was no longer attractive. Despite all the craziness, I still think about getting back online nearly every day.

The Sex Addict's Beliefs and Addictive Cycle

Sex addicts have a set of core beliefs very similar to those of many partners. According to Patrick Carnes, author of *Out of the Shadows: Understanding Sexual Addiction*, these beliefs are: (1) I am basically a bad person; (2) No one would love me as I am; (3) My needs are never going to be met if I have to depend on others; and (4) Sex is my most important need.[8] Sex addicts typically come from a dysfunctional family. One (or sometimes both) parents may be alcoholic, workaholic, mentally ill, emotionally disturbed, physically ill, disabled, or abusive. No matter what the details, the child comes to feel unloved and unworthy. He or she feels isolated and different. He may take on the role of Family Hero, Scapegoat, Lost Child, or Mascot. He often learns to comfort himself sexually. If he or she is told that sex is wrong, as many children are, then he finds himself in the double bind of knowing that what is so comforting to him is no good. This further lowers his self-esteem. As he grows older he feels different, that he doesn't belong. He feels like an outsider. By the time he reaches adulthood he truly believes he is a worthless person whom no would want if they really knew what he was like inside.

This belief leads the addict into a repetitive addictive cycle. In an attempt to cover up his painful feelings, he begins fantasizing. After being preoccupied with thoughts of sex or pursuing a woman, he takes action. He may reach for his smartphone and visit his favorite sexually-oriented website or chat room. He may download "Ashley Madison" or another app in order to hook up in real-life with a married woman, or he may cruise a bar until he meets someone, connect with a woman at a party, or visit a girlfriend. At this stage, every gathering is a roomful of possibilities. Alan, for example, reports that whenever he drove to a workshop or meeting, his mind would be filled with fantasies about whom he might meet there and connect with.

During the fantasizing and acting out stages, the addict feels no pain. But immediately afterwards, the guilt and shame set in, and the addict feels at least as bad as before. His despair is relieved only by withdrawing into fantasy and preoccupation, and the cycle begins again. '

Sex Addiction is Progressive

Sex addiction, like alcohol and other drug addictions, is progressive. In the early stages, an alcoholic establishes rules for himself that allow him to believe he has control over his drinking. He may decide he will drink only after 5 P.M., or only beer but no whiskey, or only on weekends, or never alone. With time, however, he finds himself breaking all his rules. Sex addicts follow the same sequence.

An attractive older man who had multiple affairs told me:

I never thought of myself as one of those "one night stand" kind of guys. I prided myself on getting to know the people I slept with. I conned myself that the latest affair was really 'the one'. In reality, what I found was that once I had sex with a new woman, she lost that mysterious quality and I began to get restless.

I had a set of rules regarding my playing around. At first I had affairs only on business trips out of town. I had vowed not to have sex with anyone in my own city, certainly not with someone at work or in my own social circle. And I set myself a limit as to the age of the woman I would come on to. But I broke each of these rules as I began to take more and more risks. Soon being seen in public places with other women didn't seem so dangerous – I somehow thought that my wife would not find out. Then I began having girlfriends visit me at work even though my coworkers knew my wife. I finally realized how out of control I was when I made a play for the 18-year old daughter of one of my friends. After being confronted by my friend, I decided I needed help.

For other people, the spiral of progressive involvement continues until their lives are so unmanageable that they lose their marriages and jobs. That's what happened to Virgil, a 50-year old university professor:

For years I'd had casual affairs with students, but when my wife found out and threatened to leave, I promised her – and myself – that that part of my life was over. And for a while, it was. Nearly losing my wife made her more attractive, and we worked hard at revitalizing our marriage. But then I went to an out-of-state conference and ran into someone from one of my classes. I hadn't been able to get a room at the hotel, so I asked if I could stay with her. We played around a little that evening but did not have intercourse. I thought if I didn't actually go all the way it wouldn't count. It was crazy thinking – just like the old days of the "technical virgin" when I was in college.

Later that night, she got angry about my holding out and we ended up having sex. I got physically ill and told myself this was the last time I would cheat on my wife. I spent the next year "white knuckling" it. I was still using my radar, putting out signals like a bat and listening for what I got back. That's funny, thinking of myself as a bat. I remember dressing up as Count Dracula one Halloween in college. I liked that image – swooping down on defenseless women and making them my slaves as I drained their life force.

After several near-misses, I got involved with someone even though I had promised myself I wouldn't. It started innocently. Sybil, an attractive graduate student, stopped by my office a few times after class for some help with a problem. I began to look forward to these meetings and was concerned when she didn't arrive. Her perfume would fill my cluttered little cubbyhole and I would breathe it in for the rest of the day. I began to spend more time obsessing about her, even buying my wife that same perfume to maintain the connection at home and to decrease my risk of getting caught.

When Sybil called me about a missed assignment, I suggested we get together for coffee. I did this even though it broke one of my rules – not to be seen in public socializing with my students. In fact, my department head had warned me in a friendly way that it was common knowledge I had bedded several students and there was a big push on campus over the sexual harassment issue. Not only was I putting my marriage on the line, I was jeopardizing my career.

At the campus coffee shop where we met, I told her how bright she was and how much she added to my class. Somehow, I managed to bring the conversation around to her personal life. She'd been divorced about a year earlier from a man she said she'd outgrown. I told her that my own marriage was stagnant and that my wife was so busy with her own career she didn't have time for me. I was looking for someone to make me the center of her life. I wanted to recapture the high of first love.

She seemed interested and I felt I'd been given a new lease on life. I couldn't wait for my wife to leave in the morning so I could phone Sybil. Sometimes we'd talk for an hour. One morning I lost track of the time and missed my ten o'clock lecture. I was conning myself that this relationship was different from the others. After all, we hadn't even held hands. Maybe I was really in love.

As we began to spend more time together I became more obsessed about making love with her. I arranged to go over to her apartment one Saturday afternoon when her children were with her ex-husband. I was like a nervous kid getting ready for his first date. I changed my shirt three times and doused myself with expensive cologne. I drove around the block twice and smoked a joint in the car.

When I finally got the courage to knock on her door, she opened it and we fell into each other's arms. I found myself being pulled into a whirlwind that eventually cost me my bid for tenure, my marriage, and my children. I knew almost from the start I couldn't continue the relationship with Sybil. She began to make more and more demands on my time and her own course work suffered. She assumed she wouldn't have to do any more work for her class with me. When I suggested that I had to pull back from my involvement, she threatened to tell my wife and my department head. She eventually told a classmate who told my boss. It was at that point I realized my life was unmanageable.

The price that sex addicts pay for their sexual activities is guilt and shame. Unlike a sociopath, who feels no remorse for his actions, addicts are at times aware of their dishonesty, ashamed of their lies, and feel guilty for the pain they are causing their spouse or partner. Although they are unwilling or unable to stop the behavior, they judge themselves at least as harshly as others do. In their guilt and shame, they promise themselves to do things differently next time, and then feel twice as bad when they can't keep their promises.

Shortly after Troy, the recovering cocaine addict, was divorced by his wife, he found Lisa, a new girlfriend to whom he felt very close. Nevertheless, he soon found himself sexually attracted to a nineteen-year-old girl and became involved with her.

My life is again unmanageable. I'm living in dishonesty and fear of getting caught. I tell one I'm somewhere else when I'm with the other, I tell the other I'm somewhere else when I'm with the first. There's fear and dishonesty in both relationships. I love Lisa and I don't like lying to her; she deserves bet-ter than that.

Despite his guilt feelings, Troy is still seeing both women.

As mentioned in earlier chapters, both men and women can become addicted to sexual behaviors. Sex addicts of both genders have many similarities, but there are also some differences in their activities and preferences, and the consequences in their lives.

The Male Sex Addict

When Bruce was six years old, his mother became ill and died, and his father began drinking heavily. Bruce and his older sister were pretty much left to themselves. Here is Bruce's story:

In the alcoholic family, I was the Lost Child. I spent a lot of time by myself. I didn't know how to make friends. I was angry almost all the time. At night, when Dad drove me home, he would stop at a bar and leave me wait-ing in the truck. I'd sit in it until he got through drinking, which might be two or three hours. I spent a lot of time sitting and waiting. Finally, when I was eight or nine, I decided to walk home instead of waiting. It was scary walking home in the dark. That's when I began making plans to get away from Dad.

By age fifteen I had a job and was driving a car. I was very lonely, espe-cially on Saturday nights. The filling station where I worked was in clear view of the baseball stadium and the lights and the crowd. I'd be over there pumping gas and listening to the crowd and wishing I could have been at the stadium with some friends.

Dad got a DWI [driving while intoxicated] citation nearly every month and his name was often on the front page of the newspaper. He was the town drunk. I was embarrassed and ashamed, but I kind of repressed it. I learned not to feel. My friends didn't say anything to me – nothing like, "Your Dad's name was in the paper again," or anything like that.

After college I became a hospital social worker. At a church dinner I met my wife, who was friendly and nice. Barbara came from a stable family, and her folks were really good to me. Her home was my home, and I was there all the time. We got married and had a couple of kids. I didn't realize how difficult it was for a mother with two small children. I had a very responsible job at the hospital, helping a lot of people, and I was in my glory, getting all the strokes I'd never had. Meanwhile, she was at home with two kids, getting more and more angry. The angrier she got, the more I withdrew. I was unhappy with my marriage, but because I had my job and I was in my glory, I was able to make it.

After several years I realized I really wanted to be a minister, so I went to seminary. To work my way through, I got a job as a night watchman. I spent all day at the seminary, stopped by home for dinner, and then I'd be out until 2 A.M. walking the floors. I had no fellowship with the other seminarians; after class they'd meet at one of the local pubs and drink some beer, but I had to go to work. My life was strictly studying and working. I was an absentee father. Barbara had to handle everything at home, and she became angrier and angrier.

I was so happy to graduate from seminary! When I got to my first congregation, I didn't realize there were so many needy women; but there they were, both married and single. That's where I began my affairs. The church was a ready-made place because people were allowed to go there without suspicion. There were a lot of women there.

One day a woman came in for marriage counseling. I tried to get her husband to come but he refused. She kept coming back and one day when she cried, I hugged her, and that was my undoing. That was what she had wanted all along. Every woman I was involved with told me later on she'd planned what was going to happen. So they sensed something in me, a loneliness. Their vibes picked up whatever was going on for me. I wasn't enough in touch with myself to know that I was putting out those signals, but evidently I was.

After that there were others. With each one, when she first came in I was serious about wanting to help her. When I saw it wasn't going to work, the husband wasn't interested in counseling, I think I just gave up. The women didn't come in with counseling in mind. I'd realize that when I did the holding and they responded. I knew it was wrong. I don't know what was happening in terms of my own values and morals, but they took a backseat. My thinking went out the window and my emotions took over. When one woman would come in and we'd get something going, I would stay with her until something would happen, and she'd decide or we'd mutually decide to stop seeing each other. We'd have sex right on the floor in my office. I think Barbara suspected, but she never said anything. She just wanted me home more.

I was very busy, very involved in community activities as well as the church, but I would get this longing. It would come over me almost like a hunger, and I'd call someone and ask, "Can you come over?" And they were always obliging. They were as codependent as me, and as lonely. I kept that up for ten years, until the woman I was then having an affair with told her best friend, who told her husband, who told the woman's husband who was on the church council.

I had to resign. After I left my job there was a hearing, and the result was that the church administrative body took my ordination from me. I can never go back into the ministry again. So all those years that I worked nights, all that effort in school, all that has been taken away from me. It's down the drain.

After that I went back to the hospital job. It was bad for me, because I met a lot of needy women there too, and although I managed to stay straight for a year, soon I was getting involved with women again. That's when I realized it was more than just loneliness. I met a woman — if I was ever in love with anyone, it was with her. And while I was going with her, I went out on her with someone else. This woman was at my beck and call, but I couldn't stay faithful to her. I realized that I just couldn't get enough love, it was like an addiction. The more people who loved me and stroked me, the more I wanted. It wasn't that I was oversexed; many times we'd just talk and hold each other. With all those women, we had a lot to talk about. We'd spend all evening talking, and would end up by celebrating with sex. My relationship with every one of them was a very intimate one. They were very interested in what I was doing and what I had to say, so I felt important.

I am still tempted by the many lonely women I meet professionally, but I am determined to remain faithful to Barbara. She has told me if I have another affair she will leave me. I just don't want to hurt her and the children any more. And I feel too much guilt for what I've done in the past. During those years, although I enjoyed the relationships with the other women, I went through inner turmoil and guilt. I knew what I was doing was wrong. Had I not been in the church it would still have been wrong, but in my position as a pastor, I can't think of anything worse than what I did. I was crazy to do that. I know the church will always remember the years I was there and how I left. Even though in every other area I was a straight-forward, honest person, the black mark against me is what they remember.

Some people might say that Bruce was just a lonely guy in an unfulfilling marriage who was getting comfort where he could find it. What makes him different from countless other men who have affairs? Despite the guilt Bruce felt and the risk to his job and marriage, he continued to have affairs with his parishioners until inevitably he did lose his job and, even worse, was kicked out of the ministry. Bruce was also guilty of professional sexual misconduct – he abused his position of trust and responsibility and took advantage of those in his care.[9] Bruce's life was unmanageable because of his sexual behavior.

Another example will illustrate this point. In a periodic police round-up, a prominent faculty member of a university community was arrested for soliciting a prostitute. His name was on the front page of the newspaper, causing great embarrassment to him and his family. One month later the man was again arrested in the same neighborhood for soliciting a prostitute. He then resigned his university job and moved away. Many men have sex with prostitutes, so his first arrest might be considered as bad luck – he happened to be in the wrong place at the wrong time. But the second arrest strongly suggests that he could not control his compulsive behavior. He was unable to desist finding a hooker even though an outsider could see it was clearly against his best interests. Despite the arrest, the pain to his family, and the risk of losing his job, he returned to the same location only to be arrested again. This is addictive behavior.

Bruce's story contains many of the typical elements of the sex addict's background. Bruce grew up in a dysfunctional family – his father was alcoholic and his mother was absent for most of his youth. In his family of origin, feelings were covered up and were not discussed; problems were not confronted. Bruce felt lonely and isolated. He compensated for his feelings of worthlessness by working very hard and suppressing his feelings. In his marriage, he continued the pattern of avoiding problems rather than dealing with them. When his wife became angry, Bruce withdrew further into his work.

In his ministerial work, Bruce found a ready-made way of being valued and accepted – sexual involvement with the many needy women who came to him for help. It is to Bruce's credit that he recognized that although the women came to him, *he* was sending out signals that encouraged them to pursue a personal relationship with him. Bruce became addicted to the affection and validation he received from the women, and as his addiction progressed he found himself unable to be faithful even to the girlfriend he thought he loved. That was the event that caused him to seek help.

Bruce's guilt over his many affairs has so paralyzed him that he feels he will never be able to leave his wife – he is hoping she will make the decision to leave.

She'll have to be the one to kick me out; I won't leave. I'm hoping she'll meet some charming man at work who's divorced and he'll say, "Let's you and I try to make it," and she'll come home and say, "Well, I've found someone else. Good-bye."

Because his wife has buried her head in the sand for so long, it is unlikely she will leave him. Bruce was able to stop his sexual acting out by shutting down his emotions and becoming chronically depressed, a poor solution to his problems.

Bruce's story is not uncommon. Members of the clergy are at high risk for extramarital affairs. In *Avoiding the Scarlet Letter*, Dr. Louis McBurney lists several reasons for this:

Men in ministry are especially vulnerable to sexual temptation because they work in what is often a female subculture, the church. Simply their presence on the job exposes them to potential romantic or sexual relationships.

Another reason for the increased vulnerability is the similarity between spirituality and sexuality. In both, we lower personal barriers, encourage intimacy, become open and vulnerable, and experience profoundly moving emotions. Some individuals compare their deepest spiritual moments to sexual climax. Both provide an intense response, a loss of ego boundaries, a sense of oneness with those who share the experience.

Our personality also makes us more vulnerable. As sensitive, caring, giving persons, we resemble a warm living room for the lonely and dependent. Thousands of people, single and married alike, seek closeness. Most married women name as their primary marital problem their husband's insensitivity to their emotional needs. It makes them desperate for a companion who will talk with them and listen.

Enter the minister, the model husband. As long as they don't consult our wives, women may see us as ideal – strong and capable, yet gentle, warm, and loving. The church even encourages us to be that sensitive person to everyone in need, which includes many lonely women, whose activity in church masks a hunger for attention and affection. Both our personal warmth and our professional calling put us in jeopardy. . . . .

It's also critical that we know our particular vulnerability. Only I am aware of my individual sexual thoughts and drives.

I may have frustrations with marital sex or doubts about my potency. I may find certain female physical characteristics particularly tempting. Midlife transition may raise questions about what I've been missing or how long I can continue to function successfully. Any of these issues may contribute to my vulnerability in an affair[10]

In other words, the clergy is a profession where there is often the combination of a need to help and to be needed, coupled with limitless opportunities. The need may arise out of childhood woundedness and deprivation. This results in *narcissistic entitlement* - the expectation that one deserves special treatment and rewards for his or her actions. In his professional setting such a clergy person may exploit parishioners who expect warmth, kindness, and connection. This doesn't mean that a person would choose the ministry in order to have opportunities for sexual contact. On the contrary – most young people become ministers, physicians, or counselors out of a sincere desire to help people. But for the budding sex addict who finds himself in the ministry, the opportunities are plentiful for carrying out his compulsive behavior. The same is true for the physician, psychiatrist, counselor, or other members of the helping professions.

Sex addiction does not affect only professionals. The approximately six percent of Americans who are sexually addicted come from all areas of society. Certain careers may appear to be overrepresented among men who have affairs because provide endless opportunities for meeting women. One of these is the police, as Ted's story illustrates:

Ted was the oldest of three children. In his childhood he witnessed his alcoholic father beating up his mother. Ted was the responsible child at home, cooking and cleaning for his younger siblings. Even in adulthood, his sisters seek him out when they have family problems. Ted knew his father was cheating on his mother, and soon began to imitate him. In high school he went steady with six girls at the same time, until they all ended up at the same party, compared notes, and gave him back his rings. Ted recalled,

I was going steady with all of them, and I was juggling schedules and making excuses and lying about where I was going and what I was doing.

Ted barely got through high school, and was frequently in trouble with the law for fighting, siphoning gas, and other minor offenses. A stint in the military straightened him out, and upon his discharge he became a policeman. He married a shy, pretty girl, who soon bore him a son. Then he was assigned a night shift.

I got teamed up with some other cops who were single and I started thinking like them. Whenever they wanted to go and do something, they'd say, "Oh, come on, Ted, you can't let your wife run your life for you." I let myself be persuaded to go to bed with a girl at a party. After that first time, it was like I just fell back into my old routine in high school. . . . I knew what I was doing was wrong. Today, whenever I get a chance to talk to a guy who's just gotten married, I tell him, "Don't do it." It's like taking dope. You take your first hit and like it, it gives you a high, and then you're hooked. You'll never be able to quit, no matter what you try to do.

Ted began having one casual sexual encounter after another, always being careful not to get involved emotionally. He became such an expert on cheating that once, when he had to give a lecture on a topic of his choice in a class on public speaking, he spoke on "How to Cheat on your Wife and Get Away with It." After the class, several men came up to talk with him to ask him for specific tips.

The first crisis in Ted's marriage came when his wife found lipstick and makeup on his clothes and confronted him. They separated, but soon they reconciled. He continued to have casual affairs, but when his wife found out about the latest, Jan, Ted decided he was really in love with Jan. He felt so torn between the two women, so full of guilt, that he considered suicide. Eventually he leveled with his wife and broke up with the girlfriend. Currently he is trying to become more involved with his wife and children and thus avoiding temptation. However, he doesn't give himself much hope of staying straight:

You could say I'm addicted. Sometimes when I'm driving home I get to feeling desperate, like I'm going to explode, if I don't call Jan. I know I have to get home and be around my wife and have her touch me and put her arms around me so that I don't call Jan. You know, guys get the bad rap for this, but there are also a lot of women who know how to innocently put across the message that they're available, and the guy who's streetwise knows how to pick up on them. Guys like me, we're streetwise. I grew up with it, it was my basic training. And when I have my low periods I say, "What the hell, I guess I'll pick up on the messages that this girl or that one puts out. Why don't I give her a call?"

You know, we're nice guys, we're easy to get along with. And we're probably the world's greatest liars. We're probably the hardest on ourselves, being the liars that we are. If I could have the ideal situation I would like people to like me just for me. I would like to be able to talk to women without getting those messages. But then I wonder sometimes if I'm not sending them without knowing it. I just want people to like me. I'd like to tell them I'm married, and be treated as a married person, to clean up those signals I'm sending. But it doesn't work that way. I go to a party; there's always someone who has to hang on just a little longer than necessary.

When it comes right down to the sexual act, I've never believed the act was the high. I think it's everything that goes with it. In fact, sometimes the sexual part of it can be very disappointing. Sometimes it's been so disappointing that I've asked myself, Why? Why did I do this? I didn't want to. You make these little promises to yourself like, I'd never mess with a friend's wife. But if a friend's wife comes on to me like any other woman, then I rationalize by saying, "Hell, if I don't do it, someone else will."

Ted is uncertain about his future with his wife. He loves her, he considers her his best friend, and he feels guilty about the pain he has caused her. In frustration he exclaims, "I wish there was a pill to make me stop thinking and feeling this way!" Ted used to drink heavily, but has hardly touched a drop of alcohol in fifteen years. He compares his sexual addiction with alcoholism:

In time maybe I'll come around. It's like the alcoholic – he never says he's cured or that he's not an alcoholic. He may be dry and he's trying. I'm at that point now sexually; I'm dry and I'm trying, but. . . I don't know.

I think the reason I'm still with Theresa is that I would never tell myself I don't love her. I could never walk away. When the guilt caught up with me, when I realized how much I was hurting her, that's when I got into crying spells and thought of suicide. Theresa's been through some real tough times. She stuck it out with me through thick and thin. And I kept trying to lay a lot of blame on her. So now I'm trying to concentrate on Theresa and the family.

Ted describes Theresa in martyr-like terms, hoping this picture of her will help him stay away from other women. But he realizes it is unlikely he will succeed. That's because Ted is depending on his willpower to accomplish this. What has helped sex addicts like Ted recover in the long run is to obtain sex addiction counseling and to get seriously involved in a Twelve-Step program for sex addicts. Chapter Six, "The Elements of Recovery," introduces the reader to the Twelve Steps and describes how the program works. The same program is the most effective recovery tool for alcoholics, sex addicts, other types of addicts, and their partners.

Bruce, the former minister, is attempting to steer clear of affairs primarily because of guilt over his past behavior. Ted, on the other hand, has a loving wife who doesn't believe him when he says he's a sex addict, thinks his affairs are always the other woman's fault, and keeps trying in every way to make him stay at home. Ted's pain comes from his recognition that his control over his behavior is very tenuous. Neither man is an abuser of alcohol or other drugs; both came from dysfunctional, alcoholic families and have chosen affairs as the means of dealing with the pain and the isolation of their youth.

As an aside, although both Bruce and Ted's fathers were alcoholic, many dysfunctional family systems don't necessarily revolve around alcohol. Some, for example, revolve around the meaning of money, working, and the chase of success. You can read more about this in Debra Kaplan's 2013 book, *For Love and Money: Exploring Sexual & Financial Betrayal in Relationships.*

The Female Sex Addict

Like alcoholism eighty years ago, sex addiction is often presumed to be a man's problem. Sex addiction in women is judged more harshly than it is in men. A man who has multiple affairs is called a "Don Juan," "ladies' man," or "skirt-chaser." A woman who has many sexual partners is likely to be called a "whore" or "slut." Clinicians working with women sex addicts have observed that they experience more shame than do men sex addicts, and women sex addicts are considered more shameful. Hard data about the prevalence of sex addiction in women are difficult to come by, but we do know that about one-third of the members of Sex and Love Addicts Anonymous (SLAA) a Twelve-Step recovery programs for sex addiction are female. It's likely that sex addiction is almost as common in women as in men, although the forms it takes differs in men and women. Sexually addicted women are likely to seek fantasy, romance, and serial relationships. In a survey published in 2011, of 261 self-identified female sex and love addicts, 64% identified as a love and relationship addict, whereas only 34% considered themselves to be sex addicts.[11]

In their information statement on, "Women and Sex Addiction", the Society for the Advancement of Sexual Health (SASH) lists the following behaviors suggestive of sex addiction in women:[12]

1. Compulsion, or unsuccessful attempts to control a sexual behavior:

   - Changing relationships to control sexual fantasy and/or activities.
   - Swearing off relationships, only to give in to the next "right" lover"
   - Breaking promises to self or others to stop abusive fantasy or sexual behaviors
   - Switching to caretaking others, workaholism, overeating, or romance novels to take the place of a sexual relationship

2. Continued behavior despite negative consequences:

   - Unplanned pregnancies, abortions, sexually transmitted diseases, or violence
   - Terror or shame resulting from sexual activities
   - Decreased productivity at work due to sexual behavior with self or others
   - Relationship problems resulting from extramarital affairs or excessive time spent on sex-related activities
   - Depression related to inability to change sexual patterns or their consequences
   - Substance abuse or eating disorders to numb shame and other negative feelings related to sexual activities

3. Obsessive thoughts in planning or obtaining sex:

   - neglecting family, relationship, or career because of time spent preoccupied with sex or sexual partners

Addictive sexual behavior patterns in women may include:

   - Excessive flirting, dancing, or personal grooming to be seductive

- Wearing provocative clothing whenever possible
- Changing one's appearance via excessive dieting, excessive exercise, and/or reconstructive surgery to be seductive
- Exposing oneself in a window or car
- Making sexual advances to younger siblings, clients, or others in subordinate power position
- Seeking sexual partners in high-risk locations
- Multiple extramarital affairs
- Disregard of appropriate sexual boundaries, for example, considering a married man, one's boss, or one's personal physician as appropriate objects of romantic involvement
- Trading sex for drugs, help, affection, money, social access, or power
- Having sex with someone they just met at a party, bar, or on the Internet (forms of anonymous sex)
- Compulsive masturbation
- Exchanging sex for pain or pain for sex

Relationship symptoms typically reported by female sex addicts include the following:[13]

- a history of short, failed relationships where sex is the primary bond
- a pattern of returning to or remaining with partners who are abusive or emotionally unavailable
- masturbating compulsively to romantic fantasies of past or potential partners, romantic books, fictional characters, television shows, and movies
- a pattern of inappropriate sexual relationships—with married men, bosses, or subordinates
- consistently having sex as a way to feel wanted, loved, and validated
- taking money or encouraging gift-giving in exchange for sex but not viewing this as prostitution

- giving money to unethical massage therapists and physical trainers in exchange for sex, but not viewing this as hiring prostitutes
- excessively and consistently abusing food, exercise, and spending to "feel better" when lonely or not in a relationship
- secretly acting out fetish behaviors with casual or anonymous partners while in a primary relationship
- a pattern of seeking emotional validation through online or in-person encounters (new relationships) while already in a primary relationship

Like men, many women sex addicts view pornography on the internet, although women often prefer chat rooms and other ways to actually interact with men. The internet is a powerful medium for fueling fantasy-based interactions, and for feeding the romance addiction to which women are particularly susceptible. This is undoubtedly why, as my research has shown, women cybersex addicts (those whose sex addiction involves the internet) are significantly more likely than are men to seek real-life meetings with their online sex partners.[14] Other women become involved in intense fantasy romantic relationships online, which often spill over into real life. Broken marriages and pain for their husbands and children can result. Here is the story of 35-year old Janice, a public relations manager:

I spend about 20 hours a week on Facebook, in chat rooms, and using smartphone apps to meet men. Time that I used to spend with my husband and kids, I now use to meet men online and chat with them, sending IMs, texting, sexting, and fantasizing that they're the perfect guy for me. Eventually we arrange to meet in person, usually at a motel or some other place where we can have sex. By then of course I'm already attached emotionally, and that scares the men off. They just want sex. I can't seem to develop a meaningful relationship with any of them. Basically we just have sex a few times, and then it's over. None of the relationships have lasted more than a month.

Meanwhile I'm completely unavailable emotionally to my husband, and I've even withdrawn from my kids. It feels like I've abandoned my family, but I can't stop what I'm doing. I keep imagining that someday one of these men will really love me. . . I love the sex, of course, but what I really crave is the attention.[15]

Many women sex addicts were sexually abused in childhood. They learn that sex is the way to get power and love from men. A woman who had multiple affairs during both her marriages related:

With the affairs, by the time we got down to the sex part, I just wanted to get it over with. I was never orgasmic with any of the other people I was looking to get even, to get revenge. It was a real power thing to be seductive. When I was a teenager, my girlfriends would say you can't have sex unless you're in love, that it has to be special. But the men would talk about getting it however they could, and they'd say whatever it took to get sex. I used to say to myself, I can be like any man. If a man can do that, so can I.

Recalling the women she met during her treatment, a woman who had affairs in her first marriage and fantasized a lot in her second marriage commented:

Women addicts seem to be more focused on the attention, the feedback, not so much the sex. In fact, the orgasm seemed to be optional for most of the women, unless they were into masturbation. It seemed to be the power of getting the man, getting the attention, the chase, and the capture.

Some Addicts Are Reluctant to Marry

Sex addicts have difficulty integrating their sexual wants into the larger world of human relationships. Sex addiction is basically an intimacy disorder; sex addicts have difficulty trusting another person enough to become vulnerable and reveal their true selves. Sexual activity is not perceived as part of a committed relationship, but rather as an end in itself. Not surprisingly, monogamy – and the intimacy it implies – is a fearful prospect.

Some sex addicts spend their lives jumping from relationship to relationship, fleeing when they feel too crowded by their partner's demands. In middle age or even older, these playboys are still photographed squiring some attractive new woman who changes every few months or years. They never "settle down." Other sex addicts agree to marriage only because their partner gives them an ultimatum after waiting for what seems like forever. They may remember their wedding as something they knew at the time was a big mistake.

Ted, the policeman who married at nineteen, remembers:

I don't even know how we ended up married. I know I asked her, and then I went overseas as a soldier. When I came back, all the arrangements had been made. I thought, wait a minute! Things are going too fast! I know I asked her to marry me, but I wasn't quite ready yet. In fact, on the morning of our wedding I couldn't get out of bed. I couldn't wake up psychologically. But I went through with it.

Frank, a married wealthy businessman with a younger mistress, recalls:

My wedding was a terrible experience. I didn't want to marry her. I probably did it because the option of not having her was the immediate hurt that I could define; the other seemed too far away.

For Frank, however, marriage was not the end of other relationships. Troy, the recovering cocaine addict, says:

Tina and I lived together for ten solid years. During that whole time there were other women in my life. She finally pressured me into getting married. I'd asked her what she wanted for Christmas and she said a ring. So I got her the ring. I don't know why I married her. I remember all the way to the wedding my dad was saying, "Okay, this is your last chance. You don't have to go up there." And I remember the feeling in my gut, even though I was totally wrecked. I'd been doing tons of cocaine the night before and all that day, and drinking. I remember my gut saying, don't do it. And I said to myself, if it doesn't work, I can always get a divorce.

John, an insurance salesman who had multiple affairs, went through two weddings reluctantly. Recalling the first one, when he was 24, he says:

I tried everything I knew to get Lucille to call off the wedding. I became morose and deliberately picked arguments with her. I "forgot" to make reservations I had agreed to make. I objected to whatever arrangements she suggested. I told her I didn't want my parents at the wedding. I wanted her to take the responsibility of canceling the wedding. I repeated this pattern in my marriage. It was important to me not to be the one to end the marriage, to fail. Lucille finally kicked me out after catching me in bed with another woman in our house.

I didn't want to get married the second time either. Melissa and I had been living together for a few months, under ideal circumstances. Her kids were living with her ex, and we could just enjoy each other. I couldn't make up my mind to make a commitment to Melissa. Finally she said, "If you can't decide when there's just the two of us, how will you ever know once the kids are back with us?" She knew it would be even harder for me with the stresses of parenthood. She said, "If you can't decide by the end of this year, that will be the end of our relationship." I knew she meant it, and I couldn't stand the thought of losing her. So I agreed to get married. But I remember standing up there at the wedding, as the minister was reading the service, and thinking, my God, I don't know how this is going to work. But then I comforted myself with the thought that even it it lasts only a year, at least she'll know I tried.

Some Addicts No Longer Want or are Unable to Have Sex with a Live Partner

You are undoubtedly aware that the spectrum of eating disorders, which are a type of behavior addiction, runs the gamut from compulsive overeating to *anorexia*. Anorexics are obsessed with being thin and severely restrict their consumption of food. Similarly, the spectrum of sex addiction ranges from compulsive sexual activities –such

as compulsive masturbation, pornography viewing, and multiple partners – to *sexual anorexia*, which has been defined by Patrick Carnes
as "an obsessive state in which the physical, mental, and emotional
task of avoiding sex dominates one's life.[16] Anorexic sex addicts often
have an avoidant attachment style, meaning that underlying their
addiction is a fear of intimacy. This style of attachment and therefore
avoidance of intimacy may have its roots as far back as childhood. It
may be due to experiences of abandonment by their caregivers, which
may have led them early on to conclude that the safest way to protect
themselves from further pain was to avoid emotional closeness with
others. When it comes to sexual expression, some avoid any sexual
activity. Others may have never learned how to be sexual with a live
partner and instead find an outlet to be sexual and avoidant of personal contact with masturbation to pornography.

Two unexpected but increasingly common consequences of
online pornography addiction are a loss of interest in partner sex and
actual sexual dysfunction in otherwise healthy young men. In Japan,
a study published in 2010 reported that among teens aged 16-19,
36.1% had no interest in having sex with a live person, or else actually
an aversion to doing so. The same was true of young men aged 20-24,
of whom 21% were uninterested in partner sex.[17] These rates were
significantly higher than a similar survey conducted 2 years earlier.
It is believed that the reason is that they prefer technology-assisted
sex which they consider to be cleaner, quicker, and less complicated.

Other men who are extensive users of internet porn report that
when having sex with a live partner they have delayed ejaculation
or even that they have erectile dysfunction (ED) and can no longer reach orgasm other than via masturbation.[18] Mark, 26 years old,
described this phenomenon:

*My long-term girlfriend and I are both graduate students, but at separate
universities. We typically spend weekends together. Our sex life was great
until about a year ago, and I'm not sure what happened. I used to look*

forward to her visits because I knew the first thing we would do was hop in bed and make love. But lately I struggle to reach orgasm when I'm with her. What I can't understand is why I'm ready, willing, and able when I log onto my favorite porn sites, but I can't function when I've got the real thing right there in front of me. My girlfriend is incredibly sexy, and I'm not at all bored with her. I just can't perform with her the way I'm supposed to.[19]

A new book called *Your Brain on Porn*, and a website with the same name, advises such men on how to reverse the situation: Basically, they need to stop masturbating to porn, thereby giving their brain a chance to "reboot." Their sexual function will likely gradually return.[20]

The Role of Other Addictions

As we have seen, alcoholism plays a prominent role in the families of origin of many persons who have multiple affairs. In adulthood, alcohol is often an important factor in the lives of sex addicts. Alcohol (and other drug addictions) and sex addiction tend to reinforce each other. Approximately 60 percent of sex addicts in an inpatient sex addiction treatment program are also addicted to alcohol. Approximately 70 percent of cocaine addicts in an outpatient treatment program were also addicted to sex.[21] Other addictions that may coexist with sex addiction are food and money. One sex addiction therapist reported to me that most of the male clients in her therapy group have gained weight because their new coping mechanism became food.

Compared with non-sex addicts, sex addicts have an increased likelihood of concurrent chemical dependency and other addictions, and also are likely to substitute one addictive behavior for another if the first is no longer available. Patrick Carnes has noted that "one of the greatest unacknowledged contributors to recidivism [relapse] in alcoholism is the failure of treatment programs to treat multiple addictions." Carnes has written about these various combinations, which he terms "addiction interaction disorder."[22] It is now widely understood in chemical dependency treatment programs that sobriety from drug addiction is difficult to maintain until all addictions are treated, and most such programs assess for food, sex, and gambling addictions as part of their intake process.

An example of the interaction of multiple addictions was seen in the case of a young lawyer who, after six years of sobriety from alcohol, was found by a colleague drunk in his house after he failed to show up to work one day. After going through treatment again for the alcoholism he said:

The real problem isn't alcohol – it's my sex addiction. I felt so bad about what I was doing sexually that I started drinking again to feel better. If I could get that part of my life straightened out, I know I'd have no trouble staying away from alcohol.

When one addiction becomes very problematic in one's life, it is easier to switch to another than to learn non-addictive ways of dealing with life's problems. It is much more difficult to make a fundamental change in one's coping strategies than it is to find a new way to avoid facing reality. Thus, at an Al-Anon meeting, a young woman tearfully described how her husband had begun pursuing young women after he came out of a treatment program for alcoholism. He had no difficulty finding needy women at his A.A. meetings. Infidelity had not been a problem during his drinking days. Now sober from alcohol, he had switched addictions from a mood-altering chemical to a mood-altering experience.

Not all sex addicts have abused alcohol or other drugs. In Alan's family, for example, there is no history of alcoholism. Nor have chemicals ever had much appeal for him. "Women were always my drug of choice," he says. Nevertheless, in recovery from sex addiction he recognized that alcohol lowers his resistance to interacting with women. In order to remain monogamous, he realizes he needs to have his brain functioning at full capacity when in potentially enticing situations, so he has decided to avoid alcohol altogether when at parties.

For other sex addicts, workaholism is the addiction that coexists with affairs. Both Frank, the wealthy businessman, and Bruce, the former minister, were non-drinking workaholics. Both are now working harder than ever and claim that this relieves their obsession with women. This solution, however, is only temporary. Should they experience problems on the job, each of them is at risk for turning once again to their drug of choice – other women.

The addiction interaction disorder also speaks to money and work, not just alcohol, food and drugs. In her book, *For Love and Money: Exploring Sexual & Financial Betrayal in Relationships*, Debra Kaplan delves into the elements of sex, money and power, yet an additional facet of multiple addictions. Kaplan writes, "Money for sex and sex for power can play out across many relationships, cultures, and demographics. There is no one socioeconomic stratum – be it profession, personality type, gender, ethnicity, sexual orientation, age, education level, or any other identity – that has cornered the market on exploitation. The battle for power and control by way of sex and money is universal. Sexual compulsivity at its core is a disease of the self-absorbed, and so is exploitation. Thus these two phenomena often travel hand-in-hand."[23]

In summary, addiction to affairs and/or online pornography can be thought of as similar to addiction to alcohol. Fantasy is the first drink to the sex addict. The endless ruminating about the other woman or man, the pursuit, the risk taking – all of these are important elements of the addictive mood-altering experience. To many sex addicts, these elements are at least as important as the sex act itself.

Sex addicts often realize they have a problem. They may be reluctant to get married because they anticipate that their sexual options may be limited. They are aware of society's moral values but are unable to square them with their own needs, impulses, and desires. Their own moral values become fuzzy and compromised as they attempt to justify their behavior to themselves. Their confusion and conflict result in guilt and shame, but the only way they know how to cope with these feelings is to do more of the same. They are thus caught in a vicious circle. Eventually, if their life becomes sufficiently unmanageable, they may seek help.

Sex addicts do not live in a vacuum. As we have seen, they are adept at finding a needy person who wants to care for them and who is often willing to join them in their addiction. The couple's life together becomes a vicious circle which is described in the next chapter.

CHAPTER FIVE

The Roller Coaster Ride of Living with Sex Addiction

In her book, *Stranger in Two Worlds,* schoolmistress Jean Harris writes about the collection of gold cuff links, gold watches, gold tie pins, and needle-pointed vests and slippers that her boyfriend, noted cardiologist Herman Tarnower told her were gifts from "grateful patients." It did not occur to her that "grateful patient" was a euphemism for the latest woman in is life. Some of those women pursued Tarnower by letters, phone calls, or in person even when he was on vacation with Jean in another continent. (These days, of course, texts and emails would also have piled up as well!) Even when he kept disappearing from their hotel room at the romantic getaway on some flimsy excuse, "I didn't suspect a thing because I didn't want to and I didn't want others to."[1] Like many women whose partners are cheaters, Jean Harris ignored the evidence of Tarnower's involvement with other women because she preferred not to know. Moreover, because they were not married, she felt she had few rights in the relationship and therefore could not confront her lover when she did find blatant evidence that he had other women in his life. Her repeatedly suppressed feelings eventually led to the showdown with a gun that killed Tarnower and landed Harris in prison for many years.

In the relationship between Harris and Tarnower there were elements that are typical of the interaction between a sex addict and his partner. He often treats her with disrespect and she responds with denial and excuses. She explains away the bad times and cherishes the good. She hangs on to his loving words and gestures, believing they represent the real person, and she makes excuses for his hurtful actions. Her core belief that she is an unworthy person prevents her from realizing she deserves better treatment. Although she does not realize it, his mood swings are what keep her hooked in the relationship; she is attracted to excitement and unpredictability. There is always hope, she believes, that *this time* he will show her some real evidence of his love.

A pursuit-withdrawal cycle is also an element of the relationship. When she attempts to win him over with love, attention, and gifts, he withdraws. But should she finally get fed up with his uncaring behavior and talk of leaving him – or worse yet, actually walk out – then he will redouble his efforts to win her back. He will be as charming, tender, and loving as when they first were dating, and will promise to make whatever changes she desires. But once she is safely back in the fold, however, the cycle will begin again.

Because of the partner's fear of abandonment, she does not dare to tell her mate how she really feels about his behavior. Instead, if she does not completely deny to herself that there are problems, she is likely to develop resentment and anger, which she keeps buried inside. Afraid of confronting her mate, she lives in fear of disaster striking in the form of another woman. In an effort to prevent him from straying, she may give in to his sexual demands, no matter how uncomfortable they may be for her, and eventually she may begin to wonder whether she herself is a sex addict.

Partners the Sex Addict Chooses

Just as a needy person somehow seems to find an addict to marry, so the sex addict usually manages to find an insecure person with whom to connect. Frank, a wealthy 40-year old businessman, muses,

I've always been attracted to women who have screwed-up home lives. I don't know if it's conscious or unconscious, but I always have. They're so intense, especially the ones who have no father. I'm everything to them – the lover, the father, the whole nine yards. They're extremely dependent.

Frank's wife came from a single-parent family; her father abandoned the family when she was very young. The father of Frank's current girlfriend left his wife for a younger woman. At age 25, Frank's lover already has had three divorces.

Alan, the remarried businessman, was like "a kid in the candy store" during the years between his two marriages. He seemed to have a knack for picking out needy women in a crowd. I asked him how he did it.

I'm not sure exactly – it was just an intuitive thing, a kind of radar. People carry themselves a certain way. Perhaps they're a little overweight or they sit hunched over. They have a certain insecure look. They're also the women who are really touchy-feely; they hold a glance too long, their eyes are also sweeping the room. It's just something I developed.

Alan had a long series of relationships with needy women. Alice, his second wife, was very dependent on him emotionally and was devastated when she eventually learned of the affairs he had during their marriage.

Sex addicts don't always choose a partner who is insecure. In her book *Relationships in Recovery: A Guide for Sex Addicts Who Are Starting Over*,[2] Linda Hatch has a chapter titled, "Identifying How You Choose a Partner." She emphasizes that "there is not necessarily anything wrong with the partner types described below, but it is what they signify to the addict that is useful to look at." She describes several types of partners, but notes that the types frequently overlap. They may include:

- The unreliable partner: This is a partner who liked to live in the midst of high drama – impulsiveness, intensity, conflict, break-ups and getting back together. The chaotic nature of relating to an unreliable person allows the addict to justify his/her own lack of commitment.
- The checked-out partner: This is a partner who lives his or her life separately without sharing their innermost self. The partner is often focused on their work and look to their work for their identity and self-worth. The relationship has very little intimacy and often very little sex. The addict feels free to pursue a secret life of sexual acting out.
- The fleeting or fantasy partner: This is the partner who is willing to have sex with the addict from time to time, either online or in person. This situation allows the addict to believe he or she has a "real" relationship, but in fact, the need to distance themselves fairly quickly overtakes the need to seduce, and the addict withdraws.
- The partner who serves as a rescuer.
- The partner who serves as a policeman.
- The partner who has no expectation of sex or romance.

Regardless of which type of partner the addict chooses, the choice will usually help to support his or her addictive behavior.

The sex addict often gives his partner clues about his sex addiction long before their marriage. When Troy was still single, he made a pass at one of his future wife's girlfriends. "After that she never trusted me. She kept real close tabs on my activities. 'Where are you going?' 'What are you doing?' If I went somewhere, I'd usually get a call there." She knew that Troy was interested in other women, and kept checking up on him throughout their marriage because of this, yet she still chose to marry him.

Alan, who had several affairs during his first marriage, had a stormy three-year courtship with his second wife. Several times during those years he broke off the relationship, insisting that he needed more space to meet other women. Alan and Alice had many discussions about his reluctance to commit to monogamy. They talked about open marriage, swinging, and separate vacations. He even asked Alice to find another sex partner for him. Yet Alice still chose to marry him.

How They Meet

Many of us who are or were in relationships with sex addicts believe it was a matter of chance we ended up with an addict, and sometimes it is. But it's instructive for us to recall the circumstances in which we first met these people and what attracted us to them. Although we may not have known it then, sometimes clues to the future problems existed at the first meeting. Several partners report an instant feeling of knowing the person well, of being able to communicate with him or her on a deep level as though they have a window to each other's soul. In our attempt to understand the basis of our apparent knowledge of a total stranger, we might tell ourselves that God destined us for each other, or that we knew each other in a previous incarnation. Because sex addicts have to be charming and persuasive to keep their addiction to affairs going, they can make us believe these things. It's only during our recovery from our trauma/codependency that were understand that instant recognition or love at first sight is a lot less romantic – it is merely the recognition of a fellow codependent (the sex addict).

Here's how Patty, a petite, 25-year old medical assistant, describes her first meeting with her husband:

The first time I saw Peter was in church. He was a very nice-looking man, but the first time I saw him he had been in a fight, he'd been drinking too much and got mad at another guy. Peter had black eyes, his nose was broken, and his hand was bandaged. I remember when I walked by him at church I thought, How sad! And I kept walking. I don't know why, but I remember being attracted to him. When we went out on our first date I remember thinking, you're making a big mistake. This guy's twenty years older than you. But when we sat and talked, we knew each other so well, it was just unbelievable.

Patty learned soon after that Peter's first wife had left him because of his many affairs. Peter and Patty's marriage eventually was threatened by both his alcoholism and his infidelities.

Another woman who married a future alcoholic and sex addict was Ellen, a 40-year old psychologist:

I first med Ed on the sidelines of debutante parties I was chaperoning. He was hanging over the bar, drinking and talking. He was surrounded by people who loved his stories and his mind.

Ellen realized he drank excessively, but somehow assumed he would take care of it. And for the first few years of their marriage, while he was in professional school, he hardly drank at all, but in later years his alcohol consumption escalated until he finally went to A.A. for help. His affairs kept pace with his drinking, but when the drinking stopped the affairs continued.

Some may ask, "Isn't it possible that a young, inexperienced, naïve girl can unknowingly marry an addict, or even someone whose alcoholism or sex addiction only becomes apparent years later? Isn't it blaming an innocent woman unfairly to suggest that she must take some responsibility for choosing a partner who later made her so unhappy?" It's true, what we know today from past experiences would have been difficult for us to perceive back then. Interviews with women who met their spouses when they were teenagers show that in most case, clues to their future spouse's sex addiction were present early on. These women recognize this now, but at the time they met their future spouse the clues were much more difficult to interpret.

Beverly, the daughter of an alcoholic, married a man who had multiple affairs over many years; they are now divorced:

At the time I met my husband in college at age nineteen, I had been dating a man who worshipped me and I could no longer stand the sight of him. After the first date with Brian I told myself I wanted to marry him. We had spent the night talking about his family. His mother had just died, his father – an alcoholic – had died a few years earlier, and his sister worked at a bar. I felt he needed me. Our romance was filled with his arriving late or not at all and my making special trips to bring him donuts at night or give him rides home from his job. When he would date someone else for a few weeks and not call, I walked around in a dark fog, hoping to get another chance. I told myself I would be better this time. He would want to stay with me.

I was sure Brian was not going to become an alcoholic like my father because he had come from an alcoholic family himself and had felt the same pain I had from that experience. I felt so comfortable with him even though our relationship was a series of fights and reconciliations. I felt like he was someone who would keep me in control and not let me get out of line.

All the patterns were there from day one; they didn't change in sixteen years. I guess you could say I was young and didn't know better, but I think I just replaced my dysfunctional family with an addictive marriage.

Rita first met her husband, Ralph, when she was sixteen. Having grown up in a chaotic household and having had incest experiences with her two older brothers, Rita was looking for a knight in shining armor to save her.

When I first saw Ralph across the room, he was like my karma, my destiny. I immediately latched onto him. He kept breaking up with me and I'd be shattered, and then we'd get back together. He told me he couldn't see me because his parents disapproved, but the real reason was that he thought maybe he could score with someone else. And if he did, then he'd stay away for a while and then return to the person who gave him some balance – me. Of course, I had no idea; I believed what he said about his parents.

The pattern of unpredictability that was established before their marriage continued for many years afterwards – until they both sought help, Rita for her codependency, and Ralph for his many affairs. Rita recognizes now that many of the problems that have plagued their relationship were evident very early on.

Diane, a schoolteacher and mother of a young child, had such low self esteem that what primarily attracted her to Dick was simply that he was interested in her. Once they began dating they got to know each other very quickly, and within a month they were considering marriage. Now married to Dick, Diane recalls the intensity of their immediate connection:

We just seemed to be able to communicate beyond words. There were a lot of times in those early days when we just knew things about each other that we didn't have any way of knowing.

Yet a major problem in their marriage, according to Diane, is Dick's inability to talk about his feelings and his fear that any conflict could be fatal to the relationship. The most likely explanation for this discrepancy is that the closeness and ease they initially experienced resulted from their common codependency. Their very real incompatibilities did not emerge until later.

Dick began spending many hours at the computer, and Diane occasionally walked in on him masturbating to porn. This later escalated to random sexual encounters with women Dick met through hookup apps. Diane was aware before their marriage that Dick had a problem with pornography, but

It didn't seem like any big deal to me. I don't know if I thought that when we were married it would be better; it certainly didn't seem to me as big a difficulty as Dick made it out to be. He acted like it was a big problem and maybe I just chose not to believe him. I remember thinking it was kind of cute that he was so embarrassed about telling me. I didn't ask him for details, so maybe I didn't want to know.

In her view, her perception that they shared a deep level of communication with Dick more than made up for any potential little problems.

Alice, the biologist, first met her husband, Alan, at a singles party.

What first attracted me to Alan was his good looks; he was by far the best-looking man I'd ever dated. He also came across as very sincere, very caring. He really seemed interested in what I was saying. He wasn't aggressive sexually, which I liked; I had the feeling that he wanted only what I wanted. But I was so attracted to him sexually that we made love on our third date. He was gentle, considerate, experienced, and interested in my reactions. He asked me what I wanted and if what he was doing was pleasing to me. I'd been to bed with a few men before, but it was nothing like this. The next morning he called me up at work and his first words to me were, "Do you still respect me?" It was such a charming reversal of the usual roles that I was totally won over; I knew right then that this was the man I was going to marry.

Our next three years together, before we got married, were very stormy. At times he was the caring, considerate lover I had fallen in love with. But at other times he was inexplicably distant. Whenever we got too close he would ask for distance. But when in response to his dating other women, I would get close to another man, he would suddenly become the ardent wooer again and I would once again be won over. I knew by then that he'd had affairs during his first marriage and that he was having trouble staying in a monogamous relationship with me, but I assumed that somehow he would work this all out as soon as we got married. I really shouldn't have been surprised that after our marriage he wasn't faithful.

In Alice's mind she hung on to the good times they had and assumed that the bad times would vanish after the wedding. But the very traits that appealed to Alice about Alan – his excitement and his unpredict-ability – made it likely there would be difficult times ahead. After the wedding she ended up with exactly the same type of relationship she had endured before the marriage, and eventually they were divorced.

Problems After the Wedding

When the sex addict marries, there are often misgivings on both sides. As you saw in Chapter Four, because they realize that monog-amy is a problem, sex addicts may be reluctant to get married. They anticipate there will be problems, but they believe that the alternative is to lose the partner. Partners, too, may have misgivings. They were often aware before marriage that there were problems in the areas of sex, alcohol, and/or relationships, but denial, being charmed and won over by the sex addict, and a reluctance to trust their own feelings combined to make them believe that everything would turn out fine.

For some couples the honeymoon period is truly that, but for oth-ers the problems begin quickly. Nancy, now a 40-year old mother of seven children, had the following recollections:

Nick and I got married about three months after we met. Right from the beginning it was bad. We had serious arguments on our honeymoon. About a week after we got back we went on a hayride with the church, and he paid all sorts of attention to some little teenaged girls. I just couldn't believe it. I thought when we got married he wasn't supposed to even look at anybody ever again! One day I went to his college with him to sit in on a couple of his classes, and a girl came up to him and said, "Oh, man, are you married?" and he said, "Yeah," and she commented, "Well, you don't act married!"

We had several separations in the following years. I left him when I was pregnant with my second baby, but I returned following the baby's birth. Nick was so supportive that I was sure everything would be wonderful. But within a couple of months he was treating me like dirt, so I left again and went back to my parents' home. Nick wooed me back again, and the cycle continued. We had seven children over a dozen years.

Our life was pretty bad. I never knew what he was doing. There were times I had an uneasy feeling, a feeling of disquiet, that something was wrong. But these periods were interspersed with times when he was getting himself right again. He might be a really nice guy for three or four months, and I'd think he's changed, whatever the problem was, he had dealt with it. And then he'd start going out again and being mean to me.

I tried to change myself for him. I dyed my hair different colors. I gained weight, then I'd lose it. I did anything sexually he wanted me to, and I'd do anything to get him to make love with me. For me, when he was having sex with me, somehow that validated me. That was how I was all my life – if someone was having sex with me, then they really loved me.

Nancy's story illustrates early difficulties following marriage to a sex addict, the partner's denial, her attempts to please her spouse, and her core belief that sex is the most important sign of love. Certainly, Nancy's behaviors are unhealthy and misguided. However, they are not uncommon among partners.

Another woman, who suspected but had no definite evidence that her husband was having affairs, became afraid to deny him sex, convinced that this would be inviting him to get it somewhere else. She also believed she could control his sexual behavior by making sure he had good sex at home. To this end, she always arranged a romantic, sensual encounter the night before he left on a trip. Because she believed that her mate's sexual interest in her was the most important sign of his love, and thus evidence that she was successful in keeping him happy, she would wait to see how anxious he was to make love to her upon his return from the trip. She also used his desire for her as a clue to whether or not he'd had sex while away. She ignored her own sexual needs and desires; all that mattered to her was pleasing her husband.

Whether the problems are present initially or begin after some years after the wedding, the situation worsens with time. Partners react by intensifying their efforts to understand their mate, to please him or her, and to control him or her. They seek reasons for the mate's behavior, and when they think they have found one, will eliminate it and hope that this will make the mate change. Because addicts can find a new excuse as fast as partners can rectify the previous one, partners become involved in endless, fruitless attempts to please the mate. Unaware of the actual cause of the mate's behavior, partners increase their efforts to please the mate – with the result that their resentment and anger at the lack of success grow.

Financial and Job Problems

Chronic job dissatisfaction often accompanies sex addiction and can cause financial problems that add an additional burden to the marriage. Some sex addicts crave excitement and novelty on the job as well as in their sexual relationships, and quit a job when it is no longer new. Others are so preoccupied with their sexual activities that they perform poorly at work and keep getting fired. For some, this includes repeatedly using the work computer for sexual gratification, an activity that can get them fired. Others' work suffers because they use office time to sext, text, or surf hookup apps on their smartphones. Some addicts have an affair with a coworker and then change jobs to get away from her or him. Still others hope for a geographic cure for their problems and repeatedly move their families to new cities. One woman, whose husband had multiple affairs, reported the following:

My husband hasn't worked steadily in years. He can never seem to get along with his boss, and keeps quitting his job. We have three small children, so I haven't been able to work. We've been on the verge of bankruptcy several times. Each time my husband has asked me to talk to my parents. Each time, even though I felt humiliated, I swallowed my pride and asked my parents to bail us out. We now owe them thousands of dollars; I don't know how we'll ever pay it back.

Another woman told me that, because her husband kept getting new jobs, they had moved cross-country ten times in the previous ten years. Each time she would get a job too, but because of the frequent moves she was never able to build up seniority in any one position. The family was chronically short of money.

The fiscally irresponsible man may marry a responsible, caretaking rescuer who lands a good job and becomes the financial support of the family. Because she seeks his approval and fears abandonment, she is likely to turn over control of the funds to her husband. Many partners have difficulty spending money on themselves. Resentment may build up inside the self-denying family breadwinner as they see the money passing quickly through the mate's hands.

The spouse who does the family accounting may find certain sums of money unaccounted for, or may notice charges for dinners or hotel rooms in other cities. One young wife found a $300 credit-card charge for "ABC Services" after her husband returned from an out-of-town business trip. His explanation to her seemed contrived, so she phoned ABC Services, which turned out to be a massage parlor where one could get "full service" for exactly $300.

Even when family income is adequate, money can become a pawn in the game of control that a couple plays. For example, the partner may spend money for revenge for the mate's affairs, or to make up for his lack of attention to her. One woman described buying a very expensive pair of shoes to punish her husband for his latest affair.

Debra L. Kaplan addressed the interplay of sex, money and power in, *For Love and Money: Exploring Sexual & Financial Betrayal in Relationships:*[3]

The veritable fact is that power and money may be two of
the most potent sexual stimulants known, perhaps even more
effective than chocolate and Viagra combined. Since the first
caveman learned to make fire men and women have been
playing power games. Fast-forward several thousand years
and power, influence and wealth are still making a difference. Although money and power can provide financial stability, it may lag far behind in the emotional security department. While many of those surveyed report dollar-and-cents
arousal, like most things new and novel, aphrodisiacs will
eventually dissolve and go the way of short-term attractors.
Therefore, healthy longer-term relationships need more than
just money and as we've seen from so many examples in this
book – plenty of money does not make for love or affection.

Betrayal of partners by sex addicts often involves both sex and money.
Kaplan goes on to say:

Many betrayed spouses first encounter evidence of sexual
betrayal when overlooked or discarded credit card receipts,
phone bills, or work vouchers are discovered. In the early
phases of betrayal there may not be any sign that a partner
is withdrawing or allocating time and money toward another
person, behavior, or addiction. A fluctuation in mood due to
work, family, or emotional stressors is a common event in anyone's life. But, when the baseline behavior for an individual is
noticeably changed for an extended period of time, the awareness of something amiss can become too strong to ignore.
Mounting warning signs that something is NQR (not quite
right) often leads a betrayed partner to question if something
is happening in their relationship, and at this point will go
to great lengths – if not any – to learn the truth. Often this

results in "detective"-type behaviors – checking phones, bills, pockets, purses, expense reports, and the like – that uncover the truth (or at least part of the truth).

Effect on the Sexual Relationship

Beverly, the child of an alcoholic, married a dashing, exciting man who, although she didn't initially recognize it, had an active sex life outside their marriage:

A few years into our marriage, the sex in our life changed. Brian said he wanted to try new things so I bought new underwear, then lotions, then he bought a dildo, then we watched porn movies online, then he started to tie me up, then he wanted me to tie him up, then he wanted blindfolds and gags, then he purchased a box of props – leather belts, whips, and chains. This took place over a period of about three years, and in the meantime we had two more children, which meant my attentions were now turned to taking care of babies. I was exhausted and felt angry at being asked to do all this.

I know what it's like to be sucked in by the seduction of a sexual fantasy because in my attempt to please him I joined him as a sexual coaddict. I let him call me "cunt" and "whore" as we made love, and for a short time I found it exciting, but then crushingly degrading.

By this time he had also started to have affairs. Right after the birth of one baby, and when I was pregnant with the next, he stopped coming home at night. I felt very vulnerable. I felt I couldn't compete with someone else who must be more beautiful, intelligent, and was certainly new and available.

At the end of three years he was having sex with me very early in the morning, then I would iron a clean shirt for him and he'd put on after-shave lotion for his luncheon date. He'd call me about 4:30 to tell me he was going out for a beer, and he'd return at about 7 P.M. (to a dinner I had kept warm for him), smelling of perfume. At night he'd get up around 11 to "go back and finish some work at the office." It was a nightmare come true.

Although during this time I had many arguments with him and often made threats to leave and gave him ultimatums, I never followed through or took any action. As I look back on it now, I was more comfortable coping with the chaos in my life than taking the risk of my changing and his changing. I knew I was good at being the "wronged woman." I knew I was good at taking care of him, but without these roles I had to be myself, and I had lived my life so much for him that there wasn't anything left of me.

Beverly's story illustrates denial, endless efforts to please her husband, comfort with the martyr role, participation in her spouse's sexual activities, and unwillingness to risk change.

In an attempt to hold on to their mate, partners may even agree to swinging, group sex, or sex with strangers. Ellen, the 40-year old psychologist who for years had only infrequent sexual relationships with her husband, was glad to have an opportunity please him when he finally told her what he liked:

We did a whole thing of sadomasochism. I tried all kinds of things to satisfy him. We did the whips and chains, the leather, anything and everything. Then he asked, "May I watch you with another man?" So I'd have sex with younger men in front of the fireplace while he watched through the window.

Beverly's and Ellen's reactions to their husbands' sex addiction are not uncommon. In a chapter about the effects of a spouse's sex addiction on the partner, Dr. Omar Minwalla listed the following effects on their sexuality described by some of his patients:[4]

- They avoid, fear, or lack interest in sex
- Sex feels like an obligation
- They participate in compulsive or inappropriate sexual behaviors
- They experience negative feelings when touched - such as anger, disgust, or guilt

- They have difficulty becoming aroused or feeling sensation
- They feel dirty and contaminated
- They feel emotionally distant or not present during sex
- They experience intrusive or disturbing thoughts, images, and flashbacks
- They have trouble establishing or maintaining intimate relationships
- They have vaginal pain or difficulty achieving orgasm
- They have body image issues
- They feel secrecy and shame
- They feel responsible for this victimization

These reactions can be summarized as constituting sexual trauma, one aspect of the relational trauma experienced by partners who've been betrayed. A period of abstinence is usually recommended for sex addicts early in their treatment, and the same strategy, taking a break from being sexual, can also benefit partners.

As for women who have participated in unusual sexual activities at their husbands' requests – and enjoyed it – they sometimes wonder whether they too are sex addicts. Some partners who have come to self-help recovery groups for spouses of sex addicts (S-Anon and COSA) have wondered whether they belong there or with the addicts. A key factor is the *goal* of the behavior. The goal of the female sex addict is the mood alternation that comes from having power over another person, and from living out the chase, the conquest, the new experience. The goal is not to please another person.

In contrast, coaddicts by definition are addicted to their mate, and will do practically anything they believe will keep him from abandoning them. The spouse of an alcoholic will sometimes drink with him to keep him at home. Similarly, spouses of sex addicts may join them in their behavior, which is sexual. The partner may enjoy it – after all, sex is usually pleasurable, but the partner's goal is to hold on to the mate by satisfying his needs. Security, not sexual gratification, is the partner's primary aim.

Effect of Cybersex on the Partner and the Relationship

Like other forms of sex addiction, cybersex is time consuming. Many hours per week are spent at the computer or on mobile digital devices, hours that might otherwise be devoted to the spouse and children. Partners of compulsive cybersex users often feel lonely, ignored, unimportant, neglected or angry because the user prefers to spend so much time on the Net. What makes it worse, however, is that most cybersex addicts withdraw from the partner emotionally and sexually, preferring computer images and conversations with fantasy women or men to their real-life partners. As a result, the partner feels abandoned, betrayed, and hurt. Cybersex addicts usually lie about their activities; the spouse begins to distrust the mate and becomes suspicious of their solitary activities. When the mate promises to stop but then resumes the online activities, the distrust increases. It seems impossible for partners to measure up to the idealized images on the computer screen, and their self-esteem falls.

Partners' reactions include feeling sexually inadequate, unattractive or ugly; doubting one's judgment and even sanity; and severe depression, even suicide attempts. Some partners engage in extramarital affairs or encounters, either to shore up their own self-esteem and validate their attractiveness or desirability, or else to get revenge on their cybersex-using mates. A 34-year-old woman, married 14 years to a minister, said,

He's never been physically unfaithful, but he has had online real-time experiences with others. I feel cheated. I never know who or what he is thinking of when we are intimate. How can I compete with hundreds of anonymous others who are now in our bed, in his head? When he says something sexual to me in bed, I wonder if he has said it to others, or if it is even his original thought. Now our bed is crowded with countless faceless strangers, where once we were intimate. With all this deception, how do I know he has quit, or isn't moving into other behaviors?

As demonstrated above, some partners try to compete by agreeing to new sexual activities, even ones that make them uncomfortable. Some volunteer for these activities, whereas others succumb to pressure by the addict. One potential problem for partners is that the internet offers an endless smorgasbord of sexual activities. No matter how unusual or deviant the activities, one can always find a group of people who enjoy that activity and support its use. Sex involving urine, children, animals, threesomes or foursomes, domination and bondage, fetishes, whatever – it all starts to feel "normal" to the person who participates in it for some time with others who encourage the activities. In comparison, the previous sexual activities with the spouse become boring, "vanilla sex." The addict is then tempted to pressure the partner to try out the new activities. A 31-year-old woman, married 3 years, related,

The kinky and perverted behaviors shown all over the internet fuel his beliefs and give him ammunition to say that I am the "weird one" for not wanting anal sex. "See all of the women out there on the Net who are just crazy about it!" he says.

Some cybersex users blame their partners for being unwilling to engage in these behaviors. Some partners may also blame themselves and begin to question their own judgment and values, wondering whether they are indeed too uptight or old fashioned. Out of guilt, they may give in to the addict's wishes and then berate themselves and feel shame for having engaged in those activities.

Compulsive cybersex use by one member of a couple usually has significant adverse effects on their sexual relationship. Approximately two-thirds of couples have less sex with each other after one of them gets hooked on the Net. This is most often because the cybersex addict is not interested in real-life sex with his partner, but sometimes it's the spouse who is too upset, repulsed, or angry to want sex.

A typical example of the sexual problems experienced by couples is that of a 34-year old woman who had learned of her husband's cybersex involvement only weeks earlier:

I realize now that many of the things he most liked and requested when we made love were re-creations of downloaded images. He is unable to be intimate, he objectifies me, he objectifies women and girls on the streets, he fantasizes when we're together. I feel humiliated, used, and betrayed, as well as lied to and misled. It's almost impossible for me to let him touch me without feeling really yucky and/or crying. I tried to continue being sexual with him initially (and in fact, being more sexual, trying to fix it by being sexier, better than the porn girls), and I couldn't do it. We have now been consensually abstinent for 3 weeks.

A 34-year old woman, married 10 years, related,

He's not interested in sex with me and blames me. He told me it's his way or no way. He wanted me to participate with him on the Net. He is up all night on the Net and then is tired and unavailable. I feel like I'm making love to a corpse – he doesn't really participate.

In my study of cybersex addicts[5], the partners frequently mentioned the following problems:

- The cybersex addict makes excuses to avoid sex with the spouse: not in the mood, too tired, working too hard, has already climaxed and doesn't want sex, the children might hear, his back hurts too much.
- The spouse feels hurt, angry, sexually rejected, inadequate, and unable to compete with sexy computer images and online women (or men) who are willing to do "anything."
- During sex with the spouse, the cybersex addict appears distant, emotionally detached, and interested only in his or her own pleasure.

- The partner ends up doing most or all of the initiating, either to get her own needs met, or else in an attempt to get the addict to decrease his online sexual activities.
- The addict blames the partner for the couple's sexual problems.
- The addict wants the partner to participate in sexual activities that the partner finds objectionable.

Some partners don't want to participate, but continue out of fear of driving the addict further into online activities. Other partners are too repulsed or turned off. A 44-year old man married to a cybersex-addicted woman related,

At first we had sex more than ever as I desperately tried to prove myself, then sex with her made me sick. I get strong pictures in my head of what she did and lusted after, and I get repelled and feel bad. I used to see sex as a very intimate loving thing. We always had a lot of sex and I thought we were intimate. Now that I found out my wife was not on the same page, I can't be intimate or vulnerable – sex for me is now more recreational or just out of need.

Partners who no longer are interested in sex with the cybersex addict report:

- Initially increasing the sexual activities in order to "win back" the mate. This early response is usually only temporary.
- Feeling repelled and disgusted by the addict's online or real-life sexual activities and no longer wanting to have sex with him.
- No longer tolerating the addict's detachment and lack of emotional connection during sex.
- Feeling too angry over the addict's denial of the problem to be interested in sex.
- In reply to pressure or requests by the addict to dress in certain ways or perform new sexual acts, feeling angry, repelled, used, objectified, or like a prostitute.

- Fearing catching a disease from the user, or already caught one.

The Partner Attempts to Control the Mate

In her excellent book, *The Booze Battle*, Ruth Maxwell describes the misguided thinking and actions of the spouse of the alcoholic. Exactly the same can be said of the partner of an unfaithful mate.

> Virtually every wife who is responding to the disease of alcoholism by herself is guided by two specific principles that set the tone for all her actions and that ultimately guide her toward her own destruction. First, she attempts to control her husband's drinking, and second, she concentrates on his reasons for drinking and attempts to eliminate them.
>
> With every attempt at controlling her husband's drinking, the wife creates new sources of anger for her husband to use against her and as reasons for further drinking., . . . By attempting to control her husband she is setting herself up as a target for his frustrations and is granting him the very justifications for drinking that he is looking for.
>
> Wives of alcoholics spend an inordinate amount of time and energy trying to discover the reasons, past and present, for their husbands' drinking. They become preoccupied with events, circumstances, people, places, and things in their husbands' lives. They believe it is forces in this outside world that are somehow causing it all, and, sadly, they often assign themselves first place among these causes. They do not see the addiction that has to be fed at *any* cost, no matter what is or was taking place in the life of the alcoholic.[6]

Partners of sex addicts often suffer from the same thought disorder as do partners of alcoholics. They mistakenly believe that external factors are responsible for the mate's behavior and that through their own efforts they can control him. Partners believe that if they can keep a close eye on the addict, they can prevent him or her from interacting with other sexual partners and getting into trouble.

One woman who believed she was ideally situated to keep track of her husband's activities was Patty, a beautiful but very insecure woman who for a while worked as a dental assistant for her dentist husband.

I loved working in Peter's office, because I thought I could monitor every woman. If I was in the reception area and saw the best-looking patient who came in that day, or a woman of the type he was usually attracted to, I'd go to her chart and I'd look up how old she was and whether she was married. Then I'd start up a conversation with her. I was very good at getting people to reveal things about themselves. I'd get them to talk and tell me about their lives. I'd never let them know I was his wife; I kept my maiden name. I had a terrific personality and came across great with people. I would try to stay in the room while he was treating her so I could see what the interaction was and if it was a threat or not. If I couldn't be there, I'd find out from the other dental assistant how he acted around the patient.

I did much the same thing at parties. I'd look around the room and find the woman that he'd be most attracted to and I'd watch them carefully. I'd look at his eyes to see if he met hers. It was like a prison, I was so consumed with his behaviors.

Despite Patty's vigilance, her husband managed to arrange meetings with other women. All of Patty's efforts to scout out the competition did not prevent her husband from doing exactly what he wanted to do.

Attempting to control the partner and the environment constitutes partners' way of trying to cope with the unmanageability of their life and to feel safe. The less control they have over their life, the harder they try.

It is very common for the wife of a man who has affairs to attempt to control him through sex. Nancy, the mother of seven, recalls:

If there was going to be a problem, I knew I could smooth it over by having sex with him. If I had to tell him the checkbook was all out of whack or I'd overspent our budget, then I could ease into it with sex. I'd get him into a good mood first. If one of the kids did something wrong, which he always thought was my fault, I'd always try not to tell him about that until after we had sex.

Interestingly, the sex addict who recognizes his partner's need to control him can turn this behavior around to his own benefit. For instance, he may ask his partner to help him by policing his behavior. He probably does feel a genuine sense of the compulsivity of his behavior and a desire to stop it, but part of the reason he involves his wife in being the policeman is to reassure her he won't do it again. In other words, it's a con and she's buying it. She thinks he must really be sincere, because he's so remorseful. With his wife now believing it won't happen again, the addict is free to pursue new relationships.

This scenario most commonly happens early in the addict's recovery, when he will invite the partner into the recovery process by asking her to help him avoid his triggers (i.e. situations that can lead to a slip or relapse). This can create the illusion that the addict is trying to get better, even if this is untrue. The risk to the partner is not only being deceived, but should the addict relapse or have a slip into his bottom-line behaviors, the partner is likely to blame herself for not doing "a good enough job." This is why therapists often tell the addict to choose an accountability partner other than the spouse – for example his sponsor in a Twelve-Step program or the therapist.

Is Online Sex Cheating?

When President Bill Clinton was asked on television whether he'd had sex with White House intern Monica Lewinsky, he said no, and later defended his lie by explaining that to him, receiving oral sex does not constitute "having sex" or cheating on one's wife. It's amazing how many Americans agree that if you haven't had intercourse with someone outside your marriage, you haven't committed adultery. There is still disagreement about what constitutes sexual relations. Nowhere is this more true than with cybersex. When a married person engages in real-time online sex with someone else, especially when digital cameras are involved, most spouses react as though skin-to-skin adultery has taken place. Two partners described their reactions to their husbands' cybersex involvement as follows:

My husband is using sexual energy that should be used with me. The person on the other end of that computer is live and is participating in a sexual activity with him. They are doing it together and are responding to each other. It is one thing to masturbate to a two-dimensional screen image. But to engage in an interactive sexual encounter means that you are being sexual with another person, and that is cheating.

People who don't think cybersex hurts the spouse should try it for themselves one time, and see how it feels to be less important to their partner than a picture on a computer screen! They should see what it feels like to lie in bed and know their partner is on the computer and what he is doing with it. It's not going to do much for the self-esteem. My husband has actually cheated on me, and it feels no different. The online "safe" cheating has just as dirty, filthy, a feel to it as does the "real-life" cheating.

Partners who have experienced the sense of betrayal that comes from being rejected in favor of an online image, and the lying and covering up by the addict that usually go with it, want desperately to have other people – friends, therapists, family – understand and validate their feelings. This was confirmed in a survey-based study I carried out with Robert Weiss and Charles Samenow[7] and which was published in 2012. The online survey was completed by 29 women and 5 men who described their reactions to their mate's cybersex behaviors. About half (55%) believed they had been traumatized by the user's online sexual activities. One question we asked was whether the partner believed that the mate's behaviors were limited to online or if they included physical contact with another person. Much of the distress experienced by partners related to the uncertainty about the user's sexual activities. One third (32%) of partners believed that physical contact had indeed occurred, and another third were uncertain. Only 38% believed that only online sexual activities had taken place. Moreover, only 22% of the cybersex addicts had voluntarily disclosed their activities before the partner discovered them. To obtain more information, many partners resorted to "snooping behaviors." As one partner wrote, "If you suspect something, try to find out because not knowing is more hurtful and worrisome than anything; use spyware or any other method to learn the truth." Betrayed partners often express the need to know more and more details in order to understand the past and avoid future pain, i.e., to have control over an out-of-control situation.

After experiencing the pain of uncertainty, of betrayal, and of being lied to, partners are slow to trust and fearful of recommitting. Repeated dishonesty on the part of the mate, who often denies the partner's questions, gut reactions, and instincts, is indeed traumatizing and traumatic. Repeatedly faced with discrepancies between their internal emotional experience and thee minimization or outright lies told them by the addict, spouses report feeling "crazy," finding it difficult to trust their own judgment and conclusions. By the time the facts are known, these partners often expressed feeling victimized not only by the user's sexual behavior, but also of emotional abuse in the form of deception and denial.

In our study, 71% of the partners reported having lost trust in their mate. Some of them wrote, "Trust has been **shattered** beyond belief." "His behavior obliterated the trust in our relationship. I no longer believe a single thing he says." "Smartphones dramatically worsened his addiction by having this material available 24/7, while at the same time making it harder to locate and track his activities." "I have been traumatized by the repeated discovery of his deception and betrayal of me with these activities."

One clear conclusion from this study is that lying is just as traumatizing as the sexual behaviors themselves. So to answer the question, "Is online sex really cheating?" we can start by defining infidelity as *the breaking of trust and the keeping of secrets in an intimate partnership.* We wrote,

> Betrayed partners of cybersex abusers and sex addicts consistently report that it's not the cheating itself or any specific sexual act that causes them the deepest pain, it's the lying, denial of their own reality, and inability to maintain relationship trust. The most agonizing part for those who are being cheated upon is the betrayal of their trust in their mate. While some couples may choose to negotiate an open relationship or integrate internet porn into their lives, it is the man or woman living a hidden sexual life who will cause the most harm to their loved ones.[8]

What are the Costs of Infidelity?

Resentment

A feeling commonly shared by both members of the couple is resentment. The partner who suspects or has evidence of her mate's real-life or online affairs resents him for having fun while she picks up the pieces – caring for the children, often juggling career and family, doing her best to make her spouse happy, and getting little in return. Her overt reaction may be to assume a martyr role. From this role she can obtain the sympathy of her friends and can hope to make her spouse feel guilty.

The addict, meanwhile, probably feels guilty about his actions, and finds that the same sexual activities no longer make him feel as good as they used to. He is likely to resent his partner for her martyr role, her attempts to control his behavior, and her assumption that she is the only one who is suffering. They are each likely to deal with their resentment by doing more of the same: the partner will try even harder to make things right, while the addict will devote himself even more to his addiction in order to escape the bad feelings.

The Emotional Roller Coaster, and Tolerating Emotional Abuse

Depression, anger, resentment, guilt, confusion, physical symptoms, a feeling of craziness – these are all common features of life in an addictive relationship. At a time when she was separated from her husband but still involved with him emotionally and sexually, Beverly tried to make sense of her life by figuring out the pattern of her interactions with Brian. Even after she divorced Brian, she realized she was still addicted to him. Beverly told me:

Brian's cycle is about three weeks long. It has six stages, the last one leading back to the first. I call stage one "on the make." Brian has an intensity of purpose in his walk. He takes pride in his clothes and acts aloof and distant. This stage corresponds to the "preoccupation" stage of Patrick Carnes' addictive cycle. I find Brian very attractive in this stage. I try to get him to go to bed with me, especially if he has an appointment elsewhere. If he does so, I feel validated – he loves me; he puts the rest of his life on hold so he can be with me.

In stage two, Brian is on top of the world. He used to bring me flowers; now he phones and sounds as if we're best friends and still married. He's in Carnes' "retreat from reality" phase. I have a gut feeling at such times that he has just connected with someone else, but if I confront him with that he is explosively angry so I am afraid, confused, and angry.

When we were married, stage three consisted of Brian arriving late smelling of perfume. He made sure I knew he had just slept with someone. Then almost immediately he'd become morose and would begin lying. My response was anger. I hated him and felt very bad about myself.

In stage four, "the hook," Brian would give me a look of love and need and tell me of his genuine feelings for me. Now in Carnes' phase of "sincere delusion," he would promise not to do it again, and said he would change. I felt very confused – my gut reaction was that he was sincere, but I also knew he'd soon be acting out again.

Next, in stage five, Brian would be mildly depressed. He'd be critical of me, trying to get me to feel down too. My reaction was to feel strong. I was glad he felt down, and I hoped he'd now change and not do it again. I wanted to get him into a program so that he would change.

Stage six was the stage of "terminal loneliness." Brian was obviously experiencing low self-esteem. Wherever he was, he wanted to be somewhere else. I tried to hook him in, to make plans so he'd be busy with something he liked. I tried to make him happy but I never succeeded. Brian would finally snap out of this by going on the make, and the cycle would begin again.

Notice Brian and Beverly's dance, which greatly resembles the cycle of domestic violence. The similarities between addiction and domestic violence was described almost 20 years ago by Richard Irons and myself. We listed the following parallels:

1. Loss of control: The abuser is contrite after the abuse, promises not to do it again, yet inevitably the abuse recurs.
2. Continuation despite adverse consequences: The victim experiences emotional, sexual, and [possibly] physical damage and loss of self-esteem; abuser experiences remorse and guilt at times, but the abuse continues.
3. Preoccupation or obsession: abuser is preoccupied with controlling the victim and (if sex is involved), maintaining access to sexual gratification.

4. Development of tolerance: Initially a testing of the abuse; the victim gets desensitized and tolerates increasing levels of abuse, which escalate in frequency and/or intensity and/or diversity.[9] [10]

Beverly's feelings and reactions were a response to Brian's mood and behavior of the moment, and she was so focused on him that there was nothing left of the real Beverly. Because the couple shares three children with whom Brian is actively involved, interactions between them continue. Beverly found her analysis of Brian's cycle and her responses to be helpful in changing her own behavior. Recognizing that some particularly attractive behavior on his part is but a phase in his cycle has helped her avoid being hooked in. In the past, Beverly and Brian repeated the same cycle dozens of times; currently, by identifying his actions as a predictable part of the cycle, it is easier for Beverly to remain detached emotionally from him.

Because the partner's life is so focused on her spouse that existence without him is intolerable, the partner is willing to put up with abusive behavior which a person with more self-esteem would not tolerate. Cynthia Koestler, the healthy 55-year old woman who committed suicide together with her very ill, elderly husband Arthur (a well-known novelist and journalist), described their relationship in her autobiography. Her father had committed suicide when she was ten years old, and at age nineteen she was still complaining of "a paralyzing lack of self-assurance."[11] When Cynthia first met Arthur, she was an insecure, unassertive, self-effacing 22-year old who was thrilled to have obtained a job as secretary to a well-known writer. Arthur Koestler was then 44 years old, an arrogant man with violent moods, frequent depression, and a thirst for new female conquests. All this was clearly apparent to Cynthia in their first few meetings. She writes that he appeared to be quite enraged at some minor transgression by the housekeeper. He drank a great deal, was arrested once for hitting a police officer while drunk, and had hangovers. About a year after they first met, he married another woman. On his wedding night he got drunk, argued with his bride, and drove away to spend the time alone.

Arthur was often depressed. His low self-esteem led a friend of his to comment, "We all have inferiority complexes of various sizes, but yours isn't a complex —it's a cathedral."[12] He apparently compensated for this with compulsive sexual activity; every new woman was a potential conquest. He recognized this in himself, reported that he had "a persistent and well-nigh pathological streak of promiscuity in my youth and early middle age." He collected women, referring to them as his harem. He complained in is diary that "my harem is wearing me out."

Titling part of his notebook, "Chronology of an Obsession," Arthur Koestler described his despair when a certain woman turned him down. He recovered from this terrible experience by seducing a different woman: "Whilst sitting at a table in a crowded bar he saw an Italian girl with her fiancé sitting at the far side of the room, and was unable to take his eyes off her. He carried her off for the night and was thrilled by this feat."[13] Undoubtedly what added to the thrill was that he won her over from another man. Later, when Cynthia, his lover, arrived in London for a brief stay, Arthur asked her to find a room for the Italian woman for the night. In her journal, Cynthia documented this and other episodes in an accepting and nonjudgmental way. In fact, she reacted to Arthur's story about stealing the woman away from her fiancé by asking for details because Cynthia was "thrilled by the exploit."

Despite the clues that Cynthia had about Arthur from the beginning (or perhaps because of the clues), she found herself very attracted to him. After their very first meeting she wondered vaguely what he would be like in bed. His friends warned her against falling for him, but to no avail; she had already made him the center of her life and had given him the power to make her happy.

When Arthur left, I existed somehow. In the mornings I got
up; at night I went to bed and cared not whether I slept or did
not sleep. I was conscious only of a pain in my heart which
seemed to radiate to my lungs, stomach, and liver. Could a
heartache be experienced not only figuratively but literally as
well?[14]

When he didn't pay attention to her, she wrote, "Worst of all, the
brief illusion of being at times close to him faded, died, and was sup-
planted by a fathomless void."

During this time, Arthur was married to another woman. Cynthia
was sorry when his wife decided to leave him: "Life would never be
the same again without her there. Like a devoted dog, I was happiest
when I was together with both of them." Cynthia considered herself
Arthur's slave; she signed her letters to him, "your slavey." To be with
him, she followed him from city to city, giving up jobs to return to
him as soon as he asked for her. She attempted to do everything for
him perfectly, and felt "filled with guilt" or "black with guilt" whenever she thought she had displeased him. Her moods swung from
high to low depending on where she thought she stood with him.

Arthur Koestler knew very well how Cynthia felt about him.
How did he treat her? "Abominably," wrote George Mikes, a friend
of Arthur's. He humiliated her in front of others, emphasizing her
mistakes. But "Cynthia did not insist on being a person; she was content to be a function.[15] Arthur's opinion of Cynthia's devotion was
that it was boring. "Cynthia – toujours la [always there]," he wrote in
his journal.

Cynthia never knew where she stood with him, which must have
added to the attraction he had for her:

As always, he was unpredictably unpredictable and this side
of him, fascinating though it was, had the effect of scattering
my poor feelings in all directions, as if a whirlwind had been

through them. I was constantly receiving some sort of jolt, of which Arthur of course was quite unaware. Sometimes I felt happy, at other times I went home with a sinking heart.[16]

She constantly sought his approval. "When he told me in a joking way that I was the favorite, I felt awestruck." But Cynthia recognized deep down how relatively unimportant she was to Arthur. She wrote,

I often wondered whether he knew who was beside him at night, for sometimes an arm reached over to feel or he turned his head in the semi-darkness, as if he wasn't sure. I vaguely pondered the mystery. Perhaps I should have felt jealous, but I only felt lucky to be sharing his life.[17]

Although Cynthia coped with her pain primarily through denying to herself his ill treatment of her, she did have episodes of depression and melancholia.

In 1965, sixteen years after they first met, Arthur and Cynthia were married. For the next eighteen years she continued her slavish devotion to him, and he continued treating her like a slave. Harold Harris writes in his introduction to the Koestlers' book, "It is hardly an exaggeration to say that his life became hers; that she *lived* his life. And when the time came for him to leave it, her life too was at an end."[18] This is a sad and telling epitaph for a relationship addict.

Like Cynthia Koestler, schoolmistress Jean Harris also gave up her life for the man who so often mistreated her. After accidentally shooting Tarnower in 1980, Harris spent twelve years in prison, suffered two heart attacks there, and was released in 1992 when the governor of New York State commuted her sentence. (She died in 2012.) Even before Tarnower's death, Harris was living her life through him. The thinking of this competent, intelligent woman was so distorted that she believed this treatment was indicative of her lover's love for her. She constantly excused his behavior and tried to persuade herself that he was really there for her emotionally. She believed when she was with him she was safe, whereas away from him she was vulnerable.

Despite Tarnower's maltreatment of her, Jean viewed him through rose-colored glasses and attributed wonderful qualities to their relationship. She considered Tarnower her "sounding board, my oasis, my warm and reassuring friend. . . . Touching base with Hy gave me a feeling of safety and stability so I could cope with whatever traumas life tossed my way."[19]

Not surprisingly, the contrast between fantasy and reality threw Jean into periods of depression. Tarnower gladly provided medical treatment by giving her amphetamines. At one point she considered consulting a psychiatrist for her depression and got as far as phoning one. But her unwillingness to talk about her feelings overcame her intention to seek help. Instead, she bought a gun with the idea that she could kill herself if life became unbearable. Harris did eventually attempt to use the gun on herself, but killed Tarnower instead.

In thinking about why women choose to stay with emotionally abusive men, some skeptical readers may still believe that economic considerations predominate – that women stay primarily because they have no other financial options. This might be true of some women, but then one might expect a financially independent woman to leave the relationship if the going got bad. But in fact, many women who have their own income remain in troubled relationships far longer than any reasonable person would do. Clearly, finances are not the deciding factor. Here again is Beverly, the wealthy society woman, talking about her relationship with her philandering husband, Brian:

I was lucky to have enough money to do all the things I wanted to and to feel financially independent, but the truth is I never used my money to be independent. Instead I gave all my money to Brian so he could be in a business by himself and to establish himself. I figured then he would support us and I wouldn't have to feel guilty for the money I used to keep us going. Near the end he invested "our" money to the point that we didn't have enough left for groceries. He spent it on things like political campaign contributions to impress one of his girlfriends.

He never in fourteen years brought home enough money to support us, but when he realized I was getting ready to leave him he found a job that paid over $50,000 per year. This was after bringing home no more than $2,000 in any one year previously. At tax time he'd have a fit because he had to face that reality. We both always had the means to become financially independent but chose to lean on each other and we dragged each other down in a pit of low self-esteem.

In their addictive relationship, Brian never had to use his skills to earn a living because Beverly was always there to bail him out financially. Only when she was considering divorce was he forced into supporting himself.

For her part, Beverly saw her family's money as a means of holding on to Brian and making his life more comfortable. As Brian's affairs became more obvious, Beverly funneled more and more money into his business in the hope of showing him how much she cared. Although she had the means at any time to leave the relationship, she did not do so until things became intolerable, after fourteen years of marriage.

Emotional and Physical Illness

One of the costs of living in an addictive relationship is the pain endured by the partner who suspects that the mate is cheating. Long before partners learn for sure about their mate's affairs (most partners never know for certain) there is often a nagging suspicion. Partners expend enormous energy in proving to their mate that they are the only person the mate needs. Additional energy is spent in denial. Partners tell themselves they must be mistaken, since there is no definite proof of the mate's infidelity. Unable to explain their feelings of pain and their foreboding of doom, they conclude there must be something wrong with them.

The addict usually agrees it is the partner's problem, and may even suggest they obtain a psychiatric evaluation. Since partners are more likely to believe their husband than their own feelings, they may well concur that they must be crazy. When the addict colludes in convincing the partner that she is mistaken or deluded although her observations are in reality true, this is called *gaslighting* (after a classic 1944 film called *Gas Light* in which the husband of a newly-wed, played by Ingrid Bergman, attempts to make her doubt her own perceptions and her sanity). One can imagine how angry the partner is likely to be over the mental abuse when the truth finally comes out!

Whereas some women develop emotional or psychiatric problems in response to life in a chaotic family, others may develop physical symptoms. Many physical ailments are greatly influenced by the emotions: headaches, muscle spasms in the neck and shoulders, back-aches, stomach aches, asthma, irritable bowel syndrome, hypertension, colitis (inflammation of the lining of the colon), chest pains, and menstrual cramps. In addition, depression, fatigue, and insomnia are influenced by one's emotions. Obesity can result from emotional problems, and can itself cause an array of physical problems including diabetes, hypertension, and knee pain. Smoking, which is often increased by stress, can result in lung cancer, emphysema, and bronchitis. People who are very stressed are more susceptible to viral illnesses and to heart attacks. Autoimmune disorders such as rheumatoid arthritis and systemic lupus erythematosus (lupus) can flare up at a time of stress. In brief, a chaotic home life predisposes a person to illness.

Studies have indeed confirmed that spouses of addicts have more office visits to their doctor and higher medical costs per year than do other people. For example, a large population study of Kaiser-Permanente patients in California found that family members of persons addicted to alcohol or other drugs had medical costs of $490 more per year than family members of comparable but nonaddicted patients. Family members of addicts had a higher prevalence of behavior problems, depression, headache, low back pain, sexually transmitted diseases, substance abuse, and trauma than did family.[20]

Nancy, who had to cope with an unpredictable husband as well as seven children, experienced physical and emotional illness throughout her marriage. When one week after their honeymoon Nancy's new husband used the occasion of a hayride to flirt with a couple of teenage girls, Nancy reacted by developing sharp chest pains and hot flashes. Her symptoms immediately brought Nick's attention back to her. But Nancy's primary method of controlling her husband was through depression.

The main thing I did was to be really depressed. I did that even before I met him. My father did it to my mother. He was always depressed, he was always going to psychiatrists, and I hated that in him, but I did the same thing. If I needed something or if my parents weren't treating me right, I would get depressed and sick and go to bed. And then the pattern was that they would come and bring me a present or something and I'd be better. I did the same thing in my marriage. I spent a lot of time being depressed, which of course made Nicky feel guilty because he was always going out and doing something to feel guilty about anyway. He'd come home and see me there, probably nine months pregnant, in bed, depressed. I got satisfaction out of that. It was my way of relieving my tension, and it would get him back to treating me right. He'd treat me badly for several weeks, and then I'd get real depressed and he'd shape up a little and treat me better. That way I tried to control him.

Depression is in large part a neurochemical problem, resulting from an imbalance of brain chemicals. Most people don't ask to be depressed, and don't use it deliberately to manipulate others. Nancy may indeed have had an underlying organic depression. But she recognized that developing depressive symptoms was an effective way to control her husband.

Sexually Transmitted Disease

Consider the experience of Beverly:

I was pregnant and I knew my husband was having affairs with more than one woman. He came to tell me he had a sexually transmitted disease and his doctor had told him he had to tell everyone he had sex with to be checked for it. I was furious at first and then I was mortified. How was I going to face the family doctor I had known for years? I made the appointment and I went with mixed feelings: I was finally going to justifiably tell someone else what he had done. The other mixed feeling I had was I had to admit that while I was carrying this man's child and it appeared on the outside that I had an ideal marriage, I was unable to keep him sexually faithful to me.

I told the doctor the reason I had come and I cried. I was ashamed. This was not the image I had projected to my doctor in the past. He reassured me, "It happens all the time," but offered no advice. I needed to hear more. I returned to my husband and resumed sexual relations with him. I certainly knew now that I ran the risk of infecting the baby and of having to go back to the doctor, but my husband's approval was more important to me at that time.

Beverly shudders when she remembers how oblivious she was to her own responsibility for her health and that of her unborn child. At times when she is tempted to lay all the blame on her former husband, recalling this period in her life helps remind her that she was just as troubled as he was. Her addiction to her husband was more important to her than her own health or the baby's. Knowing she was risking contracting another sexually transmitted disease (STD), she nevertheless continued to have unprotected sex with him.

Beverly is not alone. Thousands of people who know or suspect that their spouses are having sex with others continue to sleep with them. They feel caught in a double bind. On the one hand, they fear catching a sexually transmitted disease (STD); but on the other, they believe if they deny their mates sex, then they will surely drive their mates into the arms of the other women or men. Given the choice between their own health and their addictive relationship, they are far more likely to give the relationship a higher priority. The lifelong pattern of these individuals is to put their own needs last, and this goes for physical health as well as happiness. Moreover, since one of the basic irrational fears of such partners is that sex is the most important sign of love, they will risk acquiring an STD in order to obtain this sign of "love" from their spouse.

This decision is easy to understand. Denying a spouse sex is not an easy choice for anyone. It is natural to want the intimacy of a sexual relationship with one's spouse, and it is difficult to decide to withhold sex. But withholding sex as punishment is different from withholding sex because of self-care. Helping the partner discern which of the two is operative (or both) will go a long way to increasing one's personal and romantic health.

The irony in the partner's fear of depriving her mate of sex is that giving sex is not likely to prevent an addict from seeking it outside the marriage. The fact is that one person cannot control another's addiction; it is part of codependency to believe that one can. Thus, by risking an STD partners cannot accomplish their goal of preventing the addict from being unfaithful. It merely forces him or her to find some other excuse besides, "My spouse won't make love with me." Meanwhile, the price the partner pays is constant worry about disease.

In my medical practice several middle-aged women came in periodically to be checked for sexually transmitted diseases. These women had chosen to continue having unprotected sex with their husbands despite knowing they were engaging in extramarital sex. They decided their current situation was preferable to getting a divorce and living alone. They were unwilling or unable to consider making a change.

In the past, when gonorrhea and syphilis were the most likely STDs that one could catch, a periodic STD check was reasonable, because both diseases are easily cured with antibiotics. Unfortunately, the STDs of the 21st century are viral, not curable by antibiotics and often permanent or even fatal. Thus, a periodic STD check is no longer a viable option for partners who value their health. Avoiding sex with a potentially infected person is the only reliable alternative.

For some STDs, visual inspection of a partner may decrease the risk of acquiring the disease. For others, use of a condom provides safety. Avoiding certain sexual practices may help prevent catching some diseases. It is my goal in this section to give you information about the most important STDs, thus enabling you to make an informed decision about continuing to have sex with a mate who is also having sexual relations with others. I will cover (1) the traditional STDs – syphilis and gonorrhea, (2) Chlamydia, an infection caused by a one-celled organism, the most prevalent STD in the United States in the 21st century, and (3) the viral STDs – HIV, herpes, hepatitis B and C, and venereal warts. I will also discuss the most common causes of vaginal discharge – Gardnerella, Trichomonas, and Candida (yeast).

Until recently, when most people heard the term *venereal disease* or VD (now termed sexually transmitted disease [STD] or sexually transmitted infection [STI]), they knew it meant syphilis and gonorrhea. Before the days of antibiotics these diseases were justly feared. Gonorrhea can cause sterility and syphilis can be fatal. The chemist Paul Ehrlich spent years searching for the "magic bullet" to cure syphilis, and thought he had found it in 1909 when he synthesized Salvarsan, a toxic arsenic preparation.

Syphilis

Isak Dinesen, author of *Out of Africa* and heroine of the film of the same name, spent most of her life combating syphilis, which she caught from her husband in 1914, shortly after they were married. She had traveled from Denmark to East Africa to marry Bror Blixen. Later she would tell a friend that she discovered, sometime after their first year of marriage, that he was having several affairs and lying to her about them.[21]

After several months of illness with high fevers, fatigue, joint pains, and depression, Dinesen returned to Europe to seek treatment. She was first seen by a doctor in France, who diagnosed syphilis. The doctor told her that she would need long and painful therapy if she were ever to be cured permanently, and there was no assurance that she could be. She then returned to Denmark, where for three months she received weekly injections of Salversan, a poisonous compound with unpleasant side effects. At the end of this period, spinal fluid tests showed the disease had been arrested, and she was no longer contagious. The following year she again made the long journey to East Africa.

Dinesen's syphilis infection was not cured, and several years later she began to experience new symptoms. The disease spread to her spine. For the rest of her life she had difficulty walking, an impaired sense of balance, severe abdominal pains, and episodes of severe vomiting. By the time penicillin became available in the 1940s, Dinesen had been battling syphilis for 30 years. Her body had sustained too much damage to be cured by antibiotics. She had several operations to try to relieve her pain, but by 1960, when she was 75 years old, the ravages of syphilis had made it too painful for her to walk or even to stand. She was grateful when death came two years later.

Syphilis in the pre-antibiotic era was a fearsome disease, a potential life sentence of pain and shame, and to forgive the person who gave you the infection must have been even harder than today, when a few injections of penicillin will cure the disease. In the antibiotic age, the worst aspect of acquiring a case of syphilis or gonorrhea is its implications for the relationship and for one's self worth.

Syphilis is forty times less prevalent than gonorrhea. The cause is *Treponema pallidum*, a corkscrew-shaped bacterium called a spirochete. According to the CDC, the rate of syphilis infections in 2013 was more than double the rate in 2000, with the greatest increase occurring in men who have sex with men. Having a syphilis infection increases by 3- to 5-fold the risk of transmitting and acquiring HIV (human immunodeficiency virus), the virus that causes AIDS (acquired immunodeficiency syndrome). About 95 percent of infections are acquired by sexual intercourse. A small percentage of cases occur from a moist kiss to the mouth of someone who has a syphilitic sore on the lips or tongue. Babies can contract the disease from the mother before birth.

About three weeks after intercourse with an infected person, a sore appears at the site of inoculation, usually the penis of the man or the labia (the vulva) of the woman, or on the lip after oral sex with an infected partner. The sore turns into a hard, painless ulcer (chancre). The ulcer teems with spirochetes and is very contagious. If not treated, it heals itself in two to four weeks. Unfortunately, the disease is not cured: Two to eight weeks after the primary ulcer heals, the person develops a flu-like illness that consists of fever, malaise, muscle aches, and a body rash. Lymph nodes in the neck, armpits, and groin enlarge and become hard lumps. This stage, called secondary syphilis, lasts a few weeks and then resolves, even without treatment. About two-thirds of people have no further symptoms. About a third, however, develop serious complications later, especially in the heart and nervous system, which can eventually cause death.

Syphilis in pregnancy can harm the baby. Treatment of the mother during the first sixteen weeks of pregnancy prevents infection of the fetus. Later infection of the mother can result in the birth of an infected child. The baby may have the usual symptoms of secondary syphilis. In addition, it might have some permanent abnormalities of the facial bones and teeth that are typical of congenital syphilis.

Syphilis is most contagious in the first year after infection, less so each following year, and is not at all contagious after four years. Syphilis is diagnosed by means of a blood test. However, the blood test is abnormal in only 25 percent of infected people in the first week, 50 percent in the second week, and 75 percent in the third week. Thus, the blood test reliably diagnoses the disease only about four weeks after initial infection. An infection can be diagnosed earlier by microscopic examination of material scraped from the painless ulcer.

In 2012, 75% of reported syphilis cases were in gay men. Married men who have sex with other men are at a higher risk of developing this disease and so, therefore, are their spouses. Men who use the internet to meet other men for sex should be aware of the increased risk of syphilis.

Syphilis is easily treated with antibiotics. To minimize the risk of catching this disease, do not have sex with a partner who has a sore on his genitals.

Gonorrhea

Gonorrhea is caused by a bacterium, *Neisseria gonorrhoeae*. Cases of gonorrhea are supposed to be reported to the Public Health Service. Since 2009, the annual incidence of gonorrhea has been increasing in both men and women; in 2012, according to the Center for Disease Control (CDC), there were 335,000 cases reported, and many others occurred but went unreported. Gonorrhea is the second-most-prevalent STD in the U.S. (after Chlamydia).

More men are affected than women. In infected women, symptoms begin two to eight days after intercourse. Only about 25 percent of infected women have symptoms, but all infected persons, whether they have symptoms or not, can transmit the disease to their sexual partner. Except for newborns, who can acquire gonorrhea infection in their eyes as they pass through the birth canal, sexual activity is the only way to acquire the disease. It can't be caught from toilet seats or towels.

Gonorrhea is spread more easily from man to woman than the reverse. A woman has a 50 percent chance of contracting the disease after exposure to an infected man, whereas a man has only about a 20 percent chance of getting it after sex with an infected woman.

About 30 to 40 percent of infected men have no symptoms, and will probably not realize they are infected. Men and women who have no symptoms but who transmit the disease to others are the major reason for the continuing spread of gonorrhea in the United States.

In women, gonorrhea can cause inflammation of the uterine cervix that can result in a vaginal discharge. Infection of the fallopian tubes, the pipelines through which the egg passes from the ovary on its way to the uterus, occurs in about 20 percent of cases and results in a disease called salpingitis or pelvic inflammatory disease (PID). PID can be caused by other organisms, but about half of all cases are caused by gonorrhea. The symptoms of the disease are fever, lower abdominal pain, and a vaginal discharge.

Infection of the fallopian tubes can cause them to be blocked off permanently, resulting in sterility. With each episode of PID there is a 15 percent risk of sterility. Salpingitis also increases the risk of a pregnancy occurring within the fallopian tubes (ectopic pregnancy), a dangerous event that can lead to death from hemorrhage (bleeding). Salpingitis is responsible for half of the ectopic pregnancies in the United States.

About 40 percent of women who develop a gonorrhea infection of the cervix also have the infection in their anus and rectum. This is usually because vaginal secretions have contaminated the rectal area. Most of the time there are no rectal symptoms. In gay men, infection of the anorectal area is acquired through anal intercourse with an infected man. Occasionally there is rectal burning, pain, and discharge, but more often there are no symptoms. Infection without symptoms can persist for months in the rectum and is probably the major reservoir of the gonococcus bacterium in gay men. An untreated man is thus potentially infectious for months.

Another complication of gonorrhea is arthritis of one or two joints. This occurs in 1 to 2 percent of people who have gonorrhea. One or two joints, often the wrist, knee, or ankle, become hot, painful, and swollen. A few days before the onset of the joint inflammation, the person often has a rash and fever. The rash and arthritis are completely cured by antibiotic treatment.

Another location for gonorrhea infection is the throat. The infection in this area most often results from oral-genital contact with an infected woman (cunnilingus) and not from kissing. There are no symptoms; however a person with a gonorrhea throat infection can transmit the disease to a man through oral sex.

Gonorrhea is diagnosed by inserting a swab into the vagina, rectum, penis, or throat and sending the swab to the microbiology laboratory which determines whether the organisms that grow out after several days are gonococci.

When a woman contracts gonorrhea during pregnancy, she risks giving birth to an infected baby. As the baby passes through the birth canal, its eyes can become infected (ophthalmia nenonatorum). To prevent blindness from this disease, almost all babies in the U.S. have special eyedrops put into their eyes at birth. Pregnant women who have untreated gonorrhea have an increased risk of miscarriage.

In recent years the Gonorrhea bacterium has developed resistance to each of the antibiotics that were previously effective to treat it. By 2012 the only antibiotic class recommended by the CDC for treatment of gonorrhea is the cephalosporins.

The chief symptom of gonorrhea in men is a thick yellow discharge from the penis ("the drip"). The discharge is loaded with gonococci. A good precaution for both sexes is using a condom, which will protect a man from acquiring the disease and from transmitting it via infected secretions.

Chlamydia

The most commonly reported STD in the United States today – and still on the increase – is chlamydia. Like gonorrhea, chlamydia is sexually transmitted. The organism can be recovered from the cervix of about 60 to 80 percent of female sexual partners of infected men. Most chlamydia infections in women are asymptomatic. Although they often have no symptoms, infected women can transmit the infection to their partners. If not treated, cervical infections in women can last over 20 months, all the while being spread to their sexual partners.

The primary symptom of chlamydia infection in women is frequent urination and burning when urinating. These are also the typical symptoms of a urinary tract infection (UTI), but urine from chlamydia-infected persons lacks the high concentration of bacteria usually found in a UTI. In addition to invading the urethra and cervix, the bacteria can travel up to the fallopian tubes and cause infection there (termed pelvic inflammatory disease or PID), a condition that can result in infertility. Infertility can be a potentially devastating consequence of chlamydia infection.

In a man, the chief symptom of chlamydia is a thin watery discharge from the penis. To minimize your risk of acquiring this infection, do not have sex with a man who has a urethral discharge. Wearing a condom will prevent a man from transmitting the infection.

About 30 to 60 percent of men who are treated for gonorrhea are also infected with Chlamydia, a frequent cause in men of nongonococcal urethritis (NGU, also termed nonspecific urethritis or NSU). Urethritis means inflammation of the urethra, the tube through which urine and semen exit the body. *Chlamydia trachomatis* is an organism that is often acquired together with gonorrhea. This bacterium is also the most common cause in young men of acute infection of the epididymis, a long tube in the scrotum.

A common scenario is the man who is treated for gonorrhea with penicillin, improves, but one to two weeks later again develops a discharge from the penis. The reason is this: The incubation period for chlamydia infection of the urethra (NGU) is one to two weeks, longer than gonorrhea. Chlamydia is resistant to penicillin and ampicillin, the drugs traditionally used to treat gonorrhea. Thus, just at the time that the gonorrhea infection resolves, the untreated chlamydia infection appears. For this reason, doctors now routinely treat gonor-rhea with drugs that are also effective against chlamydia.

Viral Hepatitis

Viral hepatitis is an infection of the liver, often transmitted sexu-ally or through needles. Its chief symptoms are fever, jaundice (yel-low skin and eyeballs), abdominal pain, and fatigue. Several different viruses cause the disease. The hepatitis A virus is excreted in the stool, which can then contaminate food (through poor hand washing) or water supplies. Sexual transmission is possible between partners who participate in oral-anal sex.

Hepatitis A is occasionally fatal, but most people recover fully; there is no chronic carrier state. Hepatitis A is very contagious, and about 40% of people in the United States have been infected and have developed immunity; most of them had no symptoms of the disease. An effective vaccine is available for people who are at risk of exposure.

Hepatitis B, another cause of viral hepatitis, has about a 5 per-cent likelihood of becoming chronic. Chronic carriers of the virus often feel well and are sexually active, but continue to be contagious. Hepatitis B is not spread through food, water, or by casual contact. It is much more easily transmitted sexually than is hepatitis A or HIV: among monogamous couples who repeatedly have unprotected sex, the risk of transmission of hepatitis B from an infected partner is 30 percent. Currently, more than half of adult cases of hepatitis B are transmitted sexually, with 25% of all adult cases related to hetero-sexual intercourse. Persistent hepatitis B is an important risk factor for development of hepatocellular carcinoma (liver cancer), the most common non-skin cancer in the world.

A very effective vaccine to prevent hepatitis B is available and is recommended for young children, health care workers, travelers, and anyone at risk. Using condoms will help prevent transmission of the disease.

A third common cause of hepatitis is the hepatitis C virus (HCV). Infection with the virus, which is usually transferred through blood, becomes chronic in 85% of cases. Hepatitis C is the most common blood-borne disease in the United States today. Because of wide-spread screening of blood donors it is rare for HCV to be transferred via a blood transfusion, but before 1992 most cases were spread by contaminated blood. Today, most new cases result from previous or current intravenous use of illegal drugs.[22]

People who have multiple sexual partners are at increased risk of acquiring hepatitis C (HCV). Transmission from men to women seems a little more common than vice versa. Fortunately, in monog-amous long-term relationships, transmission of HCV is rare. In 2010 CDC guidelines included the following: "Most scientific evi-dence demonstrates that although HCV can be transmitted sexu-ally, such transmission happens rarely. Because incident HCV has not been demonstrated to occur in heterosexual partner-pairs fol-lowed over time, condom use might not be necessary in such cir-cumstances." In other words, the risk of transmission is low even without a condom.

At least 20% of chronic hepatitis C cases develop cirrhosis of the liver, which can be fatal. This infection is a common reason that peo-ple need a liver transplant. In addition, HCV-positive people have a 5- to 7-fold increased risk of liver cancer. Because both HCV and HIV are transmitted through blood, it's not surprising that many people acquire both viruses. About one quarter of HIV-infected persons in the United States are also infected with hepatitis C virus (HCV). HCV is one of the most important causes of chronic liver disease in the United States. HCV infection progresses more rapidly to liver damage in HIV-infected persons. In recent years new effec-tive treatments for Hepatitis C have been developed. The latest is a combination of two drugs in a once-daily pill (called Harvoni) that cures Hepatitis C in 8-12 weeks in most people.

Herpes

Before the HIV epidemic, the disease that most frightened people away from casual sexual encounters was herpes "Love is for now, but herpes is forever," was a popular saying. An advertisement for a herpes medication in a medical journal showed a very sad young woman sitting alone on a park bench; the caption reads: "He never even mentioned a word about herpes. . . ." One in five adolescent and adult Americans has genital herpes.

Herpes is caused by a virus (*Herpes simplex*) which causes blisters and ulcers on the face and genitals. There are two *Herpes simplex* viruses: type one, which traditionally causes infections above the waist such as fever blisters on the lips, and type two, the usual cause of genital herpes. However, with the increase in oral-genital contact, this distinction is becoming less important because type one is being increasingly transferred to the genitals from the mouth. Each type can be transmitted both sexually and non-sexually. For example, dental hygienists whose fingers touch herpes-infected lips risk contracting a herpes infection of the fingers. About 20 percent of adult Americans have antibodies to Herpesvirus type 2 in their bloodstream, indicating that they were exposed to Herpesvirus 2. According to the CDC in 2014, among people in the U.S. aged 14-49 years, about 1 out of every 6 have genital herpes.[23]

The reason herpes infection is so feared is that there is no cure. Once people have an infection, they are likely to have it for life. After they recover from the initial episode, they are usually not cured. The virus travels up the nervous system and stays dormant for a while, perhaps forever. But then something may trigger a recurrence, and another attack occurs. In some people emotional stress, physical trauma, or the menstrual period seems to trigger an attack.

The first episode is the worst. Two to seven days after being infected by the virus, there is a prickly sensation or pain, and several hours later painful blisters appear. In the man the blisters are usually on the penis; in the woman, in the vagina and vulva (surrounding tissues).The blisters open and ulcerate, and then crust over and heal after two to three weeks. Women usually experience more pain than do men. In addition to blisters developing, the lymph nodes in the groin enlarge and become painful lumps.

Recurrent attacks are milder than the primary episode. They last less time – usually less than ten days, and the pain is less severe. After the first attack, more than 50 percent of people have recurrences within six months. Fortunately, with time, recurrences become less frequent.

A herpes outbreak is diagnosed primarily by the appearance of the lesions. The main causes of ulcers on the penis are syphilis and herpes, and an important distinction is that only those of herpes are painful. Herpes can also be diagnosed by scraping the base of the ulcer and then growing the organisms from the scrapings, or else staining the scrapings and examining them directly under a microscope. A blood test for Herpes virus can tell whether you have ever been infected – and new tests can distinguish between Herpesvirus 1 and 2 – but they cannot tell whether a person was infected recently or long ago.

Having had a couple of outbreaks, a person can usually tell when another recurrence is about to happen because of a sensation of itching, tingling, burning, or tenderness at the site of the eruption. At this stage the person is infectious (can transmit the virus to another person) and needs to avoid sexual contact. The blisters and ulcers are also infectious. Sexual contact should be avoided as long as there are *any* visible lesions. In one study, Herpesvirus particles were found in more than 50 percent of women during the first four days of a recurrent herpes attack, 26 percent on day 6, and none after day 10. In other words, none of the women in the study could transmit an infection after the tenth day of an attack, so sex would be safe at this time.

Between attacks, there is still a small risk of transmitting the disease. Up to 15 percent of men and 2 percent of women may harbor

Herpesvirus in the urethra or vagina without any visible lesions and may be infections. Using a condom helps to lower the risk of transmitting and catching herpes.

Because Herpesvirus particles lie dormant in the nerve fibers, there is no effective cure, although antiviral drugs can lessen the pain and speed healing of herpes ulcers. They can also help prevent recurrences for as long as the medication is taken, but the drugs do not cure the disease.

Herpes infection has a particular risk for newborns. A baby born to a mother who has an outbreak at the time of delivery is at high risk of developing a serious and potentially fatal systemic herpes infection. Fortunately, the risk of transmission of the virus to the baby is very low, even if an active infection is present. In a woman with a history of herpes, the obstetrician will carefully inspect the genital area before delivery and may choose to perform a Cesarian section if lesions are present.

If your spouse has herpes and you do not, it will take a joint effort to keep you from acquiring this disease. First, don't have intercourse or oral sex from the time your mate feels an attack coming on until the ulcers have totally healed. Also, because of the small but definite risk that infected cells can shed the virus even in the absence of symptoms, a condom should routinely be used, even when there is no evidence of an outbreak.

Genital Warts

Genital warts (Condyloma acuminatum) are caused by the same virus, the human papillomavirus (HPV), that causes ordinary warts. But unlike ordinary warts, genital warts rarely disappear spontaneously. They are painless but very contagious: about two-thirds of people who have sexual contact with a partner with genital warts will develop warts, usually within 3 months of contact. The warts can be found on the vagina, vulva, penis, scrotum, anus, fingers, tongue, and roof of the mouth. Depending on the size and number of warts, several treatments are available. Small warts can be removed by freezing with liquid nitrogen, or burning with a carbon dioxide laser, or with electrocautery. For larger lesions, several chemical treatments exist. Surgery may be required to remove very large warts. Although treatments can get rid of the warts, none get rid of the virus. Because the virus is still present in your body, warts often come back after treatment.

Papillomavirus (HPV) infection of the uterine cervix is very common; evidence of this is found in 1 to 2 percent of all Pap smears. There are many difference strains of HPV; some strains predispose to cancer of the cervix. A woman whose husband has genital warts should have a Pap smear every year; the Pap smear detects precancerous changes in the cervix early enough to permit easy treatment. If a man has genital warts on his penis, use of a condom will help prevent transmission of this disease to the spouse. You must avoid unprotected contact with any genital wart.

Vaginitis

Vaginal infections (vaginitis) are very common. One of the chief concerns of most women who have a vaginal infection is whether or not it is sexually transmitted. Although the common vaginal infections are not considered true STDs, it's worth describing them briefly.

There are three common causes of vaginitis; all produce a similar symptom, a vaginal discharge. The specific symptoms are sufficiently different, however, that it is often possible tentatively to diagnose which particular infection a woman has just by talking with her. The three infections are Candida (yeast), Trichomonas (trich), and Gardnerella (nonspecific vaginitis or bacterial vaginitis). All are diagnosed the same way: Using a cotton-tipped applicator, the physician obtains a sample of the vaginal secretion and examines it directly under a microscope (or sends it to the lab for an examination). Each of the three organisms has a distinctive microscopic appearance.

A woman with a vaginal yeast infection complains most about itching. She has a scanty, white, cheesy vaginal discharge. She may have recently been treated with an antibiotic. Pregnancy, birth control pills, and diabetes also predispose to yeast infections. Yeast organisms (Candida) are naturally found in the vagina and gastrointestinal tract of most women. When any of the predisposing conditions are present, the organisms can start multiplying rapidly and will cause symptoms.

Candida infections are not usually sexually transmitted, although occasionally the partner of an infected woman will develop a mild yeast infection on the skin of his penis. Effective anti-Candida vaginal creams or suppositories will usually eradicate the vaginal infection quickly. A single dose of an oral anti-fungal drug is also effective.

Trichomoniasis is a vaginal infection that is now more prevalent in the United States than most other, better-known STDs and has been linked to infertility problems as well as to HIV infection. *Trichomonas vaginalis* is a protozoan, a one-celled organism with a wiggly tail. The woman who has a trich infection complains of a yellow discharge with an offensive odor. The discharge is frothy and profuse. The disease can be easily diagnosed with a test using a dipstick. Up to 90 percent of men with trichomoniasis have no symptoms. People who have trichomoniasis are more susceptible to acquiring an HIV infection if they are exposed to the virus than are persons who do not have trichomoniasis.

Gardnerella vaginalis, a type of bacteria, also causes profuse vaginal discharge, but it is thinner and less odorous than Trichomonas. Both infections are effectively treated with antibiotics. Both infections can be sexually transmitted (Gardnerella less so than Trichomonas), but both are also found in women who are not sexually active. Because of the possibility of sexual transmission, some doctors routinely treat the sexual partner of women who have either infection. Other physicians treat only the woman. If she has a recurrence of the infection shortly after treatment, the doctor assumes it's being passed back and forth between the two partners. Only then is the man treated as well. There are usually no symptoms in men who are carriers of Gardnerella or Trichomonas. The monogamous man or woman who develops a case of syphilis or gonorrhea can justifiably assume that the spouse has had extramarital sex. Such is not true, however, for the three types of vaginitis just described. Like Candida, the Gardnerella and Trichomonas organisms may be found in the normal vaginal tract, just waiting to cause trouble under the right circumstances.

HIV and AIDS

The acquired immunodeficiency syndrome (AIDS) is the most fearsome of the new STDs. AIDS was first diagnosed in gay men in 1981. These previously healthy young men developed diseases usually seen only in people whose immune systems were somehow damaged, for example, by disease, cancer chemotherapy, or radiation. The cause is a virus, the human immunodeficiency virus (HIV), which damages the body's immune system. The virus is transmitted through blood and body secretions, much like hepatitis B. Among gay men, the virus is passed primarily through semen. In the other high-risk groups – intravenous drug abusers and hemophiliacs receiving blood products to halt their bleeding – the virus is transferred through blood. In sub-Saharan Africa, whose population is being decimated by AIDS, the most common mode of transmission is heterosexual intercourse.

The symptoms of AIDS are varied. Often there is weight loss, fatigue, coughing, and a severe pneumonia. Purple or brown patches or nodules may appear on the skin. Widespread fungal or viral infections or tuberculosis may appear. One infection tends to follow another, and many victims eventually succumb. In other cases the virus directly infects the brain, causing early dementia and neurological abnormalities.

HIV disease is currently a massive world epidemic. The CDC reported in 2014 that in recent years there have been about 50,000 new HIV infections in the U.S per year. Worldwide, by 2011 34 million people were living with HIV and almost 30 million people had died from AIDS-related causes since the beginning of the epidemic. New HIV infections are still a huge problem, affecting primarily the younger generation. Intercourse is the primary way women are infected, often by having sex with men whose HIV infection is unrecognized.

Although there have been a few cases of HIV carriers who eventually were apparently cured, and there have been HIV carriers who never developed AIDS, most people who have been infected eventually become ill, usually after 6-10 years. Until the mid-1990s, AIDS was considered a fatal disease. Fortunately currently a whole new generation of anti-HIV drugs are available which have significantly prolonged survival and have changed AIDS in developed countries from a rapidly fatal disease to a chronic illness lasting years. Unfortunately, most people with AIDS in sub-Saharan Africa and other Third World countries do not have access to modern drugs and continue to die at a rapid rate.

The HIV virus is transmitted from person to person through body secretions (such as blood, semen, and saliva). The most common ways the virus is transferred between people are sexual intercourse and intravenous drug abuse involving the sharing of contaminated needles.

The estimated risk of sexual transmission of HIV *per sexual encounter* is low, 1 in 300 for male-to-male transmission, 1 in 500 for male to female, and 1 in 1,000 for female to males.[24] However, some infected persons transmit the virus much more efficiently than others to their sexual partners, and some persons remain uninfected despite repeated exposures to the virus through unprotected sex. Some people have been shown to have a genetic resistance to acquiring HIV infection. The presence of other STDs increases the risk of contracting HIV.

During heterosexual intercourse, HIV is more easily transmitted from male to female than from female to male. This is because transmission of HIV is most efficient when there is transfer of body fluids such as semen to the mucous membranes of another person. A tear in the mucous membrane is necessary in order for the virus to gain access to the bloodstream of the recipient. During intercourse, semen contacts the lining of the vagina, which is a mucous membrane. Any abrasion in the vagina will facilitate absorption of the virus. On the other hand, when the female is the infected partner, her vaginal secretions will contact primarily the skin of the penis, which is not a mucous membrane and therefore thicker and less vulnerable to infection. To cause infection in the male, there would have to be a significant cut or tear in the skin of the penis.

Transmission of HIV is more efficient during anal intercourse than during vaginal intercourse. This is because the lining of the rectum is damaged more easily than the lining of the vagina. Abrasions of the wall of the rectum are very likely during anal intercourse, providing easy access to the bloodstream for HIV particles. This is why a cardinal tenet of safe sex is to avoid anal intercourse.

HIV infection is diagnosed by a series of blood tests. Initially a screening test (ELISA) is done. If positive, it is confirmed by a more sensitive test, called Western blot. After exposure to HIV, it may take up to 8 weeks for a person's blood to convert from negative to positive. This is why it is recommended that HIV testing be done at 6 weeks, 12 weeks, and finally at 6 months after possible exposure. It is wise to use condoms while waiting for test results.

For women who believe their husbands are at risk of becoming infected with HIV, especially if the man is having multiple sexual encounters with gay men or female prostitutes, avoiding intercourse is the safest alternative. Since the HIV virus usually cannot pass through condoms, the next best choice is to use condoms.

Summary

In the past half century, the landscape of sexually transmitted diseases has undergone a sea change, but the problem of STDs looms as large as ever. Feared bacterial infections (syphilis, gonorrhea) have become treatable and less common. But at the same time, more recent viral infections (HIV, Herpes, hepatitis B and C), continue to spread. In addition, technological advances have produced new ways of assuring the dissemination of STDs. The internet has become a potent means of accessing new sexual partners, partners who may be carrying STDs. A year 2000 study of persons attending an STD clinic in Denver found that individuals who sought internet sex partners for real-life meetings reported a higher level of other sexual risk-taking behaviors compared with those who did not use the internet for sexual connections.[25] The internet sex seekers were more likely to be male and gay, and reported more previous STDs, more partners, more anal sex, and more sexual exposure to partners known to be HIV-positive.

An old-but-still-valid medical article titled "Primary Prevention of Sexually Transmitted Diseases" advises:

> Abstinence is the only foolproof preventive measure. For sexually active persons, stable monogamy carries no risk of acquiring an STD, provided neither partner is infected. Because many STDs are often asymptomatic (gonorrhea, Herpes, hepatitis B, and infections with HIV and Chlamydia), infected persons may be impossible to identify and avoid. Simply reducing the number of sexual partners and avoiding persons known to have many other sexual partners should reduce the likelihood of exposure to an infected person.
>
> Sexually active persons may also benefit from carefully inspecting each potential partner for genital lesions, a rash, or a discharge, and asking direct questions about possible infection.[26]

Partners whose mates have affairs are justifiably concerned about their risk of acquiring a sexually transmitted disease. Becoming more informed about these diseases and about the possibility of protecting themselves from each disease is one useful step. When I advised a young single woman that she ask her new sexual partner, whom she hardly knew, to use a condom, she replied, "I couldn't do that – he might be offended!" As long as a woman is more concerned about not offending a man than about protecting herself, she is unlikely to take precautions that would decrease her risk of contracting an STD. As long as a woman is unwilling to avoid sex with her unfaithful husband, or at least of insisting on condom use, for fear of alienating him or even losing him, she remains at risk of catching from him a potentially serious disease.

In order to be able to protect ourselves, we must first have sufficient self-esteem to realize we have some real choices about our actions. Then we can make decisions based on our own best interest rather than out of fear.

The second half of this book examines the process of recovery from relationship trauma and codependency and development of an improved self-esteem. The result can be an enhanced ability to take care of ourselves, both physically and emotionally.

Male partners of sex addicts

Living with a sex addict is not a problem restricted to women. Both heterosexual and gay men can find themselves in the role of partner. Sex addiction is more prevalent among gay and bisexual men than in heterosexual men.[27] Many of these men are married to women, but many others are in primary relationships with other men. The existence of female and gay male sex addicts means, of course, that many men are suffering silently from the consequences of this disease in their mates. Men report largely similar reactions to women's when they learn that their partners have been having affairs. One difference, however, is that heterosexual men are more upset than are women by sexual infidelity, whereas women are more upset than are heterosexual men by emotional infidelity. This was confirmed in a recent study in which a large group of men and women were asked to imagine which would upset them more – their partners having sex with someone else (but not falling in love with them), or their partners falling in love with someone else (but not having sex with them.[28] Significantly more heterosexual men than women (54% versus 35%) were more jealous about sexual than emotional infidelity. Interestingly, this group of men was unique, as bisexual and gay men and all the groups of women were more upset with emotional infidelity.

In Chapter One you read the story of Matt, a policeman whose wife had had multiple affairs. Here is the story of another man who is struggling with an unfaithful wife:

Vincent's Story
A 44 year old minister, Vincent had been married for 24 years when his wife Valerie became hooked on the internet. She wrote and read erotic stories and e-mails, participated in sexually-oriented chat rooms, became involved in the dominance/submission, sadomasochism (BDSM) online community, and participated in both online and real-life sexual encounters with various men. She spent thousands of dollars on airplane tickets and phone calls, and eventually lost her job because of her online activities. She stopped paying bills or doing housework. She stopped going on family outings, locked the kids out of her room and ignored them when she was supposed to be caring for them.

Vincent is still hanging in there, hoping he can somehow help Valerie to overcome her problems. He reports,

The whole family is still suffering the consequences of Valerie's sex addiction. The kids are still hurting, and one of them is being treated for depression. I've been depressed too, and am still on medication. I got arrested for trying to rescue Valerie one night; my codependent behavior earned me a fine and 40 hours of community services. I was exposed to sexually transmitted diseases.

I began to doubt my masculinity. At first we had sex more than ever as I desperately tried to prove myself. Then the sex with her made me sick – I'd get strong pictures in my head of what she did and lusted after, and I'd feel repelled and bad. When we were making love, she was thinking of her online partners. She reported all our personal sexual activities to her online partners. I used to see sex as a very intimate loving thing. Now I can't be intimate or vulnerable – sex now is more recreational or just out of need.

Why am I still with her? I feel if I divorce her she will end up dead in a hotel room somewhere or bring perverted people into my children's lives. I'm still very codependent and I feel I have to protect her. I am also a pastor and I think I feel (codependently) that I need to protect the church from the scandal of another divorced clergy person and of anyone finding out about her.

Vincent characterizes himself as codependent. But there's a line between codependency and caring. Partners (and of course parents) of alcoholics and drug addicts or other addicts want to help those they love who have lost their way. A goal for family members who attend Al-Anon and similar programs for families of other addicts is to recognize when caring turns into enabling, when it's time to set limits or even to leave the relationship. This is never an easy choice.

Vincent and Matt (See Chapter One) were similar in several respects – neither reported having a drug or sex addiction themselves; both were in the helping professions; both tolerated intolerable behaviors and reported being understanding rather than overtly angry; both exhibited coaddictive behaviors (Vincent's rescue efforts even got him arrested); and although only Vincent reported being treated for depression, Matt related feelings of hopelessness, rejection, and inadequacy, consistent with depression. When many other men would have long since abandoned the marriage, Matt and Vincent stayed.

When a man's sexual behavior is out of control, his wife's first reaction is often to blame herself. Her friends perceive her as a victim, and empathize with her in her efforts to save the marriage. On the other hand, when a married woman has affairs, society usually blames her too, and considers her husband a fool for staying with her. We even have a pejorative name, "cuckold," for a man whose wife has cheated on him, and such a man was traditionally laughed at. The result is that husbands of female sex addicts are more likely to divorce their spouses than are women whose husbands are sexually addicted. Husbands of women sex addicts are also less likely to examine their own vulnerability than are wives of male sex addicts.

Who, then, are the men who choose to remain in the relationship despite societal support for leaving, especially when other sexual partners were involved?

To learn more about such men, Burt Schneider and I did a study in which I interviewed 24 married women sex addicts while he interviewed their husbands.[29] The women were all in recovery from their sex addiction and the men had chosen to stay with them. Our first finding was that after learning of their partner's infidelity, men were much more likely to be in touch with their anger than were women. Whereas women's initial reactions were likely to be depression, fear of loss of the relationship, and self-blame, men more often felt and expressed overt anger, often rage. Only later did they get in touch with their sadness and fear. Joe, married for 12 years, described his initial reaction:

One night my wife told me she wanted to talk with me. She told me she had been molested by her brother when she was a kid and that that was the start of her preoccupation with sex. She proceeded to tell me about several affairs, including one I had not even suspected – with a guy who had just built a bookcase for us. I immediately went into deep anger and sadness, crying and rage at the same time. I pulled the bookcase off the wall and threw it off the balcony. Then I got my axe and chopped it into small pieces. The next day, I built a fire and burned the pieces. Looking back, I realize that that helped me get rid of a lot of anger.

Joe found his way to an S-Anon group, and he and his wife were able eventually to repair their marriage.

Another man related, "When she told me about her affairs during Family Week, I went into a jealous rage. One night in a parking lot I tried to run down a man she'd been with."

A recovering alcoholic reported,

After she told me about the other men, I wanted to strike back at these people who I felt had stolen something from me that I valued highly. I felt I'd been irreparably damaged. Getting even with them was justified, if I could only find out who they were. I went through three or four weeks of intense emotional swings between my normal self and some real homicidal rage. I felt if I found out one guy's name I would have to kill him. The urge was even more powerful than the last time I felt an urge to drink. It finally died down, and hasn't come back.

According to the study of 24 couples, after the initial anger stage, the way men reacted to their partners' sexual addiction depended in large part on two factors, (1) whether or not they themselves had an addiction history, and (2) whether or not the spouse had actually had extramarital sexual contact rather than just flirtation or perhaps kissing. (Because the study was done before the internet existed, we did not have information about husbands' reactions to wives' online sexual activities). Seventeen of the 24 husbands (71%) were themselves sexually addicted or chemically dependent. Most had attended Twelve-Step programs and were still, or had been, involved in therapy. Because they had experienced powerlessness over their own addictions, they tended to be more understanding than men who had no experience with addictions. They were more willing to talk openly with their wives about the wives' struggle with sex addiction. Husbands who were sex addicts (10) tended to be the most supportive of the wife's recovery program.

At first I thought I might not be a good lover. I fell immediately into my coaddict mode. I started asking her a lot of questions about it, the same as she asked me when I came home from my first meeting. I felt the roles changing very fast when she told me she was a sex addict! Now I realize she is, and I'm 100% behind her.

Another wife of a sex addict told him she had a problem with emotional affairs and fantasizing about other men and women. He said,

My first reaction was not to believe she had an addiction. She certainly didn't have it as bad as I did, and I certainly didn't want her going to my meetings. But after a while I realized that if I expect her to understand and accept my addiction, then certainly I need to understand and accept hers. In some ways it's made me feel less guilty about my past behaviors, because she's done some of those things too.

Husbands who were neither sex addicts nor alcoholics were the most likely to rationalize and excuse, understate, and discount the wife's addiction, to attribute the behavior to underlying issues, and to assume that if the behavior had stopped it was no longer a problem. In a response demonstrating a tendency to minimize, one man said,

I accept the therapist's explanation that she had a compulsion for relationships more than sex. I think that if my wife had been really interested in sex, she'd have had more than five partners in seven years.

According to another man,

I think she got depressed over a relationship that ended long ago, and her addiction was just a way of handling the feelings of the depression. I think she's cured. I don't think she needs to continue going to meetings.

Just as it's more difficult for women than men to admit they are sex addicts, it is more difficult for men than women to own up to being in relationship with an unfaithful spouse or partner. Men are more reluctant than women to attend Twelve-Step recovery groups and to get therapy. After the initial period of anger, those who are themselves addicts have an easier time of it, because they have a framework within which to position their spouse's behavior, and understanding of the recovery process that she has begun. Men who themselves are recovering from some addiction are familiar with the concept that "addiction is a family disease," and therefore recognize they need some recovery work themselves in order to cope with the spouse's sex addiction.

In contrast, when faced with a recurrently unfaithful wife, men who are not themselves chemically dependent or sexually addicted feel lost at sea. Unfamiliar with the nature of addiction,

- They flounder for explanations for the wife's affairs or involvement in fantasy romances
- They minimize the significance of the behavior or the effort needed to overcome it
- They don't understand the wife's need for continuing attendance at Twelve-Step meetings, believing that any sign of progress means "she's fixed"
- They tend to remain in the victim role and don't understand how they may be enablers
- They tend to believe that if they continue to be loving, caring husbands, their love will eventually make her see the light, appreciate them, and be "cured"
- They feel powerless and tend to get depressed, but may resist treatment
- They are less likely (than husbands who are themselves addicts) to attend a Twelve-Step meeting for partners or a couples' recovery meeting

Such men would be helped by getting their depression treated, by seeing a knowledgeable counselor, and by joining Twelve-Step groups such as S-Anon and COSA (see Appendix B for contact information). In the meetings they could learn about recovery from addiction, coaddiction, and trauma and how to reclaim their power. They learn how to set some boundaries for acceptable behaviors on their part and that of their partner. If they decide to stay in the relationship, it will be by choice and not out of dependency.

Husbands who are not themselves addicts fall into two distinct groups, according to Marnie Ferree, who has counseled such couples.[30] Some men are *angry*, while others are *passive*. The first group remains stuck in anger. They continue to blame the wife without looking at their own contributions to the marital dysfunction. They are not motivated to seek any help for themselves. Instead, they attempt to control her in a variety of ways. The second group tends to become depressed rather than angry. The shut down emotionally, deny or ignore their mate's behavior, and avoid dealing with the problem. They hope she will get "fixed" as soon as possible, so that they can "forgive and forget." In the meantime, they are patient, kind, and conflict-avoidant.

The second group, too, can benefit from getting help and support for themselves. On such partner was a 33-year old man whose wife left him after she had a series of affairs. Subsequently for several years he attended S-Anon meetings (a Twelve-Step program for partners of sex addicts) even though he was the only male there. He wrote,

I used to do almost anything to try to make peace, including making long lists of things that annoyed my wife and trying to remember to avoid all those things. Maybe then, I thought, she wouldn't be angry all the time. I never did succeed.

In S-Anon, I learned first that there wasn't anything I could do that was going to change her. Then I learned that that doesn't absolve me from having to work on my own issues. I realize now that my wife hungered for an emotional connection that wasn't there. I was never vulnerable with her. And when there was conflict, I withdrew.

Male partners, just like female partners, need support and validation of the relational trauma they have experienced related to their mate's sex addiction. And like female partners, they can benefit from looking at their own vulnerabilities.

Gay Men

A debate still rages regarding whether men are biologically inclined to have multiple sexual partners or whether this is a learned behavior. Regardless of the reason, it is generally accepted that men are less inclined than women to be monogamous. Not surprisingly, then, having multiple sexual encounters is an accepted part of the urban male gay culture. As therapist Robert Weiss has written, "For many within the urban gay community, public social activity remains tied to a great degree, to the use of alcohol and the seeking of sex and/ or romance. . . Gay bathhouses and sex clubs continue to thrive on men seeking anonymous, casual, sexual encounters. These broadly accepted communal activities [are] immersed in experiences that nourish chemical and sexual addiction."[31]

Because monogamy is not the norm in this community, a gay man in a committed relationship faces particular challenges if his partner continues to have sex with other men while he seeks monogamy. Unlike women, who are likely to get support and validation from friends and therapists if their significant other is unfaithful, such support may be lacking for the gay man. Yet the feelings of rejection and abandonment are just as real.

Summary

The experiences of Jean Harris and Cynthia Koestler and of people I interviewed reveal some common characteristics of life among addicted couples. Clues to sex addiction (and, often, concurrent addiction to alcohol or other chemicals) are often present when they first meet and may, in fact, be a part of the attraction. Many partners ignore the clues, or to believe they are not relevant to the relationship, or that they can live with them. The couple's courtship is very exciting, unpredictable, and intense. These elements continue into the marriage, and keep partners hooked even when the going gets rough. Sex is often very good, at least for a while. If, in the addict's search for the new and different, he asks partners to perform sexual acts with which they are uncomfortable, the partners agree because they fear abandonment. On the other hand, their sexual relationship may become more and more routine and thought of as a duty, as the addict focuses his or her attention on outside sexual activities.

In their marriage, partners never quite feel secure; there is always the fear of an imminent disaster, most likely of the mate's leaving the relationship. Needing to see the addict in a positive light, the partner tends to make excuses for the addict's hurtful behavior and tries to remember only the good times. For as long as possible, partners deny any evidence of the mate's affairs, and if confrontation can no longer be avoided, they believe the mate's promise to change. Whenever what the addict says disagrees with the objective evidence, partners are likely to believe what the addict says. They keep hoping that things will be better in the future, and usually have an apparently plausible explanation for why things are not that good at the moment.

If partners finally hurt enough to begin to pull away from the addict, the mate will suddenly find them very attractive and a new challenge. The addict may again become the ardent, sensitive, concerned lover the partner remembers from long ago and kept hoping would resurface. Believing that their wish has finally been granted, many partners give the mate another chance, only to find him returning to his usual behavior once the partner is securely back in the fold. Their friends cannot understand the partner's changes of heart, and eventually stop believing them when the partner once again talks of leaving the mate.

Sex addicts are usually just as dependent on their partners as the partner is on the mate, and the couple is likely to continue indefinitely in their unhealthy dance unless some treatment intervenes.

Part Two:
The Road to Recovery

CHAPTER SIX

The Elements of Recovery

Many years ago Patrick Carnes studied a group of partners of sex addicts and reported the stages of successful recovery.[1] These stages are still very relevant today, and Stefanie Carnes and Cara Tripodi subsequently wrote about them in greater detail.[2] They are:

1. *Developing/Prediscovery*: This is the time period before you knew for certain there was a problem. You may have been suspicious; you may have denied your concerns, believed the addict's lies, or blamed yourself; you may have tolerated and normalized intolerable behavior; and you may have tried to control the situation and make it right.

2. *Crisis/Decision/Information gathering*: You become aware of the addict's secret life and experience a crisis of trust; You may compulsively check up on the addict and seek information; you may obsess about his or her activities; you may learn everything you can about sex addiction; you may retaliate, for example by finding another sexual partner. As Carnes and Tripodi wrote, "how you respond has a lot to do with your personality and whether you suffered from prior trauma or crisis in your life." You are likely to be more reactive if you have experienced previous losses (such as childhood neglect, abandonment, or abuse.)

3. *Shock*: You experience numbness, but also anger, self-doubt, fear, and conflict.

4. *Grief/Ambivalence*: This is where you experience the full emotional impact of what has happened, especially intense pain, hopelessness, grief, rejection, and loss of your relationship as you thought it was. You also experience ambivalence about the relationship, because you start to develop self-awareness and to consider your own needs and desires rather than focusing on your partner.

5. *Repair*: In this period, which may take years to reach, you concentrate on your personal growth. You may revisit and come to more peace about negative childhood experiences and how they may have influenced your choices and decisions in your relationship. You develop your spirituality.

6. *Growth:* In this final stage, you let go of feeling like a victim. You make meaning out of your suffering and the positive changes in your life resulting from the addiction. You recognize your role in the dysfunction of your relationship. Your focus is more on your own growth, on communication skills, and on other areas in your life besides your relationship.

Successfully negotiating these steps requires carrying out a series of tasks, and is facilitated by working with a knowledgeable therapist as well as getting peer support such as is found in a Twelve-Step program. The path through these tasks are described in detail in the 2012 workbook *Facing Heartbreak: Steps to Recovery for Partners of Sex Addicts*[3]. These tasks consist of:

- Coping with the trauma of discovery or disclosure
- Managing the crisis
- Developing a plan for support and self-care
- Understanding the nature of sex addiction
- Dealing with the emotional aftershock

- Communicating effectively about the addiction
- Creating a recovery plan

This chapter will help you understand some of the elements of recovery; subsequent chapters will focus on couple recovery, on finding a therapist, and on recovery as a single person.

Partners of sex addicts often wait months or even years before seeking help for themselves. Why do they wait so long? Some reasons may be their shame at revealing to outsiders the family problems; their feeling that they may be to blame for the addict's behavior; and their hope that the problem is only temporary and will somehow improve. Unsure as they may be about what is normal behavior, they often experience a long accumulation of problems and painful episodes before finally breaking through their own denial and becoming ready to seek help.

Some partners decide to get help in the aftermath of a marital crisis precipitated by their mate's admitting to having an affair. Others who are aware of their mate's infidelity come to therapy because of chronic depression or following a suicide attempt. Some may begin attending a self-help group only because their mates have found help for themselves and urge their partners to go as well. And others, after a string of failed relationships, may eventually decide they need to find out why they always seem to choose the wrong partner.

Whatever the reason, those of us who have spent years in an addictive relationship may finally be ready to get help and improve our lives. I have described people who succeeded in making changes as being *in recovery*. What does this mean? First, to be recovering implies to be recovering from something, a disease. The idea of recovery is therefore linked to the disease concept of addiction and codependency. To be an addict or a coaddict is to have a disease, and to be a victim of relationship trauma is also a disorder; recovery from these disorders requires learning new ways of living which do not depend on a drug or an addictive relationship to solve all of life's problems. Recovery is learning to have a healthy relationship with oneself and with other people.

Models of Addictive Behaviors

Are addiction and codependency diseases? One of the major contributions of the founders of Alcoholics Anonymous was to put forward the disease concept of alcoholism, which was first proposed by a physician treating alcoholics in the 1930s. The early A.A. literature stated that alcoholics were physically allergic to alcohol, that their bodies reacted to alcohol differently than did the bodies of nonalcoholic drinkers. Research has shown that sons of alcoholics respond to alcohol differently than do sons of non-alcoholics; the former group has an increased tolerance to the sedative effects of alcohol, suggesting (1) that their bodies metabolize alcohol differently, and (2) that some of this effect is genetic. There is no evidence, however, that alcoholics are actually allergic to alcohol. The primary value of the disease concept to alcoholics in the early days, when alcoholism was considered a sign of weak character, was that it gave legitimacy to the alcoholics' problem and allowed them to seek help without further lowering their self-esteem. It allowed them to say, "I'm sick; I need treatment," and helped their families to understand that once they had taken a first drink they couldn't stop from taking another.

Acceptance of the disease concept of alcoholism was long in coming, and even today is not universal. *It makes more sense to look at addiction as an emotional or psychiatric disease rather than a physical illness.* The reference book used by psychiatrists to diagnose psychiatric illnesses, The Diagnostic and Statistical Manual of Mental Disorders, 5th Edition[4] describes criteria for alcoholism and other substance use disorders that are mostly behavioral. They can be summarized as follows:

- Loss of control:
- Continuation despite serious adverse consequences
- Preoccupation or obsession

The *disease model* describes addiction (termed "substance use disorder" in the DSM-5) as a behavioral disorder accompanied by a thinking disorder that attempts to justify and deny the irrational behavior.

An alternative mode to explain addictions is the *moral model*, which is still widely accepted. This model assumes that people have a free choice in their behaviors, so those who abuse alcohol, overeat to obesity, gamble away their savings, repeatedly have sex with prostitutes, or waste many hours on the internet engaging in cybersex are either immoral or have no willpower. According to this model, if people are shown the error of their ways they might be persuaded to reform. The threat of punishment is supposed to be another effective tool.

Imprisonment for soliciting a prostitute is a secular therapy based on the moral model of addiction. This approach assumes that transgressors have a free choice in their behavior and therefore the embarrassment or inconvenience of a jail sentence will deter them from repeating the offense. The singular lack of success of religious or secular threats of punishment suggests that the behaviors being addressed are not based on rational choices. This is not to say that addicts are not responsible for the harm they inflict on others. It is appropriate that a psychotherapist who has sex with his clients or a drunk driver who injures or kills other people should experience the consequences of his behavior. Addicts need to take responsibility for getting help for their out-of-control behaviors.

Punishment as a solution to addictive problems further assumes that the culprit is solely responsible for the offense. However, most sex addicts were sexually, physically, and/or emotionally abused as children. Should they be the only ones punished?

That many people subscribe to the moral model is readily under-standable; sex addicts sometimes *can* limit their sexual behaviors, and can even stop completely for a period of time or limit them to specific venues, such as out of town. The problem is, addicts cannot *reliably and for long* regulate their sexual acting out, just as compulsive over-eaters cannot reliably and for long regulate their eating. The moral model assumes that because people at times are able to control their addictions, they should be able to do so consistently. If they can't, it's because they are bad people.

A third explanation of addiction is the *socioeconomic model*. This model defines the factors in people's environment that are responsi-ble for their addictions. Thus, people drink alcohol to excess because their peers do, or because their jobs and home life are so dull they need an escape. The man who has multiple affairs or spends many hours per week viewing online porn is merely following the norm of American society; the woman whose identity is totally submerged in her husband's is merely living out the traditional role of the mother and wife. According to this model, women who stay in abusive rela-tionships do so primarily because they are economically dependent on their husbands and have no other choice. The socioeconomic model definitely plays a role in explaining addiction. It seems too easy, however, to use these socioeconomic factors as excuses, and they are not the most important explanation for addictive behaviors.

A fourth model for addictive behaviors, somewhat related to the socioeconomic explanation, states that having multiple affairs, drink-ing, or overeating are *symptoms of other problems* in the person's life. For example, a man is unfaithful because his wife is sexually unavail-able; a woman cheats because her husband is emotionally unavail-able. Depressed people drinks to drown their depression in alcohol. This is the model that is most commonly accepted by the addict and by his family. When addictive behaviors are considered to be only a symptom, the therapy focuses on what is considered the underlying problem – for example, the couple's sexual or relationship problems.

It is assumed that if the psychotherapy or the sexual counseling is successful, the need to have multiple affairs will disappear, as will other compulsive sexual behaviors.

Unfortunately, this is rarely the case; therapy that does not address the addiction as the primary problem is notoriously unsuccessful in bringing about behavior changes. Although the addict repeatedly rationalizes his or her behavior by pointing to external causes, the failure of traditional therapy to effectively stop addictive behaviors suggests that this model is incorrect. Yes, mood disorders, family of origin issues, and couple's communication problems need to be treated, as part of ongoing therapy, but the addictive behavior must be dealt with directly.

Finally, a fifth model for addictive behaviors is *the genetic model*, which states that the propensity for addictions is inherited. Of course, in families where addiction is present, it is difficult to sort out the contribution to the children's risk of the dysfunctional environment versus that of genetics. One way to sort this out is by studying children of addicts who were adopted out and raised by either addicted or non-addicted adults. Such high-quality studies have clearly shown a genetic component for the risk of alcoholism. If you have one parent who is alcoholic, you have approximately a 25 percent chance of becoming alcoholic; if both parents are alcoholic, your risk is closer to 50 percent. At this point there are no such studies on the genetics of behavioral addictions.

Nonetheless, it's clear that the predisposition to addictions of all types runs in families. Sex addicts who prepare a family tree of their own families often find multiple addictions in their families. It is likely that the development of any addiction is influenced by a combination of factors including genetic vulnerability, family history, situational stresses, social acceptance of the particular form of compulsive behavior, and environmental factors such as availability of the specific outlet (alcohol, other drugs, gambling, prostitutes, etc). In addition, cultural factors can predispose to addiction. For example, male patriarchy fuels male need for domination, which shows up through entitlement in sexual behaviors. The result of all these influences is that the person develops the disease of addiction.

Codependency, the common element of all addictive and coaddictive behaviors, is also a type of disease. In his book, *Diagnosing and Treating Co-dependence*, Timmen Cermak explains why codependency should be considered by mental health professionals to be a disease.

> For the purposes of clinical assessment of individual clients, co-dependence can best be seen as a disease entity. CD [Chemical Dependency] therapists speak of family members as being affected by co-dependence, or as being actively co-dependent. Such assessments imply that a consistent pattern of traits and behaviors is recognizable across individuals, and that these traits and behaviors can create significant dysfunction. In other words, co-dependence is used to describe a "disease entity" just as phobia, narcissistic personality disorder, and Post-Traumatic Stress Disorder (PTSD) are diagnostic entities.[5]

Codependent traits may be nearly universal in American society, but codependent personality disorders are not so ever-present and are amenable to diagnosis and treatment, according to Cermak.[6] When codependent personality disorder is present, it's time to get help. Similarly, when a person has had a traumatic experience, getting help can help them recover.

Getting Help

Suppose we believe our spouse's affairs are a result of sex addiction and that we have been traumatized by our mate's lying, infidelity, and/or online sexual activities – and/or that we are behaving as a coaddict in our relationship. How do we go about getting help?

Although we'd like things to be different, we're afraid of making any changes in ourselves that will jeopardize our relationship. Holding on to our significant other is probably still our number one priority. Making changes is not easy; we have to be sufficiently uncomfortable or dissatisfied with our life to be willing to take the risks that making changes involves. If we are at a point in our life when we know that change is essential, then it's time to learn about our disease and that of our mate, to investigate what resources for recovery are available to us, and to get ready to make some changes.

Learning about sex addiction and the consequences to the partner is easier than ever. Reading this book is a step you're already taking. The appendix of this book lists other resources – organizations, books, and websites. An excellent beginning point is the web site of the Society for the Advancement of Sexual Health (www.sash.net). This web site provides consensus statements on various aspects of sex addiction, lists helpful books and articles, gives names and addresses of knowledgeable therapists and counselors throughout the U.S. and some other countries, and provides contact information for Twelve-Step, self-help groups for sex addicts, partners, and couples.

The most widely known and widely available peer support groups are those based on the Twelve Steps of Alcoholics Anonymous. For partners of sex addicts, the best-known groups are S-Anon and COSA (see Appendix B for contact information). If you do not identify with codependency or coaddiction but can get past the label, you will find these groups very helpful. One of their guidelines is "Take what you want and leave the rest." But if you prefer support that is not based on an addiction model, there is Partners of Sex Addicts (POSA) (see Appendix B for contact information), which uses exclusively the trauma model and rejects the addiction/codependency model.

If you accept that group support based on the addiction model might be helpful to you, then e-mail or phone S-Anon or COSA to learn where there are meetings close to you for yourself; you would benefit from these meetings as much as your spouse would benefit from attending Sex Addicts Anonymous, Sexaholics Anonymous, Sex and Love Addicts Anonymous, Sexual Compulsives Anonymous (SCA) or other Twelve-Step program for sex addiction. If there are no S-Anon or COSA groups near you, go to an Al-Anon or an ACOA or ACA meeting to learn about the Twelve Steps.

Recovery from betrayal and codependency includes three basic elements. The first is to identify our irrational belief system and behaviors that make us uncomfortable or are against our best interests. The second is to change these behaviors. Finally, since most likely we did not get our emotional needs met when we were growing up, we must learn how to nurture ourselves and be good to ourselves so that we come to believe we are worthwhile people.

Recovery for partners (and also, of course, for addicts) is often best accomplished through a combination of professional counseling and attendance at peer support meetings. The role of counseling is described in detail in the next chapter. Some may ask, why not counseling alone? Why the necessity for self-help groups? Robin Norwood, author of the book *Women Who Love Too Much*, explained:

> Therapy alone does not offer an adequately supportive alternative to the alcoholic's dependency on the drug or the relationally addictive woman's dependency on her man. [Relationally addictive means being a relationship addict.] When anyone who has been practicing an addiction tries to stop, an enormous vacuum is created in that person's life – too great a vacuum for an hour-long session with a therapist once or twice a week to fill. Because of the tremendous anxiety generated when the dependence on the substance or the person is interrupted, access to support, reassurance, and understanding must be constantly available. This is best provided by peers who have been through the same painful withdrawal process themselves.[7]

Self-help groups based on Alcoholics Anonymous (A.A.) have several tools for recovery. These include:

- Attendance at meetings;
- Telephone and email contact with other group members;
- Having a more experienced group member as one's "sponsor" or mentor;
- Reading helpful literature; and
- Meditation.

The Twelve Steps

The self-help groups that are best suited to promoting recovery from addiction and codependency are those that teach the Twelve-Step program. These groups (free of cost to belong) meet weekly in thousands of locations across the U.S. and in many other countries. Based on the Twelve Steps of A.A., there are now also groups that address narcotic and other drug addiction, compulsive overeating, compulsive spending, pathologic gambling, and compulsive sexual behaviors. For most of these compulsions there are also support groups for spouses and significant others that function similarly to Al-Anon, the Twelve-Step fellowship for family and friends of alcoholics. None of these groups provides professional counseling; they are gatherings of people who have experienced the same problem and who have come together to share their experience, strength and hope with each other. Experience has shown that hearing what has worked for someone who has been in the same situation is a strong stimulus for change.

The Twelve Steps are a deceptively simple program for recovery originated over sixty years ago by the founders of Alcoholics Anonymous. The program consists of three elements essential to making changes. The first is to recognize that our life is intolerable as is, and that change is necessary. The second element is deciding to do whatever it takes to implement the change, and the third element is acting to bring about the change.

The Steps are the basic tools of the program. The first three are belief steps, and the last nine are action steps. In brief, the program consists of recognizing we cannot solve our problems alone; believing that an outside force (a Higher Power) can help us; admitting our problems and character defects to ourselves and to another person; making restitution for our wrongdoing whenever possible; monitoring our thoughts and behavior on an ongoing basis; continuing to seek spiritual assistance in dealing with our problems; and letting other people who need the same kind of help know about the program.

Here are the Twelve Steps, as they were adapted for sex addicts by Sex Addicts Anonymous, one of the self-help programs for sex addiction, reprinted with permission of ISO of SAA:

1. We admitted we were powerless over addictive sexual behavior – that our lives had become unmanageable.
2. Came to believe that a Power greater than ourselves could restore us to sanity.
3. Made a decision to turn our will and our lives over to the care of God *as we understood God.*
4. Made a searching and fearless moral inventory of ourselves.
5. Admitted to God, to ourselves, and to another human being the exact nature of our wrongs.
6. Were entirely ready to have God remove all these defects of character.
7. Humbly asked God to remove our shortcomings.
8. Made a list of all persons we had harmed, and became willing to make amends to them all.
9. Made direct amends to such people whenever possible, except when to do so would injure them or others.

10. Continued to take personal inventory and when we were wrong promptly admitted it.
11. Sought through prayer and meditation to improve our conscious contact with God *as we understood God*, praying only for knowledge of God's will for us and the desire to carry that out.
12. Having had a spiritual awakening as the result of these steps, we tried to carry this message to other sex addicts, and to practice these principles in our lives.[8]

Step One

Step One, as applied to sex addiction, states, "We admitted we were powerless over addictive sexual behavior and that our lives had become unmanageable." For the partner this means we are powerless over someone else's sexual behavior. One woman described what Step One meant to her when she first encountered it:

When my husband first joined a self-help group for sex addiction, he suggested that I go to S-Anon for my own recovery. I didn't think there was any reason for me to go – after all, <u>he</u> was the one with the problem! But, wanting to please him, I checked it out. What I heard at the first meeting made so much sense that I can still remember the impact it had on me. The topic was powerlessness over the addict. Until then, I hadn't realized I was powerless over my husband. On the contrary, I had been running my life for years on the principle that I had a great deal of power over him, although of course I hadn't realized I believed this.

I continually tried to keep my children on their best behavior because I thought it would keep him from getting angry. I tried to stay slim and dressed becomingly so he wouldn't want to look at other women. I didn't confront him with my suspicions and fears. And when, despite my best efforts, his moods would swing like a pendulum, I analyzed what I might have done to cause this and what I could have done differently to prevent it. I would review what he had said to me and what I had said to him, and would plan what I might say to him next time the same situation arose. I devoted an enormous amount of emotional energy to try to please him, to understand him, and to prevent his recurrent unhappiness, resentment, and complaints of boredom with our marriage. And when my efforts did not succeed, I thought I just needed to try harder.

At S-Anon, I realized how useless my efforts had been and how powerless I really was over his behavior. I learned that his craziness was not a response to me; it was a response to his addiction and to how he felt about himself. To my surprise, with the acceptance of powerlessness came a tremendous feeling of relief. I realized I could relinquish the terrible sense of responsibility I had felt until then for my husband's happiness and the blame I had felt for his failures and his unhappiness. I had believed I was responsible for his happiness; this was the core of my fruitless efforts and my obsession with him. To accept my powerlessness meant to give up that awesome responsibility. From now on I need to be responsible only for my own happiness. An enormous burden was lifted from my shoulders that first evening at S-Anon, the burden of responsibility for another person's happiness. This is the powerful message of Step One, which to me was so freeing.

Other partners have expressed the same feelings when they understood Step One. The wife of a cocaine addict who also was repeatedly unfaithful said:

I just found out this week that I'm a real person. I had hooked onto my husband as though we were Siamese twins. Now I feel a tremendous relief because I'm responsible only for myself and not for him. It's up to him whether he wants to be in the Program, and then I'll have to make my decision about staying with him.

A consequence of Step One is our ability to detach from a person or a problem. Detachment is a much misunderstood concept. It does not mean we do not care or we are washing our hands of the person. It means we recognize that we cannot solve another person's problems for him or her, and that worrying about the situation will not bring about change. Learning to detach allows us to love without going crazy. It allows us to assess realistically what we can change and what we cannot change, and to make decisions accordingly.

Steps Two and Three

Step Two – "Came to believe that a Power greater than ourselves could restore us to sanity" – and Step Three – "Made a decision to turn our will and our lives over to the care of God as we understood God" – combat the isolation we feel and the belief that we have to solve our problems alone. In working these Steps, we come to understand that we have an external source of help. Being aware that we are not alone allows us to "let go and let God." This means stopping the controlling behaviors that have been inherent for so long in our relationships with others, and recognizing that we do not have the sole responsibility of solving everyone's problems. For the partner of a sex addict, letting go can include letting go of control, of anger, and possibly even of the person.

Partners of sex addicts often have a long history of trying to control the addict's behavior. At home we may check their computer to see what web sites they visited and what emails they received.

At parties we scrutinize their expressions as they look at other women or men, and watch them across the room to see who they are talking with. We don't dare leave town or even leave them alone for the evening. We phone them at work to check on whether they are really there, go through their pockets looking for strange ticket stubs, and inspect their clothes for stains or odors.

Even after we get into a Twelve-Step program and realize we cannot control another's behavior – that the addict will always find ways to elude our control – it is hard for us to change our behavior patterns. First of all, we are accustomed to the behaviors and we're comfortable with them; they're almost automatic. Second, they served a function in the past. Facing the unmanageability in our lives would have overwhelmed us; thus, our attempts at control helped keep that reality at bay and helped us feel safe. We had the illusion that we did have some power over his behavior. We had *something to do*, and action is a strong antidote to despair and hopelessness. If we could lose weight, get our hair done, buy a sexy dress, learn new sexual techniques, or even get breast implants or a facelift, perhaps he would stop being interested in other women. To give up these attempts at control, to face our powerlessness head-on, is frightening, yet it is a necessary initial step in the recovery process. The only way to deal with this fear is to replace it with something positive – a belief that our Higher Power is watching out for us so that it is safe to let go.

Steps Two and Three allow us to take Step One without feeling total despair. We can stop trying to do it on our own, because we are not alone. The program does not require acceptance of a traditional God; all it asks is the belief that there is a source of power greater than ourselves. If we are religious, our Higher Power may be God; if we are not, it may be the strength and support of a Twelve-Step group, or else the inner resources we were unable to access until we found the Program. No matter how we define our Higher Power, its presence in our lives means we are not alone.

Many of us hold a great deal of anger and resentment toward our mate, often so much that there is little hope of saving the marriage. Those of us who have a viable relationship need to learn to let go of our anger and resentment – a difficult undertaking. Certain dates, songs, places, people, comments, blogs, newspaper articles, and situations will bring back the pain of the past. Suppressing these feelings or saying nothing about them will not keep them away. It is healthier to let our spouse know we are reliving the pain and anger. With time, the intensity of these feelings diminishes and the intervals between episodes of pain and anger lengthen.

If we believe in a Higher Power, we do not take it upon ourselves to punish our spouse for his or her past misdeeds; we will gradually learn that things somehow work out for the best without our direct intervention, and we trust that we will be shown the way to deal with negative feelings.

For many partners, an important antidote to anger is realizing how we got into the relationship in the first place. One woman said this about her marriage to a sex addict:

I was a volunteer, not a victim. It was no accident that I found myself in a situation which later caused me so much pain. I was looking for this kind of person, and I found him. If it hadn't been for this particular husband, it would have been another man doing similar things. Knowing this doesn't give me any less justification for being angry at the very real hurts I experienced, but it does remind me that I share in the responsibility of having been in that situation.

We can help ourselves by doing a written account of our past experiences with relationships. Take the time to write out answers to the following questions:

Were your previous romantic partners as loving and as nurturing as you thought you wanted?

- Were they similar to your mate in their lack of concern for your feelings?
- Were *you* the one who was usually the giver, the accommodating one, the nurturer?
- Did you feel you did not really deserve any better?
- Did you have any signs before your wedding that your spouse would not be the ideal mate you were hoping for?

Many partners who have searched their souls discovered aspects of their own personalities that helped them view their role in the relationship in a different light. One young woman related:

I saw myself as a victim my whole life. Men were to fix me and heal me and validate my existence. When people didn't meet my expectations, I got very angry. Now I realize that I'm responsible for myself.

Another young woman married to a sex addict said:

I've gathered people around me who have problems to prove I'm okay. My script has been that I'm a good person and a survivor – just look at how I get through these terrible situations! I've always lived in crisis; that is the way I define myself. Everyone tells me how wonderful I am, how strong, and how helpful. If I didn't have these crises, I wouldn't know who I am. I thought it was an accident that I kept experiencing crises, but now I see that I was using people; I've done it since childhood.

By looking at our past, we can acquire a new understanding of our own behavior; our insights are the first stage of making changes in our lives.

The "letting go" that accompanies Steps Two and Three may involve letting go of another person. Most likely we've been willing to subordinate our own needs to those of the mate. Some of us agreed to sexual activities with which we were uncomfortable in order to hold on to the other person. In doing this, we let ourselves be treated disrespectfully, perhaps because we did not believe we were really worthy of respect. As part of our recovery process, we learn to treat ourselves with increasing respect and to ask the same treatment from our mate. We need to set boundaries of what behaviors are acceptable to us and what aren't. If our spouse is not in a Twelve-Step program and/or therapy and does not believe that his or her behavior is problematic, we may need to choose between continuing to live with the unacceptable behaviors or letting go of the other person. Because a sexual relationship is so personal, it is difficult to continue living with someone who has affairs with other women or men. Recovery for us may involve removing ourselves from the situation. Letting go of a person we have been addicted to is very difficult, but may be necessary for our recovery.

Steps Four and Five

Steps Four and Five direct us to look at our own shortcomings and strengths and to admit them to ourselves, to our Higher Power, and to another person. Step Four asks us to make "a searching and fearless moral inventory." This may be our first honest look at our strengths and weaknesses in many years. We may have avoided the truth and our feelings for so long that facing the truth and these feelings is frightening. Knowing oneself, however, is necessary in order to be able to make changes.

As we take Step Four we're likely to discover that we are angry and resentful. Up to now we may have been able to justify these feelings – after all, our mate's behavior was certainly deserving of anger and resentment! But when we take a searching look at ourselves, we may find that with time we have become angry and resentful people. Anyone can be angry or resentful at times, but when we are chronically in this negative, judgmental space we become unhappy and unhealthy people who are usually depressed, have physical symptoms, or may be engaged in various compulsive behaviors. Indeed, we may need to accept that it was not only the addict who was the victimizer – we too have victimized our mate with our behaviors. Recognizing our chronic anger and resentfulness is an important prerequisite to making changes. Identifying the shared brokenness that we have in common with our mate can be an important step toward healing for each of us.

Codependent people might believe that if others knew what they were really like, these people would not respect them. According to Step Five, "We admitted to God, to ourselves, and to another person the exact nature of our wrongs." Finding a trustworthy person with whom to take Step Five may be the first time we have dared to let someone else know what we are really like. Getting acceptance from this other person, no matter what character defects we have revealed (jealousy, insecurity, anger, resentment, emotional withdrawal, criticalness) will assist us in recognizing that we are actually worthwhile people.

So will looking at our positive traits, which we are also asked to do in Steps Four and Five. Many of us are all too ready to blame ourselves for our bad characteristics, but don't recognize our many good ones. Taking an honest look at ourselves also means acknowledging our positive traits. These might include loyalty, generosity, willingness to help others, ability to follow a project to completion, competence in many areas, and commitment to being a good parent. Recognizing these strengths will help us improve our self-esteem.

Steps Six through Nine

In Steps Six and Seven, we enlist the help of our Higher Power in removing our failings and then take some concrete actions. In Step Six, we "Were entirely ready to have God remove all these defects of character," and then Step Seven, "Humbly asked God to remove our shortcomings." Steps Eight and Nine describe concrete actions: In Step Eight, we "Made a list of all persons we had harmed, and became willing to make amends to them all." Step Nine tells us to make "direct amends to such people wherever possible, except when to do so would injure them or others." Our list must include ourselves, for there is no way we can make peace with others unless we can also make peace with and forgive ourselves.

Making amends first requires facing the truth about the effects of our behavior on other people. Did our critical attitude cause those around us to feel defensive? Did our need to control cause resentment by those we tried to control? Did our irresponsibility make others have to do our work for us? Did we hurt another person by our unjustified jealousy? Did we bore our friends with our endless complaints about our spouse and then anger them by our refusal to do anything about our situation after asking their advice?

"Making amends" to others is painful; it takes courage and humility. But the result is an increased sense of self-worth and peace of mind. The objective of making amends is to accept personal responsibility for our past behavior. This contributes to our self-respect. Amends can consist of a direct apology or other sincere actions made directly to the people harmed, or it may be an indirect reparation such as volunteer work or a financial contribution to a worthy cause. An amends is *not* simply saying, "I'm sorry," and then continuing with the same behavior. "The best amends is changed behavior," is good advice.

To be effective, your apology needs to include several elements:

- Acknowledgment of the specific wrong you've done the person. For example, "I know I hurt you by my constantly questioning you about your actions. I embarrassed you by repeatedly phoning your secretary at work to find out where you were." Or, "When you were telling me about what happened at school, my mind was elsewhere, on my own problems."
- Statement of your understanding of how your behavior affected the other person. "My focus was so much on your father that you must have felt I just didn't care."
- How you feel about your actions and the effect on the other person: "I am so sorry I did these things to you. I feel really guilty and sad about them."
- An action plan for changing your behavior: "I know that in order for our marriage to work I need to treat you like an adult, not a bad little boy. You have to be in charge of your own recovery, and I have to put the focus on mine, and not on yours." Or, "When you and I are together, my full attention will be on you; you are my child and you are very important to me. If you feel I'm not paying attention, let me know."

Steps Ten and Eleven

Steps Ten and Eleven are "maintenance" Steps, designed to help the recovering person live a healthy life. Step Ten states, "Continued to take personal inventory and when we were wrong, promptly admitted it." This Step is crucial so that the partner can monitor the process of her or his recovery. In addiction to alcohol, recovery and relapse are clear-cut – a recovering alcoholic is one who does not drink; a relapse is resumption of drinking. Recovery and relapse in sex addiction can also be defined in terms of specific behaviors. But codependency consists of so many behaviors that defining recovery and relapse becomes more difficult.

To make things even harder, the same behavior may be either healthy or evidence of a relapse or slip, depending on the goal of the behavior. For example, if your mate asks you to go together to a party and you agree because you think you'll enjoy yourself, that's healthy. But if you agree because you know that an old flame of his will be there and you believe your presence will prevent him from spending time with her – this is an example of the old coaddict type of thinking. In recovery, we must be very honest with ourselves about the motives for our behavior. By monitoring our feelings and thoughts, we can then choose different behaviors.

Two years into recovery, Alice found it increasingly easier to monitor her internal monologue and correct its misconceptions. She told this story at a recovery group meeting:

One day as my husband and I were on our way to a movie, I mentioned something about our 25th wedding anniversary, which is 21 years away. He said, "Maybe we won't be together by then." Instantly my stomach flipped over, and I thought, He's planning to leave me! But in the next breath I said to myself, Wait a minute! Maybe he's afraid that I'm going to leave him. So I answered him casually – at least I hope it sounded casual – "Why, are you afraid I'm going to leave you?" He answered, "Well, yes, I do worry about it sometimes; after all, I've treated you pretty badly at times."

What a lesson to me! I had rethought my first reaction, and the revised version turned out to be correct. Meanwhile, instead of acting like a dependent, fearful wife, I had behaved as though I were self-assured and concerned about his insecurity.

I am learning that although I cannot control my initial reaction, I can choose what to do subsequently. I can evaluate that first negative reaction and if it doesn't conform to reality, I can say something positive to myself instead. I can then behave as though I believed it. Each experience like this one decreases the gap between how I behave and what I believe about myself.

We keep our bad feelings going with a constant stream of negative self-talk. If he's late, we think, 'I wonder if he's stopped off at the bar or a woman friend's house. I'm sure it's my fault. What did I do or say this morning that got him angry? Maybe if I hadn't complained about what he did yesterday, he'd be home by now. Why can't I stop being such a nag?' The negative internal monologue is part of our codependency. In recovery, we learn to become aware of the self-defeating talk, to substitute positive self-talk and to behave *as if*. The more we do it, the easier it gets.

Step Eleven, another maintenance Step, states, "Sought through prayer and meditation to improve our conscious contact with God as we understood God, praying only for knowledge of God's will for us and the power to carry that out." Daily meditation is a very helpful part of recovery. One way to do this is each day to read and think about a page from the meditation book, *One Day at a Time in Al-Anon*. This little book contains brief, thoughtful comments on subjects of concern to recovering partners such as acceptance, changing what we can, controlling, detachment, honesty with oneself, problem solving, resentment, self-deception, and serenity. *S-Anon Twelve Steps* and *Working the S-Anon Program* are additional useful books; they can be ordered from the S-Anon website, www.sanon.org. Daily recitation of the Serenity Prayer reminds us how to live our lives according to the Twelve Steps: "God, grant me the serenity to accept the things

I cannot change, courage to change the things I can, and wisdom to know the difference." This brief prayer essentially summarizes the philosophy of Twelve-Step programs.

Finally, Step Twelve states, "Having had a spiritual awakening as the result of these steps, we tried to carry this message to other sex addicts and to practice these principles in our lives." We are asked to carry the message of recovery to other people in need, and to live our own lives according to the principles of the Steps. Long ago, the founders of A.A. learned that the best way to remain sober was to work with other alcoholics. Seeing the despair and degradation that practicing alcoholics experience is a sober reminder to recovering people of what their life used to be like and how it could be again if they relapse. Twelfth Step work – that is, talking with the practicing addict or codependent about our own experiences and how we got better – is an integral part of the program.

In my medical practice, when I advised a patient to go to A.A., Al-Anon, or another Twelve-Step meeting (depending on their needs), I often hear, "But I've heard that those programs are religious – they're always talking about God. I don't believe in God and I know I'd be very uncomfortable at those meetings." The belief that the Twelve-Step program is religious is a misconception. It is not religious, but *spiritual*. It does not require a belief in God, but only a renunciation of our isolation and of the premise that we are each at the center of our own universe. The spiritual program promotes an acceptance of the availability of strength and help from sources other than our own intellect. For the atheist or agnostic, the source may be the self-help group, with its support and collective strength. A belief in God is not a requirement for membership in the Twelve-Step programs, nor is it necessary for recovery from addiction. But recovery is difficult without a willingness to develop one's spirituality.

Spirituality

Some may ask, "Why the emphasis on spirituality in the Twelve-Step programs? What has spirituality to do with recovery from addiction?" The answer is that what people seek in the addictive high can really only be found in the spiritual experience. In his book *We: Understanding the Psychology of Romantic Love*, Robert Johnson explains the confusion between romance and spirituality.

> When we are "in love" we feel completed, as though a missing part of ourselves had been returned to us; we feel uplifted, as though we were suddenly raised above the level of the ordinary world. Life has an intensity, a glory, an ecstasy and transcendence.
>
> We seek in romantic love to be possessed by our love, to soar to the heights, to find ultimate meaning and fulfillment in our beloved. We seek the feeling of wholeness.
>
> If we ask where else we have looked for these things, there is a startling and troubling answer: *religious experience*. When we look for something greater than our egos, when we seek a vision of perfection, a sense of inner wholeness and unity, when we strive to rise above the smallness and partialness of personal life to something extraordinary and limitless, this is spiritual aspiration.
>
> What we seek constantly in romantic love is not human love or human relationship alone; we also seek a religious experience, a vision of wholeness.[9]

In romantic love, the beloved is seen as an ideal being who can reveal the meaning of life to the lover. Johnson says, "When a human being becomes the object of this adoration, when the beloved has the power to 'give light to our lives' or extinguish that light, then we have adopted the beloved as the image and symbol of God.[10] According to

Johnson, because spirituality is out of fashion in our modern culture, our spiritual instinct finds expression primarily in romantic love. This is why some people tend to feel that their lives are meaningless except when they are in love.

All of us hope to find a special person to share our lives with. Brought up on childhood stories in which the hero and heroine get married and live happily ever after, it is natural for us to hope that our passion for this special person will last forever. Yet, as we acquire experience, most of us realize that this is not possible. In Sheri Hite's survey of 2,500 women, 82 percent of married women said real love is not passionately being "in love," but rather learning to know and care for the other person over time.[11] These women also felt that early feelings of being "in love" generally grow into a deeper love, defined as caring and understanding – if the relationship continues. The majority of women (59 percent) gave stability as their reason for preferring loving, caring feelings to being passionately in love.[12]

Couples who understand and accept the transition from passion to a deeper caring can experience long-term happiness in their relationships. But people who continue to expect their relationship to fulfill all their romantic expectations will be inevitably disappointed and may find themselves looking elsewhere. Johnson wrote.

> The old unconscious belief returns to haunt them, whispering that "true love" is somewhere else, that it can't be found within the ordinariness of marriage. . . . These are the terrible splits that we all carry around with us. On the one hand, we want stability and relationship with an ordinary human being; on the other hand, we unconsciously demand someone who will be the incarnation of soul, who will reveal the godhead and the Realm of Light, who will move us to a state of religious adoration and fill our lives with ecstasy.[13]

Romantic love, as described in the preceding paragraphs, is not concerned with the other person's well-being or happiness – it seeks only ecstasy, drama, and passion. It is therefore very self-centered. How, then, do we resolve the dilemma that results from the incompatibility of romantic love and commitment to another person? The answer, according to Johnson, is to stop looking for wholeness and fulfillment through another person and instead develop our own internal spiritual life. Relieving another person of the responsibility for our happiness allows us to see our partner as a real person instead of a symbol. Instead of seeking spiritual fulfillment through romance, Johnson advocates a return to spirituality, an affirmative soul-life lived day by day through prayer and meditation. Spiritual growth can be sought either through organized religion, by oneself, or participation in a Twelve-Step group.

In summary, Robert Johnson acknowledges a universal need to feel the "high" that for some people comes only by falling in love (and for some, through mood-altering experiences produced by the use of chemicals). He points out that the self-centered nature of romantic love is incompatible with long-term commitment to another person and with genuine caring. The solution to this problem is to find the same type of "high" through a spiritual inner life instead of through another person. To do this frees a person to truly love someone else. Johnson describes the kind of love that allows commitment to another person and fosters a long-term relationship.

> Loving another person is seeing that person truly, and appreciating him for what he actually is, his ordinariness, his failures, and his magnificence. If one can ever cut through that fog of projections in which one lives so much of his life, and can look truly at another person, that person, in his down-to-earth individuality is a magnificent creature.
>
> Loving is seeing another person for the down-to-earth, practical, immediate experience which another human being is. Loving is not illusory. It is not seeing the other person in a particular role or image we have designed for him. Loving is valuing another for his personal uniqueness within the

context of the ordinary world. That is durable. It stands up. It is real.[14]

Forgiving Your Partner

In order to be able to get on with our lives, we must first forgive those who have hurt us. Otherwise the resentments we feel about the wrong done to us will continue to eat away at us and prevent us from achieving serenity. The chief purpose of forgiving is to bring peace to us, not to absolve the other person of his wrongdoing. Forgiving is healing for the forgiver.

In his excellent little book, *Forgive and Forget*, Lewis B. Smedes describes what forgiveness is *not*. [15] First, forgiving is not forgetting. Just because we forgive someone does not mean we forget the hurtful act. We need for forgive precisely because we have not forgotten what someone did; our memory keeps the pain alive long after the actual wrongdoing is past. Because forgiving is healing, it will make it easier to forget. But it is not necessary to forget the past in order to forgive. What forgiving will accomplish is to heal the pain of the past.

Second, forgiving is not excusing. Excusing is the opposite of forgiving. We excuse a person when we believe he or she was *not* to blame for the wrong he did; we forgive him because we believe he *was* to blame. This is why excusing is easy whereas forgiving is hard.

Finally, forgiving is not tolerating. We can forgive someone without tolerating what he or she did. We can forgive our mate for the pain his infidelity caused us without being willing to tolerate affairs in the future. Forgiving does not imply acceptance of the behavior in the past or in the future.

In her book, *How Can I Forgive You? The Courage to Forgive, the Freedom Not To*, Janis Abrahms Spring describes four possible approaches to forgiveness.[16] The first two are dysfunctional:

- *Cheap forgiveness* is a quick desperate attempt to preserve the relationship even if the offender ignores your pain. It is premature, superficial, and undeserved. It is offered before you process the impact of his or her behavior, ask anything of him or her, or think about what lies ahead.
- *Refusal to forgive* is the approach you might take when you want to punish an unremorseful mate, when you believe you can forgive only if you are ready to reconcile or have compassion for him or her which you do not feel, or if you believe that forgiveness is a sign of weakness.

In contrast, there are two types of forgiveness which are adaptive and useful:

- *Acceptance* is a healthy response to a hurt when the addict can't or won't engage in the healing process. It asks nothing of the offender, but rather is a program of self-care, part of which is to stop "giving him free rent in your head," as members of Twelve-Step programs say. Spring calls it "clearing your head of emotional poison." Instead, you let go of revenge fantasies, ensure your emotional and physical safety, and create a relationship with the addict that satisfies your own goals, including getting along with him or her if that's in your best interest. Your may or may not choose to have any further relationship with the person. It also includes accepting that he may never change.
- Finally, *genuine forgiveness* is what can happen when your mate participates in the healing process. According to Spring, genuine forgiveness must be earned, while you allow your mate to settle his or her debt. She writes, "as he works hard to earn forgiveness through genuine, generous acts of repentance and restitution, the hurt party works hard to let go of her

resentments and need for retribution. If either of you fails to do the requisite work, there can be no Genuine Forgiveness."

What then is forgiveness? Forgiveness is healing yourself of the painful memories of the past. When you have forgiven someone, you can remember what he or she did without re-experiencing the pain. Forgiving is not forgetting or pretending that it didn't happen or that the behavior wasn't such a big deal. It was and *is* a big deal for you. As I wrote above, forgiving is not excusing nor is it condoning or tolerating. Because of what happened, you may set firmer boundaries and seek support from others as a way to protect yourself. Most likely, you will not be willing to tolerate similar actions in the future. And ultimately, you may forgive yet realize you cannot have the addict in your life.

How do we go about this? Forgiveness is a slow process that may take years. It involves several steps, the first of which is to recognize that a wrong has been done to us. As people accustomed to denying our own feelings, making excuses for our partner's hurtful actions, and taking responsibility when things go wrong, we may not find this easy. We need to acknowledge that our spouse's behavior was inexcusable, that he or she behaved in ways that caused us a great deal of pain.

The second step is to recognize that we have strong feelings about the wrong that was done to us and to *feel* those feelings, which undoubtedly include anger and hate. It is natural to hate someone who has hurt us and to feel anger toward him or her. Some women are afraid to feel such strong emotions, much less to express them. Psychotherapy may be helpful if this is the case for you.

Sharing our strong feelings is the next step toward forgiveness. It would be ideal to confront the person who has hurt us and state directly how we feel about what he did but often this is not possible – he may not be available or he may have made it clear he is not interested in our feelings. Or we may be too fearful of his reaction to risk direct confrontation, especially if he has abused us physically or emotionally in the past. In either case, sharing with our support group or therapist will allow us to express our emotions about the situation rather than swallowing them or turning them into depression.

Understanding our partner's addiction is another step toward forgiveness. We may have given our spouse enormous power over our happiness, expecting him or her to use it for our benefit. We may tend to idealize our partner, to view him as larger than life, a person with many virtues and few faults – and at the same time as a needy person for whom we have done so much that out of gratitude, if not love, he should act in our best interest. We might find it hard to understand how he could have done just the opposite. It may help if we recognize that our partner is not the romantic figure we thought we were living with; on the contrary, he is needy, fearful, and compulsive, and has a psychological disorder.

We also need to recognize that we have not been entirely the innocent victim. As you've heard earlier, most people are unlikely to marry a sex addict by accident. They often had clues before marriage of the problems to come, but did not evaluate them. They expect their mate to make them happy and then become resentful when the spouse fails to live up to their expectations. Accepting our share of responsibility for our hurt will help us to forgive our mate.

The final step is deciding what to do with our relationship with the person who has hurt us. If our mate has left and is unavailable, if he is dead, or if we have decided that as part of our recovery program we cannot afford any communication with him, then all we can do is heal our bitterness toward him and wish him well. We cannot change the facts of our mate's past actions, but we can divorce the past from how we feel about this person in the present. If they are still causing pain to others, we can say a prayer for them and hope that a Higher Power will eventually show them the way toward recovery. Forgiving will give us a sense of serenity and allow us to get on with our lives.

If both members of the couple are interested in salvaging the relationship, we have an opportunity for further healing. Forgiveness will be easiest if our mate is willing to take several steps: to see that his actions were hurtful and unfair; to feel the pain he caused us, and to feel guilty about having done so; to tell us he realizes what he did was intolerable, that he feels the pain, and that he wants to be forgiven; and to really want not to hurt us again and promise this. In this way, a couple might be able to start rebuilding their relationship.

A note of caution, however: Addicts frequently feel real remorse for the hurt they have caused. They may sincerely ask forgiveness and promise to change – but then go on doing the same things. Some of us have believed our partner's promises and then felt angry and hurt when he was gone yet another night or again showed interest in another woman. In order for us to believe he will not hurt us again, he must follow his words with actions. Ideally these will include stopping the acting out, going to counseling, and attending a self-help group.

What if our partner wants to continue the relationship but is unwilling to ask forgiveness or even to recognize that he has a role in our suffering? We still need to forgive in order to allow serenity to enter our lives. We need to understand that our mate is suffering from an addiction. We also need to remember that forgiveness does not imply permission to continue the hurtful behaviors. As part of our own recovery, we will need to decide which behaviors we can accept in our relationship and which we cannot.

For example, some partners decide to accept their mate's infidelity and to obtain the nurturing they need by having affairs themselves. (This approach will very likely eventually lead to the breakup of the marriage). Others decide they can tolerate the addict's online sexual activities, but would leave if he had another physical affair. Some people decide to stay in the marriage, but not to have sex with the spouse as long as he is being sexual with others.

Whether or not we are in an ongoing relationship, whether or not our partner seeks our forgiveness, we need to forgive them in order to be at peace with ourselves. The primary goal of forgiveness is to heal ourselves and obtain serenity in our lives.

Pitfalls When Both Partners are Sex Addicts – and How to Overcome Them

As we have seen, it's common to find two sex addicts in a marriage or committed relationship with each other. In recovery, such couples have particular challenges in the following areas:

- *Triggering each other's addiction*: Sex addicts who are in a committed relationship or marriage need to establish guidelines for healthy sexuality within the relationship. Sexual activities that can lead to acting out are best avoided. For example, a female sex addict who had engaged in masochistic activities with many partners was married to a man whose acting out had involved sadistic sex. To minimize their likelihood of S &M acting out, this couple agreed to avoid S&M activities within their relationship.

- *Attending the same recovery meeting*: It may seem convenient for a couple to attend the same Twelve-Step meeting, but those who have done so report that it is risky. One woman said, "I don't feel comfortable sharing at the same meeting as my husband. For example, if I were contemplating having another affair, I'd be reluctant to talk about it if he were present." At the very time that recovering addicts need to share their feelings with the group to try to avoid relapse, they are likely to feel inhibited if the spouse or partner is present. It is advisable for the couple to attend separate S-meetings. If only one group is available, one couple took turns attending the meetings, and at the same time they alternated attendance at open AA meetings.

- *Sponsoring each other*: A man whose therapist wife served as his Sexaholics Anonymous (SA) sponsor for a while found that it did not work. He reported,

When I bottomed out and had to go to someone for help, the one person I knew who had recovered was my wife. There was one big problem with using her as a sponsor: When the obsession would hit, my shame would keep me from going to her and I would eventually act out. It didn't work out. Don't sponsor each other.

Using your partner as a sponsor is an invitation to return to the parent-child dynamic that is so common among couples recovering from addiction–related problems. In addition, this practice has the same chief drawback as attending the same meeting: At the very time a sponsor is most needed, the addict is the most unlikely to use that resource. If a Twelve-Step sponsor is unavailable locally, you can contact the national "S" programs (i.e., SA, SAA, SLAA, and SCA – see Appendix B for contact information) and ask about a long-distance or e-mail sponsor. A long-distance sponsor can be supplemented by a local sponsor in A.A. or other Twelve-Step program Although such a sponsor may be relatively unfamiliar with specific issues related to sex addiction, he or she will be grounded in the Twelve Steps and can be another resource for your recovery.

The Infidelity is Continuing – Do I Stay or Leave?

Can we recover from our trauma and remain married to partners who are still acting out sexually online or with real-life partners? Many Al-Anon members have found serenity while continuing to live with a practicing alcoholic. They do this by "detaching with love" and avoiding all expectations of the alcoholic. They plan a separate life. If the alcoholic happens to show up at their ten-year-old daughter's birthday party, or if he or she remembers their twentieth wedding anniversary, great; if not, they celebrate without the mate. By doing this, they avoid disappointment, resentment, and anger. But – and this to me is a crucial point – they also avoid having a nurturing or supportive relationship with the spouse. The essence of a relationship is expectations; without any commitment on the part of the addicted spouse there is no relationship. They are merely occupying the same household.

Erich Fromm, in his book *The Art of Loving*, lists four basic elements common to all forms of love: (1) *care* – an active concern for the life and growth of the other person; (2) *responsibility* – the ability to respond to the needs of the other, generally to the psychic needs of the other; (3) *respect* – the ability to see the other person as a unique individual, not as an object of exploitation; and (4) *knowledge* of the other person.[17] The active addict cannot consistently show caring, responsibility, and respect to his partner and therefore cannot love them.

I don't believe that an emotionally healthy person would choose to remain indefinitely with a mate with whom there is no relationship and who cannot love their partner. To remain with such a spouse is to continue to believe that one does not deserved to be nurtured by another person. It is to let one's guilt ("He needs me – I just can't leave him") take precedence over one's needs. It is my personal bias that in most cases to remain in such a situation is unhealthy. A certified addiction and codependency counselor whom I interviewed agrees: "Detaching, yes. You're not supposed to get in there and try to change him. But, by God, if he's not changing and it's really unhealthy, then part of *your* health is to say, 'This is not for me, I don't have to stick around. I hope you get better. Good-bye.'"

Another problem with "detaching with love" is that it can be a form of *enabling* the sex addict. If there are no consequences to his or her behavior, then the addict will have no motivation to change. Allowing the addict to experience the negative consequences of his behavior, which is the opposite of enabling, might lead him to seek help more quickly. In the chemical dependency field, an accepted method of "helping the addict who does not want help" is *intervention*, which is a carefully planned meeting between the addict and the people who are important to him, such as parents, spouse, and employer. At this meeting each of these people firmly tell the addict how he or she has hurt themselves and them by drinking or drugging, and ask that they enter treatment. Because the addict cares about the people who confront him, the overall effect of the meeting is to break through his denial of the significance of his drinking; he might agree to immediate treatment.

Similarly, the person who has recovered sufficiently from her own trauma so that she is no longer willing to live with the pain of her mate's infidelity can sometimes break through the addict's denial that he has a problem by deciding to leave, thus precipitating a crisis. The fear of loss of the marriage partner has brought many addicts to treatment. However, this is true only if the partner is serious about her intent to leave, and is not using the threat of leaving as a way of manipulating her partner.

A recovering woman married to a man who is still unfaithful faces additional challenges in her own recovery. Accustomed to believing her husband's word rather than her own feelings, she may doubt that she really needs a program – after all, her husband doesn't seem to think there's a problem. Or else, in her enthusiasm for her new discoveries, she will want to share the good news with him and to help him into treatment. She must fight this tendency to continue controlling the addict and running his life. Conflict between the pair may initially increase –the mate may feel threatened as he notices the partner's behavior changing, and he may try to prevent her from attending self-help meetings.

Probably the biggest obstacle to recovery for someone in relationship with a practicing addict is his or her fear of living alone. From her discussions with other recovering partners and with her counselor the partner will soon realize that as she gets healthier emotionally she will most likely be unwilling to stay in the relationship unless the addict too changes. Terrified of having to let him go, she may decide instead to forego changing herself and maintain the status quo. This fear is probably the primary reason that partners of sex addicts drop out of Twelve-Step programs.

It is uncommon for a recovering partner who is still married to a practicing sex addict to plan to remain married if the infidelity continues. Recovering partners are either married to a person who is also in a recovery program, divorced from someone who continues to have affairs, or else are so early in their own recovery that they acknowledge their inability to get out of a relationship which they recognize they will need to leave eventually. These latter people believe that their current situation is temporary. Other partners stay for a while for financial reasons – for example, until they can finish their education and are better able to support themselves.

Unless you are in physical danger, there is no urgency in leaving the relationship. We are not in the marriage by accident; unless we understand *why* we are in it, we are likely to have to learn the same lesson in our next relationship. We will need some time in our own recovery process before we are ready to decide whether to stay in or leave. Going to a professional therapist or counselor will focus your recovery process and will help you get to the point where you are able to make real choices for yourself. If your mate is also willing to go with you for couple counseling, the chances of rebuilding your relationship will definitely improve. The next chapter will help you understand what to look for in a counselor.

CHAPTER SEVEN

Getting Professional Help

Although recovery from addictive disorders can be attained solely through active participation in Twelve-Step and similar self-help programs, counseling or psychotherapy can jump-start and facilitate healing, especially for the person who also has experienced trauma in their childhood and/or adult relationships. Twelve-Step groups provide accountability and support, and they demonstrate recovery through personal example. Members share their "experience, strength, and hope." Although direct advice is not given at meetings, sponsors can help guide you in the right direction. Professional counseling, in contrast, can be more directive. Therapy can validate your experience, address your relational trauma, and also get you in touch with the sources of your vulnerability to addiction and codependency. As well, the counselor can teach you skills that are more effective for problem–solving and healthy strategies for getting your needs met.

The key is to choose the right professional. Jessica, an intensive care unit nurse, describes what happened to her husband, Joe, when he went for counseling.

Before Joe became involved in a Twelve-Step program, he tried several kinds of counseling. He realized his life was out of control because of his cybersex activities and real-life affairs, but he didn't know how to stop. At one point he went to a psychiatrist and told him about his latest affair, but not that it was still going on. Naturally he didn't get much out of the therapy.

Later in our marriage, he found himself in a complicated affair. It had begun as a casual fling with the wife of a colleague, but when Joe found himself obsessing about her much of the time and feeling increasingly guilty about the affair, he consulted Charles, a highly respected psychotherapist, in order to get help ending the affair. They spent many hours probing Joe's childhood, our marriage, and his feelings about his current affair. Joe admitted to a one-night stand with an acquaintance some months earlier, but Charles did not recognize that affairs were a pattern in Joe's life.

One day Joe asked me to go to a counseling session with him. He told me that his therapist had thought it might be helpful to Joe's therapy to have me there for one session. The therapist, Charles, asked me several questions about my relationship with Joe. He asked what I would do if I found out Joe was having an affair, and that this was not the first one during our marriage. I gave Charles the same answer I'd given Joe on several occasions when the subject of infidelity came up – that I would end the marriage. Charles probed further, asking if there were any circumstances in which I would forgive and stay. I continued to give answers based on my assumption that these were all hypothetical questions. At the end of the session Charles complimented me in several areas, giving his opinion that I was well-adjusted, secure, and sure of my own values – none of which, as it turned out, was true of me. Later, Joe explained to me that as a result of my answers to Charles, the therapist had recommend that Joe not disclose his affair to me.

A month later, when Joe's girlfriend threatened to commit suicide if he ended the affair, he told me about it. In addition to my anger toward Joe, I found myself feeling angry at Charles, Joe's therapist. Even now, years later, I believe that his behavior as a therapist was unethical. He brought me into the counseling session under false pretenses – not because I had asked for help, but in order to assess whether Joe could risk telling me about the affairs. In order to do this, he colluded with Joe in being dishonest with me about the real purpose of the visit.

After Joe's disclosure to me, he quit seeing Charles for therapy. Shortly thereafter he learned about a Twelve-Step self-help program for sex addicts, recognized the nature of his problem, and became active in the program. He was able to turn his life around and improve his self-esteem so that he could function well without the need for validation from other women. Hoping to share his success, he phoned Charles to tell him about the program, and sent him some written material about it. Joe was hoping that the next addicted client who came to see Charles for therapy would get new understanding. But Charles never acknowledged receiving the information; he obviously did not want to be confused with new facts.

Joe spent over $1,000 and many hours in psychotherapy that was not helpful. His therapist persisted in trying to fit Joe's problem into the particular counseling framework that the therapist was familiar with. Today Joe regrets the months he spent in therapy. His marriage became more chaotic and his life less manageable throughout that period. Had Joe's affair partner not precipitated a crisis, he might still be seeing the same therapist, still involved in affairs, and still feeling guilty and worthless. This story is still very common. It points out the importance of choosing the right therapist. The wrong counselor can waste your time and money, can delay you in getting real help, and can prolong the secrecy and dishonesty that is already a prominent element in relationships where there is infidelity.

Contrast Joe's experience with that of Brian, who had a long string of affairs. Eventually he and his wife went to see a marriage counselor. When Brian admitted his affairs to their counselor, she suggested that Brian was sexually compulsive. She provided Brian and his wife Beverly with information about sex addiction and invited them both to join Twelve -Step recovery groups that met in their city. Later, the counselor attended a workshop given by Dr. Patrick Carnes, author of *Out of the Shadows: Understanding Sexual Addiction*, to learn more about sex addiction. The counselor continued to work with Brian individually, and to support his attendance at Twelve-Step meetings. She referred Beverly to another therapist for individual work. As a result of this positive experience, Beverly feels very knowledgeable about her own trauma and coaddiction issues and is making progress in her recovery.

Brian and Beverly were fortunate in having chosen a knowledge-able counselor. Working with two separate therapists worked best for this couple. And, in most cases, this is the most common and preferred course of treatment. However, there are some instances where one therapist might work with both individuals. For example, in geographic areas where there are not enough knowledgeable or skilled therapists, that option may not be available. Or, in some cases, because of specifics in the marriage or individuals involved, having one therapist know and track both sides of the therapeutic experience allows for continuity of care without an opportunity for one or the other in the marriage to omit, neglect, or manipulate information. In these two examples, it is imperative that the therapist involved is trained, experienced, and exhibits solid boundaries in working with this level of relational intensity.

In addition, it is important to have a no-secrets policy in effect so that the therapist does not become the holder of secrets and infor-mation for the coupleship. Therapists who have poor boundaries get themselves into a lot of trouble when they treat both partners indi-vidually as well as together; for example, they may obtain information from the addict which they then keep secret from the partner, at the same time counseling the partner who is unaware of the real issues.

Choosing a therapist can feel like guesswork. Therapists come from many different backgrounds. There are psychiatrists, who are medical doctors with at least three additional years of psychi-atric training. There are psychologists, who have PhDs and years of graduate training. There are clergy people, counselors with mas-ter's degrees, psychiatric social workers, regular social workers, sex therapists, certified alcoholism counselors, registered nurses, and self-taught counselors with undergraduate or no degrees at all. Some states have minimum requirements in order to hang out a shingle. In my state of Arizona, for example, one needs to have had at least 3200 hours of supervised work experience to be a Licensed Professional Counselor, or Licensed Clinical Social Worker. This supervised work experience is allowed only after the person seeking licensure has completed their Master's level education and passed the national licensing exam. In each case, the requirements to be qualified as a supervisor are carefully laid out. In other states, anyone may call him- or herself a counselor.

To compound the difficulty, the results that counselors and therapists achieve often have no relation to their degrees. Some of the best counselors I know have Master's degrees, whereas some psychiatrists, who traditionally are considered the most prestigious of those groups who do therapy, are much better at dispensing drugs than guidance.

Finally, different therapists, no matter what their degree, favor different approaches to the human psyche. Among the well-known schools of therapy are traditional psychoanalysis (now only uncommonly used), transactional analysis, rational-emotive therapy, Adlerian psychology, Jungian analysis, and cognitive-behavioral therapy. Some therapists prefer some techniques to others. Popular techniques at present include psychodrama, chair work, EMDR (eye movement desensitization and reprocessing), SE (Somatic Experiencing), and hypnosis. There is also a choice to be made between individual therapy and group therapy. Some therapists are wedded to one approach or another; others call themselves "eclectic" which means they take a little from this approach and a little from that, depending on the particular client they are counseling and the specific circumstances.

There are literally dozens of schools of thought. And, this point cannot be understated, the most important element is the rapport you have with the counselor, and his or her understanding of addictions. Is this a person who truly cares about you? Is this a person who is experienced in working with problems of addiction, trauma, and codependency?

Of significance is the clinical bond that can be forged between the addict, partner, coupleship, group and the therapist. The process of therapy requires a safe and helping relationship because the introspective work required to heal from addiction and unresolved trauma is hard and at times lengthy. It is important to remember that addicts are resistant to outside influence and have long followed their own "best advice," which is how addicts ended up entangled in addiction to begin with. Partners have no control over the therapists their addict partner chooses but it is wise regardless for either party to choose a therapist who will help hold you accountable. This is not always the case, but when the addict or partner is serious about getting help, there are qualified and skilled therapists in this field. As a good friend of mine who is a therapist is known to say, addicts who are not yet ready choose the therapist they want, not necessarily the therapist they need.

Another consideration in choosing the counselor is the counselor's gender. In most psychotherapy situations, a therapist of either sex can be equally effective. But in the area of sexual addiction, the therapist's gender can have some influence on the therapeutic process. A man who sees every woman as a potential romantic partner is likely not to take a female therapist seriously at first. Instead of focusing on the therapy issues at hand, he may concentrate on winning her over and on proving to her how charming, sincere, and psychologically healthy he is. He may tell the therapist how special she is and how much better she is for him than the previous six counselors he saw. Even if the counselor does not permit herself to be manipulated in this way, much time is likely to be lost and the real issues may never be addressed.

By now you may be a little confused about the type of psychotherapy that you may need. Perhaps you've been asking yourself, "Am I a trauma survivor? Am I a codependent or coaddict? Do I need different therapists for these different problems?" I believe that this is not an either-or situation. As I explained in the Introduction, most partners who've been betrayed feel they've been traumatized by the addict's infidelity and deception. It is important for the therapist initially to validate the partner's experience and empathize with her or him. The therapist's first step is to forge a bond with the client and acknowledge the trauma that he or she is currently experiencing.

These elements are essential at the beginning of treatment, but this is only the start of a longer process. Experienced therapists tell us that the more reactive one partner is to the other's infidelity – in other words the more traumatized they are – the more likely it is that these current adversities are triggering strong emotions related to events in their childhood or in previous relationships.

In the book, *Mending a Shattered Heart: A Guide for Partners of Sex Addicts*, which is edited by Dr. Stefanie Carnes, Dr. Carnes and Cara Tripodi answer the question, "What does my family of origin have to do with this?"

Addictions travel in families and are passed from generation to generation. Most likely, you were raised in an addictive family or a family organized around a particular family member's needs. You may have learned that chaos and secrecy were part of normal functioning within a family.

When you got older, it's possible that you sought out mates who replicated aspects of your childhood. . .For example, you may have learned to expect less and then began to seek less from a partner. By accepting less in the way of your needs you have duplicated how you were treated by your family. . . .

It's essential in your recovery that these connections be made. Only when the unconscious is made conscious will you find the capacity and insight to alter the course of your life. Having the courage to look at old hurts and challenge dysfunctional messages from childhood creates a new pathway of choice and freedom for you. [1]

Many partners of sex addicts need to work through their earlier experiences, to understand and overcome the dysfunctional coping strategies they may have developed early in their life and which now have prevented them from feeling in control of their lives and able to make good choices for themselves. They need a combination of treatment approaches – both for the relational trauma of the betrayal they experienced (expressed as minor or major symptoms of PTSD), and for consequences of their childhood or earlier adult trauma (which have been termed codependency). These two diagnoses have overlapping treatment approaches including individual and group psychotherapy, along with specific modalities for each of these diagnoses – for example, EMDR for trauma and Twelve-Step involvement for coaddiction or codependency. Partners often do best with a therapist who is knowledgeable in both of these areas.

Choosing a Therapist

How does a layperson choose the right therapist? As discussed earlier, do not be overly swayed by degrees. The exact approach to counseling is not that important either: Good results have been obtained with all of the various therapy methods. What you need to recognize first is that some therapists are better at some problems than at others. For example, check out the International Institute for Trauma and Addiction Professionals (IITAP), www.iitap.com, created by Dr. Patrick Carnes. IITAP has the largest membership of therapists trained in treating sex addiction. Their certified sex addiction therapists (CSATs) have had extensive training in using a combination of approaches to treat sex addicts and/or partners of sex addicts. In addition, check out the Society for the Advancement of Sexual Health (SASH). Their website, www.sash.net, provides a list of their professional members, by state. These are counselors and therapists from various backgrounds who have a particular interest in sex addiction problems. A more recent organization is the Association of Partners of Sex Addicts Trauma Specialists (APSATS), www.apsats.org, which trains therapists to treat partners specifically from a trauma model. Currently there are an increasing number of websites and therapists using various combinations of approaches, so it's difficult for the layman to discern the best solution for her specific needs.

If you are aware of a pattern of addictions in your family, your relationships, or both, you may wish to choose a counselor who is familiar with addictions and with the self-help recovery groups. The SASH website is a good resource. Local members of Twelve-Step programs are also often familiar with knowledgeable counselors in the community. To such counselors the Twelve Steps are a valuable tool in recovery and they will encourage clients to attend meetings.

Another approach is to ask around locally for names of therapists who are experienced in working with your issues. Talk with other people who have struggled with these same issues and who have seen a counselor. Find out how they felt about their treatment and what the outcome was. Ask your doctor or your clergyperson for recommendations. Consider whether you would work as well with a man as with a woman. Discuss with your mate whether he or she is interested in couple counseling or whether you will be going alone. And here are some thoughts to keep in mind:

1. Unless you and your mate have already discussed his affairs or online sexual activities openly, he or she may have an ongoing affair that is being hidden from you. If your therapist will be counseling your spouse as well as yourself, you need to know whether or not the therapist is willing to counsel a couple if one of the partners is concealing their sexual activities from the other. My perspective on this is described earlier in this chapter.

2. Is your therapist familiar with addictions, codependency, and trauma? Has he or she ever attended an A.A. or Al-Anon meeting? Is she familiar with the Twelve Steps? Is she knowledgeable about sex

addiction?. To sex addicts, the chase, the conquest, the clandestine meetings, the online sexual exchanges, have first priority. They cannot give your relationship the attention it deserves while they are still focused on the affair and other sexual acting out. Marriage counseling is not likely to succeed at this stage.

A psychiatrist in my community who does marriage counseling told a reporter that he thinks calling affairs an addiction "could amount to a kind of whitewash." He did not believe that sex addiction exists. How this psychiatrist would treat a couple dealing with multiple affairs is obviously different from the approach of a therapist familiar with sex addiction.

Unfortunately, even well-known experts in the field of sexuality may be ignorant about sex addiction and may do injustice to those who are dealing with this problem by suggesting it doesn't even exist. For example, Dr. Ruth Westheimer, a popular television sex therapist who is still dispensing advice at age 86 and has thousands of followers on Twitter, wrote in her column years ago, "I don't know what sexual addiction is and I suspect that it is a phony issue." She added that she does not believe an inborn natural desire for sex can be equated with an acquired need for a harmful substance. Although people at times can let sex make them miserable instead of joyous, she concluded, sexual desire cannot be an addiction.[2]. A couple consulting Dr. Ruth about the husband's multiple affairs would probably have been instructed in how to make their own sexual relationship more exciting; they would have been unlikely to get help for their addiction and coaddiction. Hopefully, with the passing years she has modified her view and increased her understanding of sex addiction.

Fortunately, in the 25 years since the first edition of this book appeared, enormous progress has been made in the awareness of and understanding of sexual addiction. Hundreds of books have been written about various aspects of sex addiction. The growth of the internet and the phenomenon of cybersex addiction (see, for example, my 2015 book *Always Turned On: Sex Addiction in the Digital Age*, co-authored with Robert Weiss) and the work-related problems it has caused has brought sex addiction to the awareness of additional millions of people. Although many therapists are inexperienced in treating sex addiction problems, by now most have at least heard of the concept.

3. Knowledgeable addiction counselors believe that group work is the mainstay of treatment of addiction and codependency. Group therapy counteracts the secrecy and isolation that are such an important part of these problems. Individual counseling is very useful at various times, especially at the beginning when many people are reluctant to go to and are fearful of group therapy. Partners who feel ashamed about particular things they have done, as well as about their spouse's behavior, and who may have been brought up with the belief that "we do not air our dirty laundry in public," may be uncomfortable talking in a group. Attendance at a group is desirable, and is a goal to be worked toward. Ask your counselor where group therapy fits into the treatment plan. Does he or she think it would be beneficial for you?

Next I've included a section for therapists regarding some recurrent issues that come up when the presenting problem is a pattern of infidelity. As the client, you may find this section of interest in talking with your therapist, or in choosing a therapist.

To the Therapist Treating Partners Affected by Repeated Betrayal:

Which model – Trauma or codependency?

Twenty-five years ago, when *Back From Betrayal* was new, the focus in the young field of sex addiction was exclusively on the addict. In parallel with the way spouses and partners of alcoholics were traditionally viewed, the partners of sex addicts were automatically considered as coaddicts and codependents, and Twelve-Step programs for families of sex addicts were founded based on this model. More recently, however, increasing attention is being paid to the partner. But in contrast to the chemical dependency professional community, a new generation of counselors of sex addicts, many of whom were themselves partners of sex addicts, came to resent the idea that partners had a participatory role in the dysfunctional family system of the sex addict, a view which they perceived as "blaming the victim." Their perception was that calling the partner a coaddict or codependent was demeaning and pejorative. They recognized that many partners were victims of relational trauma, having been betrayed and deceived by the sex addict. Their approach to treating the addict was to focus on the trauma of the betrayal. The result has been confusion among many counselors of partners of sex addicts as to which model is correct.

As I described in the Introduction to this book, I am opposed to this "either/or" perspective. I believe that the majority of partners of sex addicts can benefit from *both* therapy models – initially using the trauma model to support and validate the trauma experienced by partners, and subsequently delving into their pre-existing vulnerability and their reactivity to their current situation through the use of the more traditional codependency model. This view is favored by many experienced and knowledgeable therapists in the professional community.

Alexandra Katehakis, for example, participating in a workshop on treating partners held in October, 2014 at the annual conference of the Society for the Advancement of Sexual Health (SASH), stated that the more reactive a partner is, the more clearly she has her own regulatory problems, set long ago from early childhood trauma issues or later relational difficulties. She explained that while the reactivity is not an excuse for the addict to act out, it can derail the addict's recovery because the couple are in a dyadic dance. Their attachment systems have been severely compromised due to the strain of the addiction, making it nearly impossible to regulate or calm one another down. Untethered, the addict's tendency will be to return to his or her addiction for soothing while the partner may engage in self-defeating or destructive behaviors for regulating her emotions such as compulsive overeating, restricting food, spending, and so forth. The implication is that in addition to supporting the partner during her acute stress state, delving more deeply into her childhood experiences and the resulting vulnerabilities can help heal her own wounds as well as help the couple relationship.

When the presenting problem is the use of cybersex

When the presenting issue for a new client is their spouse or partner's involvement in cybersex activities, some are told by the therapist "it's no big deal," "it's harmless," or "it's not really cheating." Mariali consulted her pastor after she found her fiancé downloading child pornography. The pastor tried to reassure her, saying, "Marriage will satisfy his sexual curiosity, and he'll no longer need those images." The pastor was mistaken, and her husband was eventually arrested. Joyce told her counselor that it bothered her that her husband was viewing sexy women online. The counselor downplayed the significance of looking at online pornography, saying it was just entertainment. But because he did not take a thorough history, he did not realize that Joyce's husband was spending six hours nightly at the computer and had completely withdrawn from family involvement.

Lorraine complained to her therapist that her husband was no longer interested in sex with her. "He has sexual anorexia," the therapist diagnosed without actually interviewing the husband. Sexual anorexia is analogous to food anorexia, a disorder in which the person under-eats but is in fact obsessed with food. A person with sexual anorexia is obsessed with sex, but in a negative way, so that a lot of energy is consumed in avoiding sex. Lorraine's husband was not at all sexually avoidant. On the contrary, he was indulging in a lot of sexual activity, but it involved the computer and not Lorraine.

Many partners experience shame, self-blame, and embarrassment during the early days of dealing with someone's cybersex addiction. The feelings may prevent them from talking with others and appealing for help, and the resultant isolation only worsens the situation. When partners finally get up the courage to talk with a counselor about their situation, these are some things the counselor can do that can help the partner heal:

- Take the partner's concerns seriously. Ask detailed questions and get a thorough history so that you can have an accurate picture of how your client's life has been affected by the cybersex use.

- If the partner describes illegal or dangerous activities by the cybersex addict, make it a priority to help the addict stop the behaviors before he or she hurts others or gets arrested. (Also consider your legal responsibility regarding reporting such information that comes your way.)

- If you are counseling the addict, don't forget that the partner too needs help.

- Don't rush to diagnose the couple's problem as poor communication, the spouse's frigidity, or the partner's need to simply accept the internet user's activities. Take time to find out what is really going on, and become knowledgeable about sex addiction.

- Don't diagnose the absence of sex in the couple relationship as sexual anorexia, unless you're sure that neither partner is simply getting it elsewhere.

- Unless you are certain that the cybersex user is *not* sexually addicted, don't recommend that he simply cut down the time devoted to cybersex to a few hours per week (Would you advise an active alcoholic to simply cut down his drinking?), and don't suggest that the solution is for the spouse to join in the cybersex user's online sexual activities.

- Validate the spouse's feelings of loss, distrust, and betrayal, and work with her to help improve her self-esteem.

Should partners participating in couples' therapy be told about the mate's affair(s)?

Consider the position of an active sex addict whose partner is aware there are serious problems in the relationship and persuades him to go to couples' therapy with her. Many married people believe – or have been told – by the partner that the partner would leave if they found out that the spouse was having an affair. The question for the unfaithful person, then, is not only whether to reveal the affair to the partner, but even before that, whether to reveal the affair to the therapist. After all, the unfaithful person may consider it likely that the therapist might disclose this information to the partner. But, of course, if this critical piece of information is concealed and not discussed in therapy, the couple's therapy is less likely to be successful. What is the best way to handle such a situation? It is important when choosing a therapist to get clarity on the therapist's approach to this dilemma.

Some years ago I asked a dozen couples' therapists in my city whether or not they were willing to counsel a couple if one partner had revealed to the therapist that he is concealing an affair from the other partner. The replies I got were remarkably diverse. One master's level counselor felt quite comfortable in such a situation; if her counseling could strengthen the marriage bond, she told me, then the affair may become less important. On the other hand, another master's level counselor, who was also a Certified Alcoholism Counselor, insisted that couples she counseled had to agree to have no other relationships during treatment. If one of them was having an affair, he had to bring it up within two sessions, either in the counseling setting or outside; otherwise, she would terminate the therapy. Her reasoning was that intimacy issues were causing the couple problems. If one of them was having an affair, then he was not focusing his energy on the marriage relationship. If he was not willing to participate fully in the therapy, then the counseling was an exercise in futility. Moreover, this counselor was not willing to be party to a secret. If the man was a sex addict, then secrecy was part of his disease and she was unwilling to "enable" him.

Since the first edition of this book was published, a consensus has developed among most marriage and family therapists that it is inappropriate to collude with one client to keep an affair hidden from the other. For example, noted infidelity expert Shirley Glass wrote, "It is inappropriate to conduct conjoint marital therapy when there is a secret alliance between one spouse and an extramarital partner that is being supported by another secret alliance between the involved spouse and the therapist." Nonetheless, she *is* willing to see the couple without addressing the affair if the affair is first terminated.[3]

As to whether it's important to disclose not only ongoing affairs but also past affairs, even those that ended long ago, opinion is divided.

When the clients are a sex addict and his spouse, however, the situation is somewhat different. Sex addicts usually have a long history of sexual acting out and have told multiple lies. Even when the presenting problem is a single affair, there generally is a hidden history of other affairs or additional sexual acting out. Twelve-Step recovery emphasizes the importance of honesty. This is especially important in order for trust to be rebuilt after betrayal. In my book *Sex, Lies, and Forgiveness: Couples Speak on Healing From Sex Addiction*, you can read what recovering couples have to say about honesty about secrets. Chapter Eleven discusses in greater detail the question of how much information to disclose.

In 1997 my colleague Deborah Corley and I queried recovering sex addicts and their partners about the consequences of having made various choices about disclosing secrets. Almost 200 of them filled out an anonymous survey. One of the questions we asked related to threats to leave the relationship. Most spouses (60 percent) reacted just as Jessica did in the story at the beginning of this chapter – when asked "If you found out your spouse was having an affair, what would you do?" – they threatened to leave. However, when they subsequently learned that their spouse *did* have an affair, the large majority stayed. Among those couples who separated, about half eventually reunited. In other words, even if you believe *in advance* that you would leave, chances are good that when faced with the reality of an affair, you will want to try to work things out. Fear that the marriage will end should not prevent the addict from telling the spouse about his affairs.[4]

Disclosure is understandably a very stressful process for both sex addicts and their partners. Addicts reported initial worsening of the couple relationship, guilt and shame, anger from the partner, loss of trust by the partner, a cessation of the sexual relationship, and damage to other relationships such as with children, parents, or friends. Partners reported initial worsening of the couple relationship, depression and even suicidal thoughts, attempts to compensate for the pain with acting-out behaviors such as drug and alcohol use and sex, loss of self-esteem, decreased ability to concentrate and/or function at work, feelings of shame and guilt, distrust of everyone, anger and rage, fear of abandonment, physical illness, and lack of sexual desire.[5]

At the same time over 8 percent of the partners and more than 60 percent of the addicts reported that at the time of disclosure they felt it was the right thing to do. With additional time in recovery, 96 percent of addicts and 93 percent of partners concluded that it was the right thing to do. This was true even though a majority of partners threatened to leave at the time of disclosure. Positive outcome of disclosure for addicts included:

- Honesty
- End to denial
- Hope for the future of the relationship

- A chance for the partner to get to know the addict better
- A new start for the addict, whether in the same relationship or not
- Decrease in stress

For the partner, the most significant positive outcomes from disclosure were:

- Obtaining clarity about the events of the relationship
- Validation that they are not crazy
- Hope for the future of the relationship
- Finally having the information necessary to decide about one's future

This research confirms the benefits of going to counseling, having honest communication about the affairs and other sexual behaviors, and working on rebuilding the relationship. Disclosure of the addict's sexual acting-out behaviors is an important part of couple's counseling.

Keeping secrets from clients

Some therapists who see couples for joint therapy also see each partner individually. As I detailed earlier in this chapter, it is vital that the therapist involved in this triumvirate of therapy be trained, experienced, and exhibits solid boundaries in working with this level of relational intensity. It is also important to maintain a no-secrets policy. This policy requires that both partners sign a statement that they understand that information revealed to the therapist outside of the joint therapy session will not be kept out of the joint sessions. This ensures that the therapist will not be the holder of secrets between one or the other client.

Significant ethical issues arise for the couple's counselor who colludes with one member of the couple to keep a secret from the other. As Emily Brown explained:

I believe that the integrity of the therapeutic process with couples depends on open and honest communication. Nowhere is this truer than with affairs. The therapist cannot be effective while beginning to collude with one spouse over the other. If a spouse tells her couple counselor that she suspects her husband has been unfaithful, and the therapist knows that this is in fact the case but is bound by confidentiality issues, the therapist may be able to do nothing more than ask, "What makes you think that?" and advise the partner to focus on herself instead of her partner. The ethical therapist is likely to find this an extremely uncomfortable, if not untenable, position.[6]

Some therapists are willing to conceal knowledge of a client's affair if it took place before the client met his spouse, or if the affair has ended, or if the client believes it had no impact on his partner. In the context of addictive sexual disorders, however, there are several factors that significantly impact the disclosure process:

1. The nature of addiction is that the acting out is repetitive. Even when the presenting problem is a single affair, there generally is a hidden history of other affairs or additional sexual acting out (such as on the internet). This results in repetitive betrayal and lying.
2. The most widely used model of recovery from addiction, based on the Twelve Steps of Alcoholics Anonymous, requires "rigorous honesty." Disclosure is often an aspect of making amends, beginning the process of righting wrongs. This is an important element of recovery for the addict.
3. Rebuilding trust in the mate requires that he or she commit to a new behavior – that of consistent honesty with the partner. If the partner subsequently learns that information has still been withheld, the process of rebuilding trust will be significantly set back.

Frank Pittman, in his book *Private Lies,* wrote regarding betrayal that the dishonesty may be a greater violation of the rules than the affair, and that more marriages end in an effort to maintain the secret than do in the wake of telling.[7] Pittman speculated that the partner may be angry about the affair, but will be even angrier if the affair continues and the partner finds out only later. Pittman is writing about the mate's dishonesty. But the same applies to the therapist: A partner who learns that her therapist has been concealing the mate's infidelity is likely to feel betrayed by the therapist and to consider the therapeutic relationship to be broken.

This situation comes up so frequently when counseling sex addicts and partners that it's important for the therapist to have some guidelines in advance and make sure that clients are aware of this. Keeping secrets was discussed in detail in an article titled "Ethical dilemmas related to disclosure issues: Sex addiction therapists in the trenches." My co-author of this paper, Barbara Levinson, described her approach:

> When I first see a couple I tell them that I will meet with them individually as well as together and that in those individual sessions there may be things that they may feel uncomfortable divulging in the joint session. After that we'll make a decision about how to proceed. I tell them I work two ways: There are times when I'll see both, and there are times when I refer the partner out – usually I keep the sex addict. I tell them that the good news is that when I see both the couple and the individual, that I know everything. And the bad news is that I know everything. So you have to make a decision – if you opt to see me together, then complete honesty is the golden rule. If you want to see me as a couple and you tell me something your partner doesn't know and you say you're not going to tell her, I'll work with her for a period of time, but if a reasonable period of time passes and you are

not willing to disclose any acting out or slips, I will stop the couple's therapy and tell you that I believe individual therapy is better at this time. To that end, we'll have a disclosure contract before you even tell me any secrets. One of the reasons I'll decide to stop couples therapy is if one or both of you has a secret.

Another therapist reported,

I generally do not see a couple if I have seen one of them for individual therapy. But if I do, I make it very clear that by choosing me to provide couples therapy, they are forgoing their confidentiality, and that anything they have said in individual therapy can be brought up by me in couples therapy, especially if they contradict what they said in individual therapy. If they cannot agree to this, then I would not provide couples therapy.

Some therapists will see a couple only in joint therapy, thereby avoiding the possibility of being told secrets – but at the cost that the therapist may not have access to all the relevant information needed for effective counseling. This is a complicated and difficult situation, but the important point is that the therapist must have a policy in advance for dealing with it.

Male therapist or female therapist
Therapists of either gender (or any sexual orientation) can successfully treat sex addicts and their partners. However, sometimes the combination of therapist and client gender can provide additional strengths and challenges. For example, a female counselor seeing a heterosexual male sex addict must be aware of the possibility that he may be using his skills to avoid dealing with the problems. Such an approach by the client actually gives her the opportunity to bring

those behaviors to light in the session, pointing out to the client how he has successfully hidden behind them in the past, and that recovery from his addiction will require him to give up that mask and be more genuine and more vulnerable.

There are also challenges when a woman sex addict or partner sees a male therapist. The female sex addict, who may be accustomed to using sex to manipulate and get power over men, may approach a male therapist seductively and may sometimes initiate attempts to get him involved in a sexual relationship. A male therapist treating a female sex addict must have very clear boundaries and recognize that her seductiveness is part of her disease. Again, such behavior must be talked about in therapy as part of the problem, not acted upon by the therapist.

A female partner may be so anxious to please a therapist and appear attractive to him that she will not let him see her as she really is. The partner is likely to be particularly vulnerable to a male counselor's sexual advances should he approach her in this way. It's unfortunately true that sexual relations between therapist and client are very common, and are very detrimental to the client and to the therapeutic relationship. For example, a survey of 460 male physicians found that 7.2 percent of them had engaged in sexual intercourse with at least one patient.[8] A nationwide survey of American psychiatrists in 1986 found that 6.4 percent of 1,423 respondents acknowledged having sexual contact with their own patients.[9] One-third of the offenders, all male, had been involved with more than one patient.

Sexual contact between psychiatrist and patient is prohibited by the Hippocratic Oath and by the American Psychiatric Association's code of ethics. Nonetheless, in the 1986 study of American psychiatrists, only 24 out of 144 psychiatrists who had sex with patients believed that the sexual contact had been exploitative, harmful, or inappropriate. In all the other cases, the psychiatrist believed the patient had found the sexual contact "caring," "therapeutic," or "helpful." Only 9.5 percent thought their patients experienced any arm from the relationship. Most of the psychiatrists who regretted the sexual contact did so because of the adverse consequences they suffered rather than the harm done to their patients. One psychiatrist wrote that the experience "cost me my self-esteem, nearly cost me my marriage, and may yet cost me my job or career."

The survey researchers, on the other hand, concluded that sexual contact between psychiatrist and patient is always inappropriate. They stated:

> Patients enter therapy in need of help and care. . . and voluntarily submit themselves to an unequal relationship in which their therapists have superior knowledge and power. Transference feelings related to the universal childhood experience of dependency upon a parent are inevitably aroused. These feelings further exaggerate the power imbalance in the therapeutic relationship and render all patients vulnerable to exploitation.[10]

In other words, in a therapy situation, it is very likely that the patient or client will develop strong, positive feelings toward the therapist, and to take advantage of these feelings is exploitative. The attitude of the psychiatrists who were engaging in sexual contact with their patients can best be described as denial. At the risk of censure by the American Psychiatric Association, possible lawsuits, and even the possible loss of their medical license, some of these psychiatrists had engaged in sexual relations with the patients. Some of them were undoubtedly addicted to affairs.

It is not surprising that many helping professionals who repeatedly take sexual advantage of their patients or clients are themselves sex addicts. In a study carried out by Dr. Richard Irons and myself, published in our book, *The Wounded Healer: Addiction-Sensitive Approach to the Sexually Exploitative Professional*, we found that 55 percent of 145 sexually exploitative professionals (primarily physicians) who were evaluated by Dr. Irons were sexually addicted.[11]

Addiction is both a behavior disorder and a thinking disorder. The irrational belief system of addicts serves to justify their behavior and at the same time helps them to deny that they have a problem. That the small group of psychiatrists who had sexual relations with more than one patient had a thought disorder typical of addicts is suggested by the disparity between their attitudes and those of psychiatrists who had no sexual involvement with patients. Whereas only one percent of the latter group thought that sex with a patient would be beneficial to her, ten of the sixteen offenders (62 percent) who believed this were repeat offenders.[12] In other words, many of the psychiatrists who had a *pattern* of sex with patients rationalized and justified their behavior by adopting beliefs that contradicted those of the majority of their colleagues. Their beliefs were also directly opposed to the regulations of their own licensing body, the American Psychiatric Association.

It is interesting that among the psychiatrists who reported they had been sexually involved with their own therapists, most felt that such contact had been exploitative and harmful.

In *Treating the Alcoholic*, Stephanie Brown, a clinical psychologist who founded the Stanford Alcohol Clinic at Stanford University, discusses the role of the psychotherapist who is treating a recovering alcoholic. She believes that the most effective use of the therapist is as the third member of a triad that also includes the client and Alcoholics Anonymous. "Psychotherapeutic help may be necessary for some and certainly is desirable for most," she writes, "but only if the therapist can appreciate the positive ongoing value of A.A. and the importance of an integrated triadic therapeutic approach."[13] In early recovery, she advises the therapist to leave the behavioral changes and education of the client to A.A., and to provide the client with clarification or suggestions and with a supportive environment. She believes that the individual who forms a positive and active tie with A.A. may need little active intervention from the therapist other than wholehearted support for strengthening the A.A. tie. Later on, the therapist can work with the client on the strong feelings which emerge during recovery, such as anxiety and fear. The therapist can review the client's past, explore possible childhood trauma and/or unmet needs, help to understand the genesis of past behaviors, and can support the development of autonomy and the establishment of healthy relationships.

I believe that the same suggestions are valid for a therapist who counsels a recovering partner. Hand in hand with your participation in Twelve-Step meetings, an experienced counselor can facilitate your recovery whether you are alone or still in relationship. Having worked with others who have made the same journey as you, your therapist can pretty well predict how you will feel at each stage in your recovery. She can tell you, "Soon you might feel scared about what's happening." When you do, she can reassure you that this is an expected stage in the process and can discuss with you how to deal with it. She can also determine whether couple counseling or individual counseling is best for you at any particular time, and when entry into a group would be helpful.

CHAPTER EIGHT

Recovery as a Couple

At a Twelve-Step meeting for families of sex addicts, a divorced woman struggling to make it as a single parent looked enviously at one who was still married and said, "You're so lucky – your husband saw the light, recognized that he has a problem with affairs and cybersex, and is getting help. You're still together, and you can get a new start as a married couple. You don't have to be alone. My husband never thought he had a problem – and still doesn't. Now that we're divorced, he's enjoying dating lots of different women, while I'm sitting at home with the kids, feeling lonely, and trying to convince myself that I'm really okay without a man."

Recovery from trauma, relationship addiction, or coaddiction surely differs in some respects when you are married compared with when you are single. Chapter Six discussed the situation of someone who tries to recover from her betrayal while her mate is still acting out or does not recognize that his or her affairs are a problem. Chapter Nine will address the problems of those who are recovering alone. This chapter is aimed specifically at the person whose sexually addicted spouse is also committed to personal and relational change.

In some aspects the recovering couple is indeed very lucky. The pair have an opportunity to restructure their relationship and to establish a new level of honesty and intimacy – and with the same partner. They avoid the anguish of a divorce, the disruption of establishing separate households, and the pain of learning to live alone.

The children are spared the turmoil of the breakup of their family. One of the priorities of the divorced person is learning to make a better choice in subsequent relationships; the married person does not have to test herself on the dating scene.

But in other ways, the recovering couple has particular stresses and problems that the single person does not. First and probably foremost, powerful negative feelings have built up over the years that may be impossible to forget. Resentments over our mate's infidelities, dishonesty, betrayal, hurtful behaviors, and emotional unavailability have accumulated for so long they cannot be erased merely because his or her behavior has changed. Recognizing through our own self-help programs and counseling that we are not entirely blameless can help us to let go of the resentments, but this is a lengthy process and can take years. Sometimes we are unable to forgive totally, and a residue of bitterness remains. Bruce, the former minister (described in Chapter Four) who was attending a recovery group for sex addicts for two years, told me:

Sometimes I think it would be so much easier to start all over again with a new person. I can understand Barbara's resentment – all those years that I was putting out a lot of energy toward the other women I saw and none toward Barbara. She kept the family going while I was having fun and giving her nothing. But now I've been in a Twelve-Step program for two years, without a single "slip," and we still don't have a good relationship. She sees how hard I'm trying and she tries too, but I guess twenty bad years are hard to erase. I don't know if we'll ever really be close. Now that I feel so differently about commitment to a relationship, I fantasize sometimes how it could be with someone if we didn't have the accumulated burden of our past always with us. But how can we give up now, when we're both finally trying to make some real changes in our marriage?

Having interviewed women who were married 2-28 years before they and their husbands entered recovery programs, I found that those who were married for the fewest years seemed to have the easiest time letting of their resentment and anger. This is not surprising, since couples with a short history together have a shorter negative history as well. Rita has been through addiction treatment together with her husband and regularly attends Twelve-Step meetings. When I asked her whether she thinks her twenty-year marriage to Ralph will survive, she replied after a long pause, "I don't know. I know I want it to, and I know Ralph wants it to." Their relationship had contained lying, distrust, resentment, and other bad feelings for so long that it is still a real struggle for them, two years later, to turn things around.

A partner who, with her husband, was a member of Recovering Couples Anonymous (RCA), contrasted what she heard there with what single women in her S-Anon meetings were saying:

The couples in RCA who had been married a long time and said that things are better than ever did not look too happy! There just seems to have been too much pain to erase. The most enthusiastic members of my S-Anon group [for families of sex addicts] were probably the single people – they were truly getting a new start in their lives. I'm glad my husband and I found the group early in our marriage.

Couples who have been together for many years have deeply entrenched patterns of relating to one another. Even if both are willing to make changes in a recovery program, the old patterns are difficult to alter.

A second major problem for married partners is their tendency to monitor their mate's recovery program and to gauge their own actions accordingly. This is understandable as a means to feel safe. Single persons have an advantage because they are in a new environment where they can focus on their own recovery. In contrast, married people have the task of trying to make changes in their own thoughts and actions, while continuing to live with the mate they have spent years trying to please and control. Chemical dependency counselors know how difficult it is for addicts to remain sober if their environment is unchanged, even if they are working hard to change their attitudes with the help of the Twelve Steps. Partners of sex addicts have the difficult task of overcoming their relationship addiction/trauma while continuing the relationship with the person to whom they have been addicted. In those cases the Twelve-Step program of Sex and Love Addicts Anonymous is very helpful.

For those of us in recovery who see hope for our marriage, it is natural to try to make it a success in any way we can. When we see our mate attending meetings, talking on the phone with other Twelve-Step group members, and acting committed to change, our reaction is likely to be to avoid making any waves that might hurt his or her progress. We might try especially hard not to get into arguments, not to make any demands, and to overlook any minor failings or transgressions on his part. If he wants to make love and we aren't in the mood, we are very likely to along with him, particularly now that we know he is committed to monogamy.

In early recovery, no matter how many Twelve-Step meetings such as S-Anon or COSA we attend and how committed we are to the principle that we cannot control the addict's behavior, we often find it difficult to avoid trying to help in all the old ways. Feeling bad or guilty about our efforts is useless. It is better to recognize our actions as inevitable; we will be able to let go more and more as the weeks and months go by. For now, it is enough for us to *recognize* that we are still trying to control our mate, since awareness is the first step toward change.

Another behavior we often fall into in early recovery is monitoring our spouse's progress. For our own safety, we feel the need to be informed to reassure ourselves that he (or she) is seriously involved in his recovery program. We might check on whether he went to his SA or SAA meetings, and we want to know about every temptation and how he handled it. Most likely, what we really feel is that if we know everything that is going on in the addict's mind, we can control or at least influence what he or she is thinking. We probably will feel safer and increasingly comfortable about uncertainty later in our own recovery process.

Thus, for those of us who are starting our own recovery from trauma or relationship addiction, we often struggle with daily slips that we recognize but can't seem to prevent. It usually takes months to years in recovery programs before we truly believe that a mate is but the icing on the cake of our lives; until then, the part of us that is terrified of abandonment will do almost anything to hold on to our partner, and we will repeatedly act in ways that our healthier selves recognize as unhealthy. Eventually, we'll be able to recognize slips in our thinking before acting on them – and even these mental lapses will become less frequent.

There are several additional issues that couples must face together as they restructure their relationship. Some if not all of the following issues will be addressed in therapy. These include:

- Abstinence
- Disclosure by the addict of the addictive behaviors
- What to tell the children
- Changes in the couple's sexual relationship
- Setting limits and boundaries on each person's behavior
- Re-establishing trust, and
- Dealing with relapse by the addict

After the publication of the first edition of this book, Burt Schneider and I did extensive research on these issues, using anonymous surveys completed by over 100 addicts and partners who were working on overcoming sex addiction problems. Our book, *Sex Lies, and Forgiveness: Couples Speak on Healing From Sex Addiction* (Third Edition, 2004) describes what we learned. As for knowing how, when, and how much to disclose to the partner and other family members, Dr. Deborah Corley and I wrote another pair of research-based books, each of which is a step-by-step guide to this complex issue. These are: – *Disclosing Secrets: An Addict's Guide for When, to Whom, and How Much to* Reveal *(2012)* and *Surviving Disclosure: A Partner's Guide for Healing the Betrayal of Intimate Trust (2012).* Several of these issues will be discussed below.

Abstinence

Sex and celibacy – or abstinence from sex – are very closely connected. As Gabrielle Brown, Ph.D., author of *The New Celibacy*, wrote:

> Just as silence is the basis for sound, for speech, for music, celibacy is the basis for sex. . . . Celibacy can be understood in the context of sexuality as the subtlest form of sexuality – potential but unexpressed.[1]

Abstinence can occur by default – because no attractive partner is available, or because one's personality prevents the person from comfortably engaging in any sexual activity, or because one is ill – or it can happen by choice. We cannot choose to be abstinent unless we can also choose to be sexual. When sexual activity is a compulsion and not a choice, abstinence clearly does not constitute a viable option. To learn that life without sex is possible is an important part of recovery.

Inpatient treatment programs for sex addiction typically ask each patient, upon admission, to sign a 90-day abstinence agreement that prohibits sex with self or others. Maintaining abstinence gives the patient a measure of success, preventing him or her from using inappropriate sexual behavior to perpetuate the cycle of sexual dependency. It also allows addicts to practice intimacy outside a sexual relationship and become aware of their repressed feelings. Finally, maintaining abstinence lets the sex addict learn more effective ways of dealing with pain and guilt.

A period of abstinence can be very useful early in the recovery process. For people who have always believed that sex is their most important need, it is a real educational experience to find out that they *can* survive without it. "I didn't die," said one man with surprise about his experience with abstinence. Moreover, during a period of abstinence the addict can begin to view the partner as a human being rather than as a means of sexual gratification.

Sex addicts who experience abstinence, like alcoholics who give up the bottle, learn that they can manage without their "drug of choice." For the partner, however, there is a key difference between drug and sex addiction. In an alcoholic marriage, the decision of the addict to stop drinking does not force the partner to do the same. She may choose not to keep liquor in the house, but she may have a drink at a friend's house or at a restaurant. In contrast, the decision of one spouse to give up sex prevents the other from experiencing sexual intimacy.

In the past, our attention was focused on our mate's needs. Decisions were usually based on what would be good for him or her rather than us. In the sexual arena, we generally ignored our own wishes in deference to those of our mate. Perhaps out of fear of abandonment, we learned never to deny him (or her) sex. Should our recovering spouse now decide that he needs a period of "sexual detoxification," the message we may perceive is that, once again, *our* needs do not merit consideration. We might find ourselves feeling resentful that we were not included in the decision. Because we sincerely want our spouse to succeed in his or her recovery program, we feel guilty about feeling resentful. We think, Now that my mate is finally admitting the problem and doing something about it, I certainly can't rock the boat – I'll just have to do whatever is best for him. This perpetuates the previous pattern of the marriage.

Another likely outcome of the addict's abstinence from sexual intimacy is that the partner may feel rejected and unwanted. Partners who believe that sex is the most important sign of love might logically conclude that they are no longer loved when the mate withdraws sex. Their instinctive reaction will be to try to win him back sexually. This, of course, will only serve to sabotage his recovery program. Partners may realize this and stop themselves from trying to seduce the spouse. Caught in the middle of conflicting feelings, they will feel powerless and out of control.

Decisions about sex obviously affect both spouses. When the addict decides to maintain abstinence for a period of time, he needs to explain this to the partner and the partner needs to understand that many benefits will accrue to each of them and to the relationship:

1. *Partners learn that we're wanted for more than just our bodies and that we can get love without giving sex.* For Patty, the petite, attractive youthful partner, sex has been an important element in all her relationships, including her current marriage to a man who was repeatedly unfaithful in both his previous marriage and in the present one. Patty's little-girl manner and her take-care-of-me body language are what strike the observer first; it takes several minutes of conversation with her to realize she is an intelligent, articulate person who is also a successful career woman.

When Peter started going to Twelve-Step meetings, he came home and asked me about abstinence. I said, No way! I certainly wasn't going to do that; it was just too frightening to me. Eventually I agreed, but it scared me to death at first. I realized then that sex to me had been security. If things had been horrible and then we made love, I thought, Phew! He still wants me. During that month of abstinence a real bond was established between us. We knew that it was more than just sex we wanted in the relationship; we wanted each other. We learned just to enjoy snuggling. We'd wake up in the morning and we'd hold each other. I found myself able to ask him, "Would you hold me? Would you give me a kiss?" It was very comfortable.

A very different experience was had by Diane, the 30-year-old school teacher, whose husband decided on his own to avoid sex as part of his recovery program, without discussing it with her. Looking back on that period, she recalls,

I felt rejected, that there was something wrong with me, you know, the old equating of love and sex. I think if it had been an actual agreement, I wouldn't have felt personally rejected or deprived.

When two partners agree mutually to a period of abstinence and then continue to act lovingly toward each other, partners learn that their beliefs about sex were irrational. They learn that they are worthwhile people, that they are lovable for themselves, that sex is not the most important sign of love, and that they don't need to control their mates through sex.

2. *Abstinence forces partners to adopt new coping strategies and face problems directly.* Linda, the 45-year old socialite, had sexual relations with her computer programmer husband two or three times a day for most of their 25 years of married life. She rarely enjoyed these encounters because she felt like an object that was being used for her husband's sexual gratification. Before they got into recovery, Linda would overlook her husband's many affairs. Linda is slender, athletic, and expensively dressed. Her shiny black hair is brushed back into an elegant chignon. She looks relaxed and self-confident.

I used to use sex. When Lawrence and I had an argument and he was angry at me, I knew I had a tool. I could get him into bed, and as long as he made love to me everything was going to be all right. And it was. When Lawrence suggested a period of abstinence and we stopped having sex, I didn't have this tool anymore. Instead, I had to talk with him about the problem and try to resolve things instead of substituting sex for a solution.

Also part of me believed that the only reason Lawrence was staying with me was for all the sex I was giving him. During our months of abstinence I found out that wasn't true. It was a wonderful discovery. Now I know my husband doesn't need that from me – that our marriage can still go on as a happy, loving relationship without all that sex.

3. *An abstinence period can be the bridge to a new sexual relationship in which partners feel more comfortable paying attention to their own feelings.* Patty relates:

I've been learning that I've got to satisfy myself and he's not responsible for that. Both of us have experienced a real connectedness with each other. Before, I never knew where his mind was, and I was always trying to figure it out. I never really enjoyed the physical part because my mind was so involved in trying to figure out what he was thinking and what he wanted. I felt so used before, I felt he didn't really want to be there. I always let him initiate sex. If he decided to have sex, then we did, and I never said no. Now I'm beginning to ask myself, "How do I feel about making love? Do I want to, or do I not want to?"

Patty has learned that it is safe to pay attention to her own needs.

4. *A period of abstinence can allow partners to work through their own issues.* Rita, a 38-year old psychotherapist whose husband had affairs with both men and women, requested two periods of abstinence since they both went into recovery programs. The first time was immediately after she learned of his sexual activities. Rita feared contracting HIV or another sexually transmitted disease and did not want to have sex with her husband. It took her some weeks and negative STD screening to overcome this fear.

The second time Rita wanted a period of abstinence was when, in the course of counseling, she remembered something she had long repressed: in childhood she had been raped by her brother. Suddenly, when her husband touched her sexually, she found herself confusing him in her mind with her brother. She needed time out from the sexual relationship to work through the rape in her counseling sessions. That her husband was supportive of her requests for abstinence helped to improve their marriage relationship.

5. *A period of abstinence in a relationship that is committed to growth can result in renewed intimacy and can teach the couple new, deeper levels of relating.* According to Linda,

Lawrence and I used to hold hands now and then, but he hated it. He never wanted to be hugged, never wanted to be touched, never wanted to be kissed. He wanted sex, but that was as far as the intimacy ever went. Now we're trying to touch more. When I walk by him, I'll pat him on the shoulder and he's getting more comfortable with it. It's a gradual process.

Not only Lawrence and other sex addicts, but many members of American society are uncomfortable with nonsexual touching. Most Europeans shake hands on meeting someone and on leaving, and the French and Italians hug and kiss each other routinely. In the United States, nonsexual hugging and kissing are common only among women friends and between parents and children or other relatives.

Touching is a basic human and animal need. In Harry Harlow's famous experiments with baby monkeys separated from their mothers, those who had a soft, fuzzy inanimate surrogate mother in their cage to cling to for comfort developed normally, whereas those babies who had only a wire mesh surrogate grew up neurotic and were unable to form relationships with their peers. Human babies who are fed and diapered adequately but who are deprived of touching do not gain weight. Both animals and humans require touching as part of normal development. In its absence, they develop attachment disorders. Somehow in American society touching has become confused with sex. Many of us are therefore fearful that an innocent touch will be misunderstood as an invitation to sex. If our foot accidentally touches another's leg, we usually apologize. Many of us have never learned how to give or receive nonsexual touch. One of the benefits of a period of abstinence is that it gives us the freedom to explore nonsexual touching.

6. *A period of abstinence teaches that sex is optional.* Nancy, the 40-year old mother of seven, comments:

Our sexual relationship is very different now. He's there, making love with me. And we don't feel the pressure to have sex. If we start but then one of us isn't in the mood, we'll just drop it for now. Our spiritual life comes first, and we're not ruled by sex so much any more.

Gabrielle Brown provides a good description of the way a period of abstinence can put a relationship on a new basis:

Celibacy provides married couples with more choices of expression – a kind of limitless market of possible connections. It may be like "courting" all over again, but without the fear of rejection or the limitation of future goals. If a husband brings flowers to his spouse as a first step or prelude to a great night of sexual love, the meaning of the flowers becomes lost in the chain of events that follow. But flowers in times of celibacy are a thing-in-themselves – perhaps the whole expression of love for that day, not simply an offering to insure the future.

Celibacy can give the couple a chance both to re-establish pre-sexual communication of tender feelings and to open new channels of expression free from restrictive associative behavior. It can be a time for renewal of old feelings that occurred before sexual habits set in, and it can be a time to discover other modalities of loving. It can re-create and create the unbounded qualities of romance – the intensity; energy; sweetness; simplicity, and careful attention of two people falling in love.[2]

Not all couples in recovery need or want a period of abstinence. This is very much an individual choice. What is important, however, is that a decision for abstinence needs to be made with the agreement of both partners. If one member of the couple wishes a period of abstinence, the reasons should be discussed and understood. Abstinence should not be used by one partner as a way of punishing the other. Nor should it be used to avoid dealing with problems in the marriage, or as a way to avoid intimacy. When approached in a positive spirit, abstinence can be a period of spiritual growth and increased intimacy in the marriage.

Disclosure: What Should the Addict Tell the Partner About his or her Past?

When one member of a couple is unfaithful, the partner often suspects it. What brings many couples into therapy, however, is a crisis that occurs when evidence of the latest affair is so blatant it can no longer be denied. The addict is then forced to admit the affair. Some partners at this point will ask for more information, and the addict must then decide how much to reveal.

In recovery, too, there are times when a similar choice must be made. If the mate has a one-night stand after two years of monogamy, should he tell his partner? What about if a person has an online sexual encounter, or is only considering a sexual escapade – does the partner need to know about that? The whole issue of "How much should I tell my partner" is very complex. If you want to understand all aspects of this important subject, you might want to read *Disclosing Secrets* (for the addict) and *Surviving Disclosure* (for the partners), the books mentioned earlier in this chapter.

Sexaholics Anonymous, a book about addiction recovery used by members of Sexaholics Anonymous (SA), one of the Twelve-Step programs for sex addiction, cautions recovering addicts to be very careful about confessing their sexual acting out to the spouse. The book advises newcomers to the program not to discuss their sexual past with family members who do not already know of it until some time has elapsed, and even then only after discussing it first with group members. The book cautions that some relationships might otherwise not withstand the shock. Avoiding compulsive sexual behavior and working the Steps of an "S" program [such as SA, SAA, SCA, SLAA] will, it is hoped, cause improvement in behavior and attitude that the partner will see and feel. "The best amends is a changed life over time."[3]

Hope and Recovery: A Twelve-Step Guide for Healing from Compulsive Sexual Behavior, written by members of Sex Addicts Anonymous (SAA), another Twelve-Step program for sex addiction recovery, expresses the same point of view.[4] The recovering addicts who authored this book advise waiting to tell the partner until one has discussed it with the group, prayed about it, and felt it was the right time to do so.

That said, when sexual acting out, whether online or in real life has been a recurring theme in the relationship, it may be advisable to give the partner some information early on. For Alice, her husband's willingness to answer questions was a critical element in restoring trust in the relationship:

For my first two years of marriage, I lived on a roller coaster. My husband had wide mood swings which didn't seem to correlate with anything that was happening in our lives. At times when I would be feeling particularly happy with him and would tell him, he would respond in a deliberately hurtful way. Romantic vacations would be spoiled by his bad moods. Plans would be changed at the last minute. I kept trying to make sense of it all, and I kept feeling crazier and crazier.

I had no idea he was leading a separate life of affairs and fantasies and lies. One day when he tried to break off an affair, the affair partner threatened to tell me about it, so he told me first. I thought I was going to die; I could hardly breathe. But as I revived, I felt a tremendous need to put the pieces together. I asked for specific dates, for details on the ups and downs of their relationship. It was painful to hear the answers, and my husband kept trying to end the dialogue. But I insisted, and he answered everything I asked. There were things I didn't ask, because I didn't want to know.

The answers I got to my questions provided explanations for so many puzzling things that had happened, so many times I'd thought I was crazy. Now I knew why he had been so hurtful on a particular vacation. I had said, "You're so good to me," and his guilt over the affair, which was at its peak at that time, made him unable to accept the compliment; he needed to prove to me on the spot that he wasn't good to me. . . . Now I knew that I hadn't been crazy after all, that I had been right those times when I'd had a strong gut feeling that something was wrong, that he had been lying when he'd told me, "You're just imagining things."

I realized that on one level I had been aware all along of what was happening with him. To have him tell me the truth was to acknowledge the validity of those feelings. Not to have told me would have meant to keep me wondering.

And another thing: Over the years I had begun to distrust him. Things just didn't add up. Not to have told me would have kept the distrust going. By replying to all my questions, my husband began to rebuild trust in the relationship. This was a process that took many months. It is true that "the best amends is a changed life over time." But for me, the first step toward renewed trust after all the deceit was to receive honest answers from him. Evasiveness would have perpetuated the distrust.

Now, three years later, I still have no guarantees that my husband will not have another affair. But, based on that initial honesty and on the continued honesty since then, what I do know is that he will be honest with me. He will not assume he knows better than I do about what I should know. He will treat me as an adult, not as a little girl who needs protection. For me, honesty was crucial to the survival of our marriage during that crisis; I'm glad he told me about his past.

In many addictive relationships, we place the responsibility for our happiness in the hands of our mate. We give him or her the power to make us happy or unhappy, and to make decisions about our emotional life. For the addict in early recovery to decide what information his partner should have about his past is to perpetuate the old pattern, to agree that he is a better judge of what is best for her than she is herself. In individual cases this may be true, but in most cases I believe that the partner is the best judge of what is best for her or him in the relationship. This sentiment was echoed by Rita:

When Ralph asked the other guys whether he should tell me about his sexual past, everyone said, "No, don't tell her; I know a guy who told his wife and she left him." The counselors in his treatment program wouldn't tell Ralph what to do; they wanted him to make the decision on his own, but they believed he needed to tell me the truth. So Ralph told me, and I'm glad he did. It validated my sanity. I could look back and say, "So that's why that happened when it did. I really wasn't crazy!" Everything seemed to fall in place for me. All the things I'd thought, I'd suspected, were true.

I also believed that if I were going to rebuild this marriage with Ralph, the only way I could do so was to know his dark side as well as the good about him. I didn't believe then, and I don't believe today, that anyone in his recovery group has a right to know a secret about Ralph that I don't have the right to know. What I've grown to understand in my own recovery is that if there's a secret between us, there's a wall, and I don't want to live with that anymore.

An entirely different point of view is expressed by Nancy, who would prefer to have a minimum of information.

The first time Nick went out with another woman, he told me every little detail, and I spent the next fifteen years obsessing on it, thinking about it all the time. She was one of my best friends going through school. And every time I heard her name, my gut just turned over. Every time I met someone who even looked like her, I had to fight off feelings of hating her. A woman shouldn't have to bear that burden.

I think Nick was a lot smarter this last time when he had an affair. I don't know who it was, and I'm glad I don't. If he needs to talk about it with someone it should be in a group or with a person who doesn't have anything to do with her – because we codependents usually just use that information to beat ourselves over the head with. And I don't need to do that anymore.

I tried to get information out of him about the latest affair. I asked him, but he refused to tell me. At the time I thought he was just protecting her, but now I'm glad he didn't tell me anything. I don't need particulars about where or when or how. I need to know what it was in our relationship that might have contributed to it, so that we can be helped to work better together as a couple. But I don't need to know if he liked this better or that better.

And I've come to realize that the sexual things he did really didn't have that much to do with me. You see, I'm a foodaholic, and when I go to the refrigerator and pig out on chocolate cake, I don't tell myself I'm doing it to make Nick miserable, or because I like this cake better than I like him. It was an obsession with him, a sickness. It didn't mean there was anything wrong with me. He still loved me as best as he could, as best as any sexaholic could love anybody, and that's been a very good thing for me to understand. So I don't need any details. I know that I want to know it, but I don't think it's helpful for us to know it.

Nancy believes it is not healthy for her to know the details of Nick's past affairs; she would prefer to focus instead on their relationship now. With additional time in recovery, Nancy hopefully will recognize that rather than giving Nick the responsibility of denying her information she asks for, she needs to take responsibility for not digging for information from Nick that she recognizes is not good for her to have.

Obtaining information about her mate's past sexual behaviors can be part of an effort to control him, as Patty recognized:

I've heard some partners say they want to know all the details. Before I got into COSA [a Twelve Step program for families of sex addicts] I wanted to know everything. I wanted to figure out what he was doing, and I'd try to make him confess. But now that I'm in the program I don't want to go back and learn more about those affairs. I was devastated enough by what I thought I knew at the time. Also, there are things I don't want him to hear about, things I've told my [COSA] sponsor that I don't think Peter has to hear about. So I don't feel he has to tell me everything.

Sarah, a certified public accountant and an assertive person, now divorced and living alone with her two small sons, had several crises with her sexually addicted husband. He had confessed to an affair and promised to be faithful, only to begin lying again. She recalls,

I needed to know a certain amount of information about the affair. Maybe that was a part of my beating up on myself. But the bottom line was that I needed to know it was a past issue Then I could move on in the relationship, which is what I tried to do. The problem was that he would always lie to me about it. I think that if the goal is to have the relationship continue, then the partner should be told only as much as she asked for. He should tell her only what she needs to hear, and she is the best judge of that. He shouldn't just dump on her. But on the other hand, if he withholds when she asks, it's equally bad. She's asking because she has a need to know.

Some of the people I interviewed felt they needed certain details about their spouse's past to sort out in their minds the craziness they had gone through. Some women felt they needed the secrets out in the open to make a fresh start. Others believed it was in their best interest not to have more than the barest of facts; they recognized they would use detailed information to try to control their partner's behavior and to make themselves feel worse. Almost all partners, however, felt it should be *their* decision how much to be told, not the addict's. Most people did not ask for information they were not ready to hear.

I believe that if a relationship is to survive the crisis of disclosure of one spouse's sexual activities, a spirit of honesty and respect for each partner is essential. Treating one's partner with respect means letting her or him decide how much they need to know and then answering the questions they ask.

Several persons made a distinction between their need for information about the affairs the addict had *before* entering a recovery program and the information about *current* addictive thoughts, impulses, and behaviors. One young woman met her husband after he had already begun to participate in a Twelve Step "S" program. She stresses the open communication and total honesty they had from the beginning of the relationship:

When I first came into this relationship I decided I wasn't going to let any secrets go on. At first we went through a lot of disclosures. Everything had to be gone over in detail. Now, if my husband is having problems, he'll just say, "I'm having a real rough day with my urges." I don't have to know exactly how rough, or all the gory details; I just know how difficult it is.

For Alice, who wanted detailed information at the time of her husband's disclosure, the need to know has also diminished.

I realize now that part of my past need to know had to do with a feeling I had that the more I knew, the fewer surprises there would be, and that the more I knew, the more control I would somehow have over the situation. Part of my recovery has been learning to let go. Early in his recovery, Alan felt he had to be scrupulously honest with me about everything that was going on in his head. So he'd come home and tell me he'd met a very attractive girl. He had forced himself to break off the conversation with her, and he'd felt very sad all day at the lost opportunity. All that such confessions did was make me feel bad. But I listened anyway, because I thought it was important that he felt he could confide in me. Besides, there was a part of me that was glad to have an opportunity to monitor his progress.

Now I've come far enough along in my own recovery to realize I don't have to listen to stuff that makes me feel bad. I've asked Alan to tell these things to his Twelve-Step group or his sponsor. If he has some significant triumph he wants to share with me, or some particularly traumatic event that is obviously influencing his mood, then I want to hear about it. I find it's good for me occasionally to be reminded that Alan has an ongoing struggle with the temptation to connect with other women. After all, sex addiction is like food addiction; unlike alcohol, you can't give up people or food altogether – you must learn to relate to them in a healthier way. Alan has become so healthy that it's easy for me to forget that he's not "cured," and that he fights these little battles on a daily basis. But I no longer have to monitor his recovery; I realize I have no control over is behavior. Either he's working his program, or he's not. If he decided it's too difficult, he'll tell me. Otherwise, I can assume he's doing okay, and I don't have to hear about all the temptations, setbacks, or bad feelings. He can tell it to his group.

Patty, the dentist's wife, agrees:

When we were first in the program, Peter would come home and tell me, "I had a problem with lust today." And my mind would start racing – where? Was it at the office? Was it one of the patients? And I'd begin to obsess about it. I finally was able to say, "If you have a problem with that, right now I'm not able to handle it. Would you tell your sponsor or somebody else; I feel like you're dumping on me." He was just trying to be honest, but it made me feel bad. So now he tells his sponsor, and I don't have to know about it. If he tells me that he saw someone today who really drove him crazy, it might trigger the sickness back in me. So I trust him to take care of it. If he lusted after somebody, I hope he's well enough in his program that he can call his sponsor and tell him.

In summary, some of us need to know more than others do about our mate's past affairs. Most of us feel that *we* should decide how much we should be told. And we often find that the further along we get in our own recovery, the less we want to know about our spouse's present struggles. All we often really need to know is that he or she has not gone beyond the boundaries with which we are willing to live.

Establishing Boundaries

Many partners of addicts have difficulties maintaining boundaries; they are not certain where they end and the outside world begins. They are, as Anne Wilson Schaef put it, "externally referented."[5] This means they depend on others for information on how they feel, what they think, and how much they are worth. Decisions are based on what the partner believes the mate wants, not on what the partner wants.

As a result of disclosure, many partners recognize the need to work towards establishing and holding boundaries. They need to learn how to pay attention to their needs and their feelings, to be assertive about their wants and needs and to deal constructively with situations that make them feel bad. In order to do this, they must first develop enough self-esteem to be willing to risk another person's displeasure by asserting their rights. As experienced people-pleasers, many partners need to learn that they, too, deserve to be pleased.

Prior to recovery, many partners were so fearful of abandonment that they tolerated hurtful behaviors rather than risk confrontations with the mate. There always seemed to be mitigating circumstances we could use to explain and excuse the behavior. There always seemed to be reasons, however implausible, that they could embrace to avoid facing the truth.

As the partner's self-esteem improves, however, they eventually no longer believe in holding on to the mate at any cost. When the possibility of living alone ceases to feel like a fate worse than death, they are ready to consider of divorce if the mate is unwilling to cease those extramarital sexual activities. They may choose to stay despite his infidelity if they feel that the benefits outweigh the costs. One partner, for example, decided to remain married for another three years while she went back to college so she could be self-supporting. Another, who had been very poor in childhood and was now enjoying an affluent lifestyle, decided her financial needs were more important than her emotional needs. A minister decided it was most important to provide a stable home for his children; moreover, divorce was unheard of in his family. Some may not agree with the reasons why these people decided to stay in a marriage with an unfaithful spouse, but what is important is that in each case the decision was based on something other than a desperate fear of abandonment.

Couples in recovery learn to develop limits or boundaries in their relationship. Sometimes the couple openly discusses these boundaries, along with the consequences if the agreement is broken. In other marriages, one or both partners develop internal boundaries, but don't discuss them with the other. For people whose spouses have been unfaithful, the limit is often another affair. Rita, who went through a one-month inpatient codependency treatment program, told her husband at the end of her treatment, "If you have another affair, I will leave you."

Nancy initially had no boundaries in her marriage. She related,

I haven't set any boundaries because in the past I told him, "If you do this again, that's it; I'm leaving." And he'd do it again and we'd break up and then we'd get back together.

Nancy had given her husband many ultimatums in the past, and they hadn't worked. She had tried to control his behavior with threats.

Like Nancy, many other partners repeatedly threatened to leave if their partners had another affair. In our study of sex addicts and their spouses for our books *Disclosing Secrets* and *Surviving Disclosure,* Dr. Deborah Corley and I learned that 60 percent of partners who were still married at the time of the survey had previously threatened to leave should their spouse betray them. Since they hadn't left, these were just empty threats and were ineffective in changing their spouse's behavior.

In recovery, Nancy continued to confuse setting appropriate boundaries with trying to control her husband's behavior. She was confusing setting limits with giving an ultimatum. The difference was clarified by Jessica, the nurse:

When I first learned about my husband's affairs, I went through a great deal of emotional pain and a terrible loss of trust in him. I don't ever want to experience such pain again or to share him sexually with anyone else. I told him that if he has another affair I can't continue in our marriage. One of my friends said, "I, too, have given my husband ultimatums. But isn't that trying to control him? Doesn't the Twelve- Step program teach us that we cannot control another person's behavior?"

I explained to her that I'm not trying to control his behavior. What I'm doing is setting boundaries of behaviors that are acceptable to me and those that aren't. My husband can choose how to behave, and I can choose whether or not to live with that behavior. My husband's "first drink" is not sexual intercourse; it's making that first connection with a new woman. Several deliberate decisions then lead to the "tenth drink," the bedroom. He can choose to risk the "first" or the "second drink"; but if he proceeds to the "tenth drink," I will no longer be there for him. I'm not willing to experience the pain again, so I'm taking care of myself. This is my boundary; it's not an ultimatum.

Another partner's spouse used to have brief same-sex encounters. Now in a sex addiction recovery program, he still has occasional slips as he struggles with issues of his own sexual identity. She wants to stay in the marriage with him because she sees progress, they have a strong emotional bond and several children, and because she hopes he can work out his issues in favor of the marriage. Meanwhile, for her own protection, she has decided she cannot have sex with him as long as he continues to have sex with other men. She is not trying to control his behavior; rather, she is trying to avoid the possibility of catching HIV, herpes, or other sexually transmitted diseases. She has set a boundary for herself that makes her feel safe.

Although Nancy has never discussed her boundaries with her recovering husband, she is clear about them.

If Nick has another affair, I will leave him. It wouldn't be worth it to be in a relationship any more with an unfaithful partner. I'm well enough now, and I know too much to ever go back into that kind of sickness. An affair isn't just a slip, it's a long, involved process. People have to set those things up – it goes on over a period of time. It would be unacceptable for him to go out on me and then tell me, "I had an affair because. . ." Anyway, at this point I would know long before it happened. It wouldn't be like it was before, because I could spot the signs right away. I guess an affair would be the limit for me. I'm not that dependent anymore. Before, I was sure that I would starve without him, that the kids would starve. That's what Nick kept telling me too. Now I have enough faith in my Higher Power that He would get me through.

It is interesting that Nancy mentions she would not have to wait for her husband to reveal an affair to her – she would know long before. Several other people concurred, stating that their boundary would not be some particular sexual transgression by their spouse, but rather if he were to stop working his recovery program. They felt that ceasing recovery work would be a prelude to relapse to an affair and would be evident long before the affair occurred. A young woman explained:

I don't have to set any limits. My husband told me that if he stops working his program I'd be a fool to stay. Our life is so different now than before, so much calmer and more reasonable. I see evidence every day that he's committed to recovery. If he stopped, I'd know it right away and we would discuss our future before anything happened.

Patty would be willing to have an open mind about any transgressions as long as her husband was still sincere about working his recovery program:

When Peter and I were first married, I used to think that if he ever had an affair, I'd leave him. Well, he did and I didn't. Now I can't say what I'd do, but I know I would be willing to listen to him to find out where he was in the situation. Was it a slip? Does he feel regret? Does he want to continue in the program? I don't know what I'd do.

I do know I want a real relationship. Even if he never had another affair but we drifted apart and the relationship wasn't what I wanted, I would consider ending it. Whether he has an affair or not, I want more. I want us to be able to give to each other and grow together. The Twelve-Step program has shown us that we can do that.

Some may say, "It's easy to decide in advance that you'd leave your spouse if he has another affair or visits a prostitute, or spends hours per week on cybersex, but how can you be sure you'd really go through with it?" The answer is, we can't ever be totally certain of anything until we actually face the situation. That's why some of us try not to think in terms of absolutes. Linda, whose husband used to have affairs with both men and women, says:

We've never made a contractual limit. Perhaps it's because I see a man who's trying down to his toenails to be the best that he can. He's working very hard in his recovery program. Thank God that to this day there hasn't been a slip. I don't know how I would react if there was. I don't know what I would do.

Until I cross that path I will never really know. I might think I'd walk out in a heartbeat, or I might think I'd be warm and understanding and help him through it – but I might do just the opposite. I try not to think in those terms. If he comes home late from a meeting, I don't try to figure out the reason. I know he's working his program, and I have to be more concerned with me and my program.

In early recovery, partners are sometimes reluctant to be assertive about boundaries in their marriage. "I set a lot of limits in the past and always broke them," said one young woman. Another added "I don't want to be judged myself, so how can I judge another person?" Along the same vein, a man said, "I didn't even *realize* I didn't have boundaries in my marriage. Now I'm trying to set limits in my own behavior. But I'm constantly slipping, so how can I set limits for my wife?" As these people progress in their own recovery they will most likely feel more comfortable in building expectations and account-ability into their relationships.

When I first met Diane, the young teacher and mother of a small child, she was a member of the walking wounded. She had recently learned that the money that kept mysteriously disappearing from their meager savings account was being spent by her husband, Dick, on pornographic websites and on casual sexual encounters. Diane's religion, which was an important part of her life, taught her that mar-riages are created in heaven and last a lifetime. She did not under-stand her husband's behavior; she felt hurt and confused, but she was sure she would never leave him, no matter what he did. She believed her husband's problems were somehow her fault and that if she could be more understanding or more attractive, his extramarital sexual activities would cease. Dick had begun attending a Twelve-Step group for sex addicts, but Diane did not understand why he thought of himself as an addict. In her own Twelve-Step group for families of sex addicts, Diane sat and listened but said very little; she obviously disapproved of the women who spoke of the possibility of leaving their marriages.

Two years later, Diane's views on the permanence of marriage have shifted:

I don't like to confront and say this I will tolerate and that I won't. I'm always so scared of being like my mother, who was such a domineering, critical tough woman. I guess I'm also scared with Dick that if I'm too tough or too mean he'll just blow up, or who knows what horrible things might happen – he might even leave. He doesn't react well to criticism. But I know I can't live with him anymore if he has casual sex. We haven't talked about what would happen if he went back out there again, but I envision a progression of steps, where I would confront him and say, "This can't go on." And if it went on then I would call in outside reinforcements – elders of the church, for instance – and insist on counseling. I'd ask for a contract that he would not do this, or that, and if he did, then that would be the end of the marriage. I would do that, but never after one episode. I would have to see that he was genuinely not going to change, that this was his choice that he was not going to try to get better. I would feel justified then in ending the marriage.

This very important point was enunciated by James C. Dobson, a Christian family counselor with a wide radio and television following. In his book, *Love Must be Tough*, Dobson addresses the traditional Christian wife who turns the other cheek when her husband misbehaves:

Infidelity is an addiction that can destroy a life as easily as drugs or alcohol. Once a man or woman is hooked on the thrills of sexual conquest, he or she becomes intoxicated with its lust for pleasure. This person needs every available reason to go straight – to clean up his life. He certainly does not need a spouse who says dreamily, "I understand why you need the other woman, David. My goodness! I am so riddled with flaws that it's no wonder you went looking for someone else. You should see the list of my own stupidities that I'm keeping.

. . . You just go on with your other friendships for a few years while I work on myself, and maybe you'll eventually feel like being a husband again. Spend our money foolishly, if you wish, and I'll get along somehow. . . ." That approach is like buying booze for the drunk and drugs for the junkie, It is *weak* love! It is disastrous![6]

Dobson recommends a course of action he terms *tough love*. Pointing out that a partner's power to negotiate will never be greater than during the crisis of the mate's revelation, Dobson suggests she get her spouse's written commitment to participate in counseling immediately, not even waiting two or three weeks to get started.

Of several people he interviewed who tolerated their spouse's infidelities in order to try to save the marriage, Dobson says:

A key ingredient in the erosion of their homes was a kind of marital permissiveness which proved to be fatal. Upon learning that their spouses were involved in affairs, their instinctive reaction was to understand, to explain, to forgive, or to ignore the adultery occurring under their noses. These good people were motivated by committed love in its purest form, and I admire them for their compassion under the most awful pressure. Nevertheless, they each found "excuses" for the unfaithfulness of their partners, which permitted the disloyal behavior to continue unchecked.

Therein lies a fundamental problem. These loving, gracious people inadvertently shielded their wayward spouses from the consequences of infidelity. If there is *anything* that an adulterer does not need, it is a guilt-ridden mate who understands his indiscretion and assumes the blame for it. Such a person needs to be called to *accountability*, not excused by rationalization![7]

What Dobson is saying is that to turn the other cheek, to be forgiving no matter what, is to *enable* the addict, to protect him or her from experiencing the consequences of the behavior. Taking a loving but tough stance, on the other hand, encourages the addict's recovery while at the same time improves the partner's self-esteem. Having clear rules about what is acceptable within the marriage often helps to put the relationship on a new basis of mutual respect and accountability.

How Can Trust be Re-established?

One of the biggest costs of infidelity is the loss of trust it engenders. Trust in one another involves predictability, dependability, and faith. A person who is predictable will behave the same way in the future as in the past. A dependable person is someone who can be relied on when it matters. We judge both predictability and reliability by the person's past behavior. But since future behavior cannot always mirror the past, faith is the belief – based on past experience that our mate cares – that he or she will continue to be responsive and caring. According to Erich Fromm, author of *The Art of Loving*, "Faith is an indispensable quality of any significant friendship or love. 'Having faith' in another person means to be certain of the reliability and unchangeability of his fundamental attitudes, of the core of his personality, of his love."[8] The person may change his opinions, but his basic motivations remain the same.

When an affair comes to light, predictability, dependability, and faith vanish. We learn that our mate's past behavior has been very different from what he had led us to believe, and we therefore have no basis from which to predict his future behavior. We no longer feel we can depend on his concern for us. Moreover, not only can we no longer be certain of the durability of his fundamental attitudes, but we suddenly realize we don't even *know* what his fundamental attitudes and values are. All the elements of trust are gone.

For the couple who decide to rebuild their relationship after disclosure of infidelity, re-establishing trust is *the* major task. This is usually a slow process that takes months to years and requires much work on the part of both partners. My interviews with recovering couples that formed the basis of my book, *Sex, Lies, and Forgiveness: Couples Speak on Healing From Sex Addiction*, suggested it takes an average of two years for trust to be fully restored. In order to allow a betrayed partner to again develop faith in the addict, he or she must consistently demonstrate honesty, predictability, and dependability. Involvement in a recovery program seems to facilitate the process of restoring trust. Jessica, the nurse, recalls,

When I first learned about all my husband's lies, I thought I could never trust him again. It's taken a long time to rebuild the trust. I'd say that the first step was his willingness to answer all my questions about his affairs. I could see he didn't want to tell me, but the fact that he was willing to be honest about these painful things made an impression on me even them.

The consistency of his behavior is the second factor that permitted me to trust him again. In our early years together he told me so many lies and half-truths that even he doesn't know anymore whether he told me the truth or a lie about any particular event. One day I found out about yet another lie from those years and got upset. He told me, "I can't guarantee the truth of anything I told you before I got in the [Twelve-Step] program, but I can promise you that I've been entirely honest with you ever since and will continue to be so." That was a couple of years ago, and I haven't had a single occasion since then to doubt his word. He is consistently caring and loving, very different from the roller coaster life we used to lead before.

The third factor that helps me trust him is his commitment to his self-help program. He goes to meetings, he talks with program people on the phone, he reads the Twelve-Step literature. He does a lot of Twelfth Step work – when he meets someone whom he identifies as a fellow addict, he tells him about the program and about how his life used to be then and how it is now. I can see that he's so much more at peace with himself now than he used to be. He's told me, "I can't promise that I'll never have another affair. But I will tell you about it in advance. And if that happens, you won't have to leave me. I'll probably feel so bad that I'll leave first. On one level I'll be making a conscious choice; on another, I'll be acknowledging the power of the addiction."

In addition to consistently honest behavior, a consistently *caring* attitude on the part of our partner can also contribute to restoring trust in the damaged relationship. According to Nancy:

At first I didn't have any trust. When I found out there was a woman in Nick's self-help group, I thought he could still have an affair with her. He's not that much to look at, but I guess I thought that every woman was falling all over herself trying to be with him.

It's been a gradual process. He's been very trustworthy. He made sure to be home when he was supposed to. He would always phone me or leave me a note if he had a change of plans. For a long time he took a lot of care to be on that straight and narrow, even if he had to go out of his way. And then there came a time that he didn't need to do that anymore. If he was going to be late, he didn't have to rush to a phone to let me know why; I was no longer sitting at home tapping my fingers and wondering where he was if he was five minutes late. As I got better, I no longer needed all those reassurances.

Nancy's husband Nick recognized that his past behavior had contributed to her insecurity, and he bent over backwards to give her no cause for concern. As her recovery progressed, this was no longer necessary. This account illustrates that rebuilding trust is a mutual process involving changes by both partners.

Another important element is open communication between partners. This is what Diane, the young religious woman, feels has made all the difference in the survival of her marriage. In the days when Dick was having both online and real-life casual sexual encounters, Diane and Dick never talked much about their problems. Both had grown up in families where problems were not discussed; each was afraid of rejection by the other if they did not appear strong.

After we had our big talk about his sexual activities, I felt I couldn't trust him. I didn't know if I could ever trust him. How could I trust him to be honest with me? When he said he was no longer having sexual contact with other people, how could I know if he was being truthful? I had no way of knowing, and I felt absolutely no trust. But it's gradually coming back. Now I see that we can discuss things. When he slips, we can talk about it. He is seeing that people can talk about difficult things and still be connected, and not totally reject each other. Dick told me at the time that he couldn't trust me either. He felt he couldn't be himself without being criticized or judged. I guess I didn't feel emotionally that he could trust me. I think that's changing now.

Dick's fear that he couldn't trust Diane not to judge him is a sentiment expressed by many addicts. How can an addict feel safe enough to reveal his vulnerability to his partner if the result is likely to be criticism and negative feedback? Yet this is just the way many partners have learned to react over the years. Out of their fear of abandonment, they may become reactive and accusatory, contributing to the parent-child dynamic that is so common in the relationship between the addict and partner. In rebuilding trust, *both members of the couple* must demonstrate their trustworthiness over time. For the partner, this means becoming more able to listen to the addict without responding like a critical parent. Partners need to learn to listen more quietly and empathetically and take time to sort out their feelings before responding.

Rebuilding trust takes time. A period of stress and distrust is inevitable. The Twelve-Step program advises living "one day at a time." This does not mean we avoid necessary plans or not undertake projects that can't be completed today. It means not being overwhelmed by the problem, but deciding what can be doing *today* and doing that. If we approach each other with honest, consistent, trust-worthy behavior, this attitude builds upon the previous day, until a track record exists on which we can base new trust.

Relapse: Should I Stay or Leave? What Partners Have Told Us

Relapse, which is *a return to the use of addictive substances or behaviors after a period of abstinence*, is a well-recognized characteristic of addictive disorders. Some people differentiate between a "slip," which is a one-time event that happens unexpectedly, and a "relapse," which can be seen as a prolonged move back to compulsive sexual behavior. The majority of sex addicts in recovery experience a slip, and many have recurrent relapses. Partners of sex addicts are likely to discover and/or experience disclosure of relapse if they remain in a committed relationship with a sex addict.

It is advisable, therefore, for the couple early on to prepare for the possibility of a slip or relapse and to develop an action plan, including what information the partner needs to know, and what actions the partner expects to take. This is usually done with a therapist following the initial disclosure process and as part of the couples counseling that follows.

In a study published in 2012, Deborah Corley, Joshua Hook and I surveyed 92 partners of sex addicts about their reactions and decisions related to disclosure of relapse by the addict.[9] These couples had been married for an average of 16.6 years. Three-quarters of the partners (78%) reported that they did not know the mate had issues with sex addiction before committing to their relationship. After the **initial** disclosure of the mate's infidelity (perhaps years earlier than the current study), 41% of the partners separated from their mate for some time. (Another 16% moved into separate bedrooms for some time.) The separation lasted an average of 10.2 months, with a range of a few days to 2-1/2 years.

Why partners agreed to reunite with the addict after the initial disclosure of the sex addiction The main reasons that the partner agreed to get back together after an initial separation were:

- The mate got help: "He committed to recovery" 49%
- Commitment: "We're trying to make the relationship work" 27%
- Children or other financial considerations: "We
- couldn't afford to live separately" 10%
- Other, e.g. religious reasons 14%

Despite the risk of relapse and the pain of initial discovery or disclosure, partners decided to stay primarily because the addict got help and was committed to recovery. Recovery programs support behaviors of trustworthiness such as honesty, accountability, and transparency, which are important factors in promoting recovery of the relationship.

Plans for dealing with a relapse
About a third of partners (36%) reported having a plan or agreement with their mate about what each of them would do in the event of a relapse. For several couples the plan was that the mate would disclose the relapse to the partner and the couple would deal with it. For example, one partner said that "he [the addict] would be completely honest and tell me right away." Other plans included separation or ending the relationship. Still other plans depended on the specific nature of the relapse. For example, "Relapses not involving another person would result or separation or separate bedrooms, but acting out with other people would result in my leaving the marriage." Some plans were very vague, with no specified consequences: "He'd tell his sponsor and his therapist, and his therapist would tell my therapist, and then he would tell me – but he didn't follow it." Among the partners who had made a plan for dealing with relapse,

only 20% followed through, 51% followed parts of it, and 28% did not follow through at all.

Given that slips and relapses are common during recovery from sex addiction, my conclusion is that although it's uncommon to actually follow through with all elements of a plan, what is important is that couples recognize and discuss the possibility of relapse and create some plans for what to do should this actually occur. The partner often states that she does not wish to be the responsible party or the police, but she does wish to know. As a result of the addict sharing openly about what is happening, the partner gets to see change, motivation on the part of the addict in being open and sharing honestly, and a reality gut-check about how she is experiencing her addict spouse in that moment. This information will help partners make an informed decision about what they will do.

How partners learned about relapses – and the consequences
In the 2012 study by Dr Deborah Corley and myself, unfortunately more partners learned about the relapse through their own discovery rather than through the mate's voluntary disclosure. Almost three-quarters of the spouses experienced multiple relapses by their mate, so that there were several occasions when there were secrets that needed to be revealed. For the most recent relapse, most partners (65%) suspected that the mate had relapsed before his or her disclosure. Most relapses involved only the use of the internet, either to view pornography or to engage in other online sexual activities. However, 28% of relapses included a real-life meeting that the addict had arranged online.

Looking at how the manner of disclosure of one or more relapses affected the outcome for the relationship, we found that *partners whose mate more often voluntarily disclosed his or her relapse reported a higher level of relationship satisfaction and trust.* This finding turned out to be a very important factor in the future of the relationship, as we will see in the next section.

Why partners chose to stay or leave following the addict's relapse
The partners in this study were also asked to describe the reasons that kept them in the relationship despite the most recent relapse and what would make them decide to leave. Here are the reasons for staying, and some explanations for them. (Note that some partners had reasons for staying that fell into more than one category):

- The value of the relationship: "I believe that we can work through this, and that the relationship is worth it." "I love him and we've been together for a very long time – and I do believe he is committee to staying sober." "I love him regardless of what he has done and am able to view the addiction as a real illness." 26%

- Mate was committed to recovery: "I'm only staying because he has agreed to intense therapy and has begun showing progress." "He has been active with Twelve-Step groups, and has been doing serious therapy. I also understand that the addiction isn't about me. We have four beautiful children together. I am in therapy for myself and attend support groups." "He's going to an intensive, improving his recovery plan, and definite improvement on intimacy and honesty issues." "He *is* a great man, we have a 4-year old daughter, he's really working hard on his recovery." 23%

- Children or finances: "I'm currently pregnant and can't get a divorce in this state." "Finances, children, caring if not love." "I stayed for a while because of the children and to get my own schooling finished and establish financial stability." 23%

- Hope or faith: "I hope that a better marriage is coming." "We have many years of marriage; I'm willing to wait and see." "I hope that he finally hit his bottom." 7%

- Other: "I live one day at a time, I practice my own recovery." "God's promises; reading the Bible." "My husband's addiction has nothing to do with me." 20%

These reasons for staying are similar to the ones that partners gave for staying after the initial disclosure of the mate's sex addiction. What is particularly interesting, however, is what would make partners leave:

- Specific relapse behaviors: "Sex with another woman." "Contact with a prior acting-out person." ""One more emotional affair will take me over the edge." "Contact with a 'live' woman rather than what he does now." 48%
- Dishonesty: "Discovery of lying." "If he refused disclosure." "If he was not honest about things that would greatly affect my future." "Not believing he can or will be honest." "If I catch him lying about anything significant." 29%
- Cessation of recovery work: "If he ceases active recovery." "Failure to work his program." "If he's unwilling to work on the problem." "If he doesn't get medication [for his psychiatric disorder]." 26%
- Spousal abuse: 6%
- Other: 19%

Surprisingly, fewer than half the partners mentioned relapse as the primary reason they would leave, and even those partners tended to specify particular behaviors that would cause them to leave, whereas other sexual activities would not. More than half the partners focused on the addict's dishonesty or unwillingness to become seriously engaged in recovery work, which are often basically the same thing. This tells us that *what was most important for so many partners was the mate's motivation to change and honesty in the relationship.* One partner wrote that she would not leave if her husband was unfaithful, but *would* end the marriage if he didn't admit his actions to her and she would learn about them from another source. As we wrote,

> At the time of the most recent relapse/disclosure, these partners were in long-term relationships with an average length

of over 16 years. Partners had a great deal invested in the relationship, both emotionally and logistically. Many of the partners were now supported by counselors, friends, and involvement in Twelve- Step support groups. Many had worked on their own recovery. Partners could be expected by now to be well informed about the nature of addiction and to have a more nuanced approach to the relationship. This was seen in the responses, now focused on the addict's recovery attempts, efforts to work through problems together, and commitment to the relationship rather just on relapse.

Many addicts stumble on the road to recovery. The findings of this study give hope to couples who find themselves dealing with relapses, and provides guidance to the addict: The best advice for anyone who has a slip or relapse is to *be honest with your partner and demonstrate your commitment to recovery work.* As for partners, if you have made a decision to stay in your relationship despite your mate's difficulties, this study demonstrates that this does not have to be a sign of your "relapse to coaddiction" or wishful thinking, or a sign of weakness; rather, if your mate is committed to his or her recovery it can be a legitimate and reasoned choice which can strengthen your relationship and have a positive outcome.

What to Tell Our Children

All addictions involve secrecy. We make attempts to keep secrets from our spouse, children, parents, neighbors, employers, or significant others. Much of the time we have only an illusion of secrecy. In alcoholic families, for example, Dad's drinking is often well known by the neighbors and the employer despite the family's efforts to keep it a secret within with family. Certainly the drinking is no secret from the partner.

When the addiction is to cybersex or real-life affairs, secrecy is even more common. Our mates have probably tried to keep their sexual activities secret from us. If we know, we will almost always avoid telling the children. As discussed in earlier chapters, we often feel that our mate's affairs or use of digital devices for sexual acting out are somehow our fault; the fewer people know about it, the less chance there is that they will think badly of us. The unfaithful mate most certainly does not want his children or his parents to know.

Because addictions are considered a family disease, recovery is most effective if it involves the whole family. Addiction rehabilitation programs routinely include a "family week" when concerned others – spouses, children, or significant others – interact with the addict and work on their own issues. Teenagers are encouraged to attend Alateen, an Al-Anon program for teenagers, where the impact of the parental addiction on the children is discussed.

But what about recovery from sex addiction? What should the children be told? What should their own involvement be? Divorced parents, who generally have grievances against each other, have always struggled with the issue of what to tell the children about the other parent. Couples who are recovering together have had to work out their own guidelines.

Sex is a difficult subject for parents to discuss with children. It may be harder for an addict to disclose his or her sexual acting out to the child than to the spouse or parent. Factors that dissuade parents from disclosure to children include shame, anger, fear of alienating the children, fear that the children might be harmed by the information, and concern that they might tell others. Based on interviews with recovering sex addicts and partners, Burt Schneider and I recommended age-appropriate disclosure. In our book, *Sex, Lies, and Forgiveness*, we wrote,

> People who are unwilling to share with their children often assume that the children did not know what was going on. In fact, children often knew. They may have overheard telephone calls, arguments, and conversations, but kept the

information to themselves. Even if they didn't know the details, they may have sensed the stress and tension between their parents. Telling older children about the addiction and recovery can validate the children's feelings. Furthermore, it gives them permission to talk about what they may have felt and experienced during their parents' acting out.[10]

Children as young as 8 to 10 are likely to be aware of what is going on in the home and deserve some explanation about the nature of the problem and of the meetings that their parents so frequently attend. Evasiveness with children is likely to continue the legacy of secrecy, which promotes addiction.

As Dr. Deborah Corley and I explained in our books *Disclosing Secrets* and *Surviving Disclosure*, what kids want to know depends on their age. Preschool children (ages 3 to 5) have often been witness to fighting or have heard addiction discussed and don't know what is happening. They want to know: Are you going to leave me? Am I in trouble? Do you love me?

Early elementary-school age children want to know: Is the fighting my fault? Will something bad (like divorce) happen? Why do you seem different now than before recovery?

Children ages 9-13 ask: Am I normal? Will I get this addiction because I have sexual feelings or have masturbated? What will happen to me if you get divorced?

Teens and young adults want to know: How could you do this to Mom/Dad (i.e., to the partner of the addict)? To the family? How does this specifically relate to me? (You've ruined my life!)

In a survey of 89 adolescents and young adult-age children who had experienced disclosure from a sex-addicted parent, Black, Dillon and Carnes[11] found that prior to disclosure, most of the children (60 out of 89) knew of their parent's behavior or suspected it. Although the parents had undoubtedly wanted to protect their children from pain, what really happened was that the children had to keep unwanted secrets, sometimes for years. Although many of them said that eventually they were glad they were told, many children reported feeling angry at the time. This was primarily because their lives had been turned upside down. Some began to fear a parent who they now thought might be a pervert or a child molester. Others tried to take care of their parents emotionally. Some children reported initially feeling validation, confusion, anger, and mixed messages from their parents.

Black and her group suggested four reasons to disclose to children:

- To validate what the children already know
- To explain the situation to them thoughtfully before they find out from others
- To break the generational cycle of addiction often present in families
- For the children's safety, if they are at risk of being exposed to sexual behaviors by the addicted parent.

In our survey of 57 parents regarding disclosure to their children about sex addiction problems, Deborah Corley and I [12] found that the circumstances of disclosure affected the outcomes. Some disclosures were forced by events, such as public exposure of the affair or other sexual behavior, threats by others to reveal the information, or insistence by the other spouse. Some disclosures, usually by the partner "outing" the addict to the children, were impulsive, unplanned, and out of anger. Other disclosures were planned, with one or both parents involved and sometimes with the participation of a therapist. Planned disclosures generally had the best outcome.

Here are two examples of a planned disclosure. One woman remembered:

Disclosure took place during my husband's treatment, and included both of us, my 14-year old daughter, and the therapist. My daughter was tearful, but we had talked about it some before Family Week. She is very mature but said she did not understand why her father did what he did. She has missed him so much, and I think he sounded so sincere to her – it was hard for her to be mad. Later she got mad at me because I was being so negative. Sex addiction is an open subject like many others in our home. At first I was really angry and tried to control everything, but I got a handle on that.

Different circumstances were related by Nancy:

A few weeks ago Nick took our oldest daughter out to dinner and talked with her about his sex addiction. Later she told me, "That was the most wonderful night of my life. We just had the best talk!" We've been trying to help her because she's in a bad situation with a boy. She's me all over again. She's codependent, she's addicted to this boy she's living with, and it's been awful! When I hear her talking about how badly he treats her, I feel so bad for her. Her talk with Nick allowed her to see her own problems in the context of the family problems.

I don't think Nick has talked with our sons. But they've talked with me, they've asked me about certain things, and I was amazed to learn that some of the kids hated me more than they did him. They hated me because of the times I was always in bed, depressed, not taking care of them. They blamed me for a lot of the stuff that was going on. That was a real eye-opener.

For Nancy and Nick, talking with their children about their addiction-related problems opened the way for better understanding between parent and child and gave their oldest daughter insight into her own relationship addiction. Nancy is hopeful her daughter will recognize her own codependency sooner than Nancy did and will get help much earlier.

Earlier recognition by young adults of their own addiction or codependency can be a valuable outcome of the parents' sharing the family secret. Ralph, who had multiple affairs, shared his story with his two teenagers as part of his recovery process Some months later the seventeen-year-old son told his mother that he recognized he was using sex compulsively. Had the parents not been so open with their son, it might have taken him another ten or twenty years to recognize that he had a problem with his sexual behavior.

When Alan and Alice's eighteen-year-old daughter, Tracy, chose as her first serious boyfriend an unreliable young man who broke as many dates as he kept and had two arrests for drunk driving before he was nineteen years old, Alan decided it was time to talk with Tracy about his own recovery program from sex addiction. Alan had always been a hero to Tracy, and he feared she would begin to hate him if he told her he had been unfaithful to her mother. But Alan was very aware that addiction and codependency are family diseases; Tracy had been very much the "responsible child" in the family, and he could see her now beginning a life-long pattern of addictive relationships with men.

Much to Alan's relief, Tracy did not reject him after he talked with her about his past and his Twelve-Step program. On the contrary, she thought it was courageous of him to have told her, and she admired him for the changes he had been able to implement in his own life. Alice talked with Tracy about her own previous addiction to Alan and, at Alice's recommendation, Tracy read Robin Norwood's book, *Women Who Love Too Much*. Tracy began attending Al-Anon and also started seeing a therapist who specialized in alcoholism and codependency counseling. After some months she was able to break off her relationship with her alcoholic boyfriend, although she is still struggling with feelings of loss. Alan and Alice are convinced that their openness with Tracy has been helpful to her in her own recovery.

with the children about the parents' problems also serves to validate the children's own observations. Nancy explains:

Sometimes people think kids don't know what's going on, but they know! You have these arguments in the bedroom and somehow you think the kids aren't hearing it. It's insane! They're listening as hard as they can, wanting to hear what's going on.

In a dysfunctional family where feelings aren't discussed, the children may listen and absorb information for years, drawing their own conclusions without ever discussing it with their parents. Meanwhile, the children may be told that everything's fine. Discussing the "family secret" with them and allowing them to explain their beliefs about what was happening in the family as they were growing up can help them realize they weren't crazy and can correct any misconceptions they have formed. Letting them voice their feelings – anger, hurt, disappointment, validation, relief – can give them the message that open communication and expression of feelings are okay in this family, even if they weren't encouraged in the past.

Of course, telling our children about our past is risky; children do tend to be judgmental, and the relationship between parent and child may become strained as a result of the new information. This is what happened to Joe, whose wife divorced him many years ago because of his affairs. Two years into recovery and in a new marriage, Joe decided to tell his seventeen-year-old daughter, Laurie, about his sex addiction and his recovery program. Laurie had always felt very close to her father, whom she admired greatly. On the other hand, Laurie had a stormy relationship with her mother and could never seem to get along with her. When Joe told Laurie he'd had affairs during both marriages, her first reaction was to express sympathy for what Joe's current wife, Jessica, had been through. Later that day Laurie told Jessica, "I feel terrible now about how I've treated my mom all these years. I've always somehow assumed that the divorce was her fault, not Dad's, and I've tried to punish her by being deliberately mean to her and trying to hurt her. Now I realize I've done her a terrible injustice."

Laurie spent the next several weeks patching up her relationship with her mother. At the same time, she withdrew from her father, ignoring him when they happened to be in the same room. Eventually she told him how angry she was at him. Although this was a difficult period for Joe, he still thinks telling Laurie was the right thing to do.

Her relationship with her mother has definitely improved as a result of the disclosure, and Joe is optimistic that he and Laurie will be able to re-establish a bond, although he realizes that Laurie will no longer have the same idealized image of him that she had in the past.

Cara, a 32-year old pharmaceutical representative, began having affairs after learning of her alcoholic husband's same-sex relationships. Cara and her husband now attend A.A. and Al-Anon, but each has continued to betray the other. When Cara shared her story with her teenage daughter, the daughter began confiding in a relative who happened to dislike Cara. As Cara explained, "She exposed me to the entire family. It caused a lot of friction between me and the rest of the family. I don't blame my daughter – she did what she had to do – but it really messed me up with the family."

This situation in this family was complicated, of course, by the fact that the affairs were ongoing and that neither parent was addressing their sexual and relationship issues in constructive ways. One has to wonder what were Cara's motivations in confiding in her daughter. Our reasons for disclosing sensitive information to our children need to be carefully considered before we do so. Adolescent and adult children are likely to be less judgmental when it's evident that the parents are committed to working on their problems.

Nonetheless, there is always the risk, when sharing information with children, that other people we would prefer not to know about these things will find out. This is even more of a problem with sex than with alcohol, since sex is such a personal matter. It is best to wait to talk with our children until we are truly convinced that our addiction or coaddiction is a disease, not a moral failing, and that we can handle the situation if others find out about it. Covering up the family secret is very much a part of the disease of addiction. Therefore, we should not share any information with our children about our progress in recovery if we want them to keep it a secret. Being open with our children is part of *our* recovery; allowing them to share with whomever they want is part of *their* recovery.

Disclosing to Parents and Others

In addition to deciding how much to tell the children, couples in recovery sometimes also need to determine what to tell their parents. Often, the decision is to tell them nothing or very little. But if the couple feels that it is appropriate to share with parents, they may in return receive information that is helpful in their recovery. Andrea's father and stepmother learned of her husband's addiction early on; they came to visit, noted how unhappy Andrea appeared, and asked for information. At the time, Andrea knew only that Carlos spent unexplained time away from home and he was unwilling to account for some of his expenditures; she suspected that he was having sexual contact with other people. Andrea's parents urged her to get more information and to get help. The result was Andrea's and Carlos's first honest talk about his problem. Andrea remembers,

As a result of getting a little prodding from my folks, we sat down and talked in a lot more detail than we ever had before. I insisted that he get tested for various STDs before we had any more sex because I was suddenly afraid, and he agreed. It was a very good talk. He was able to open up and admit various things and I think it was because I was being nonjudgmental; I was just looking for information. I could do it because I felt supported, I didn't feel alone in it. I knew that if I looked at his betrayal and it was much more awful than I thought, my parents were there for me. It was not the end of the world. If it was the end of my marriage, I would survive. I would have some help with it.

Shortly thereafter, Carlos read Patrick Carnes' book *Out of the Shadows*, recognized himself in it, and found a Twelve-Step recovery program for sex addicts. Andrea's father continued to be supportive. He told her that he himself had been involved with other women during his marriage and that both parents had been swingers during their early years together. He said "I thought since you were having some problems in your marriage it might be helpful for you to know that I've had some problems in that area too." Andrea's parents had gotten divorced when she was sixteen and she had never known why; she has very little recollection of her childhood. It was very helpful to her to have this new information about her parents.

Patty told her parents about her husband's affairs at the time that she was considering ending the marriage. Now that she and Peter are both in Twelve-Step self-help programs, she has tried to give her parents information about the meetings:

My family is very much into denial. They think Peter and I are really funny, being in programs. They think you should be able to work things out for yourself. But they do see the change in the two of us. They've said to us, "You're so much better with each other, you're so much freer, and you laugh." My father is a practicing alcoholic and my mother has a terrible eating problem. She's one of the most unhappy people I've ever met. I've tried to get her to go to Al-Anon or to Overeaters Anonymous, but she won't go. My S-Anon program has helped me deal with both my parents.

Patty's parents are not very interested in information about her recovery, but her ability to share with them has improved communication between them. Different parents react differently.

One word of caution: Before deciding to share with your family members information about the sex addiction and about your recovery, it is crucial for you to examine your motives for doing so. Some acceptable motives are: to become honest with your children or parents, to allow them to understand what was happening in the family, and to encourage open expression of feelings. But some people use their children inappropriately as confidantes, seeking allies in a struggle with the mate and complaining about the marital partner's transgressions. Telling a child about the affairs may be used as a way of getting back at the addict. The result can be increased disharmony in the family, or even alienating the children from one parent or the other. In any case, the decision should not be taken lightly, as there is likely to be initial disappointment and anger toward the parents as the children learn that their parents do have clay feet.

In summary, recovery as a couple has unique challenges. But it also provides a wonderful opportunity for us to start over again with the same person in a relationship of increased intimacy, honesty, and communication. Working through problems together, sharing the experience of spirituality in a Twelve-Step program, learning to communicate in the language of the recovery program, and making new friends who are also in recovery – all these shared experiences can create a new, powerful bond between us that might give us a better relationship than we ever had before. Moreover, we will both be in the marriage by choice and not because we need another person in order to feel whole. Says Alice: "I know now that I would be okay living alone, but I love Alan; he's my best friend and I like being with him. As long as the good outweighs the bad I'll continue to be in this relationship, enjoying the good times and working on the problems."

Changes in the Couple's Sexual Relationship

When someone who uses sex to feel good marries a partner who believes sex is the most important sign of love, sex is likely to constitute a very important part of their relationship. By the time both are in enough emotional pain to seek treatment, about half the couples have significant problems in their sexual relationship. The remaining partners are likely to say, "Our sex was so good, I don't understand why he had to have affairs." Entering a recovery program can cause major changes in a couple's sexual relationship. In my study of many addicts and partners recovering from sexual addiction,[13] I found that two-thirds of the couples were having some new sexual problems, originating sometimes with the addict, sometimes with the partner, and in a third of cases with both. You can read in detail about these problems and how they were handled in the book *Sex, Lies, and Forgiveness: Couples Speak on Healing from Sex Addiction.*

Most couples have unspoken rules about their sexual relationship. For example, some men are always the initiators. Many women never say no. In the recovery process, the rules that formerly governed many aspects of the couple's life together are replaced by new rules. In the sexual spheres, these rules may take some getting used to; things may get worse before they get better. Judy, a 35-year old social worker, confided:

In my family, no one talked about sex. In my 16 years of marriage, George was always the aggressor. I never talked with him about my sexual feelings – I just didn't know how to talk about these things. Now George wants to know how I feel. He's trying to be more sensitive to my needs. He wants me to be more actively involved and to initiate our lovemaking. I just don't know what to say or do, but I want to learn because I really like the new George.

In the past, partners' sexual feelings might have been enhanced by the fear and uncertainty in their relationship. The unpredictability of the mate's behavior added excitement to their lovemaking. If they argued and then reconciled by making love, the energy of the argument was experienced as part of the excitement of the sexual activity. The sex was more about *intensity* than *intimacy*. For such couples, sex during recovery may be less intense than it was before. Jessica, the intensive care unit nurse, remembers:

In the old days, sex with Joe was always very exciting. I expected that when he stopped having affairs and our life together straightened out, then the sex would be even better. But that's not what happened – we've grown closer in many ways and are now experiencing real intimacy, but our sex is just not as intense to me as before. It took me a while to realize that the intensity I used to feel was all mixed up with the craziness of my life. When I'd spent all day obsessed with thoughts of Joe, worrying whether he still loved me, naturally it was very exciting to fall into bed with him. I no longer feel that panic and uncertainty. Our lovemaking is calmer, more intimate. It's different from before. Joe and I are really there for each other. We're making love to each other, instead of just using sex to feel loved or to temporarily forget bad feelings.

Here is Joe's side of the story:

I used to do a lot of fantasizing in bed. My body would be making love to my wife, but my mind was miles away with some attractive girl who had recently crossed my path. Jessica thought I was a terrific lover, but she didn't realize it wasn't her I was really making love to. Things are different now. I don't allow myself to fantasize about other women – I want Jessica to be the woman in my mind as well as in my bed. This wasn't easy at first; I had to really retrain my mind to focus on Jessica. Fantasizing about other women may be okay for most men, but not for me. What it did was isolate me from Jessica. Now I feel much closer to her emotionally, and I feel a lot better about our lovemaking.

The key to successful restructuring of the sexual relationship is a willingness to talk to each other about feelings. It is not easy for most couples to discuss sex, and it is especially difficult for many people who grew up believing it's not okay to talk about feelings. Both in counseling sessions and in Twelve-Step meetings, people are encouraged to express their feelings. As they hear others doing so, they begin to believe that the group is a safe place to risk emotional vulnerability. With improved communication about feelings, couples can deal with many sexual problems that may occur.

Several couples I interviewed agreed that their sexual relationship was better now than when the addict was having affairs. They attributed this to the overall improvement in their relationship. They now felt less isolated, more connected, and more concerned with the other. As the level of trust in each other increased, so did the intimacy and sharing in their marriage. Sex became for them an enjoyable affirmation of their commitment to each other rather than the most important element in their relationship; sex was now more about intimacy than intensity.

Learning From Other Couples: Recovering Couples Anonymous
One of the most important benefits of attending a Twelve-Step program – or any support group for that matter – is that it provides an opportunity to learn from the experience of other people who have been through a similar adversity in their lives. Fortunately, such a resource is available for couples who are committed to improving their relationship in the aftermath of disclosure of infidelity related to a mate's sex addiction. Recovering Couples Anonymous (RCA), founded in 1988, is a Twelve-Step program for couples dealing with all addictions, but the majority of the members have a problem with sex addiction. Couples' meetings follow the same format as other Twelve-Step meetings, except that when one member of the couple shares at the meeting, the other member then has an opportunity to speak. Couples in the earliest stages of recovery get to see and hear how other couples have dealt with issues of disclosure to partner and children, feelings of betrayal, rebuilding trust, restructuring the sexual relationship, improving communication, and other couple issues that are not usually discussed at separate meetings for addicts and partners. These meetings can be a powerful source of hopes for couples who are new in recovery.

The RCA philosophy is summarized in this quote from their book, *Recovering Couples Anonymous: A Twelve-Step Program for Couples:*

> In RCA we think of our lives in coupleships as being represented by a three-legged stool: Commitment, communication, and caring. All are important "legs" to the serenity, stability, and intimacy we each seek. The legs can also represent our individual recovery, our partner's recovery, and our coupleship recovery.[14]

RCA emphasizes the mutual responsibility of each partner for the problems and progress of the relationship, and the importance of each partner's individual recovery and development as necessary for recovery of the coupleship. Contact information for RCA is found in Appendix B, "Resources."

CHAPTER NINE

Recovery as a Single Person

In the previous chapter you read about couples whose relationship was able to survive, at times despite the addict's slip or relapse. However, there are many partners who find that ending the relationship is their healthiest or even the only option for them. This is often a very difficult decision. This chapter will help you get through this difficult time and will give you hope. Let's start with the story of Beverly, the wealthy mother of three who was married for fourteen years to an unfaithful man, and who had to learn to live alone:

The first time Brian admitted to me in a rather smug way that the reason he had been gone all night was that he was sleeping with someone else, I felt as if he had just taken away my "happily ever after" fantasy. I was furious. It's not that I hadn't accused him before of cheating, but he had always denied it, and I had let myself be convinced. I guess you'd say it was a classic case of denial.

From that time on the process of pulling out of my denial and really admitting to myself that he was addicted, and that I too had a problem, was a very slow and painful one. At one point he confessed to me all the lies he had told me. I needed to have him tell me because I needed to know that my instincts were right. I had come to the point where I was so confused that he could tell me he took a shower at his office (not at a girlfriend's house) and even when I checked the tub in his office and there was dust in it and he still had wet hair, I doubted myself because he was so adamant.

Now I had to catch him in lies, even if he denied them. I had to learn to trust my instincts. That sounds so simple, but it's not when your whole world is upside down and you feel that maybe getting back together wouldn't be so bad – at least you'd have him. But once that fantasy world of denial is broken, you can only step back into it briefly.

Brian moved out and we had a few holiday reconciliations but gradually, over a four-year period before and after our divorce, we've separated emotionally as well as physically. I can now see him and talk to him, and not get hooked into crazy behaviors, but it took many failures to do it. I used to run after his car after he left the kids off. For a long time I wanted him to sleep with me "one more time." In retrospect I guess I wanted to feel like the most special person in his life and then it wouldn't hurt so much.

The next stage, after the period of pursuing him, was a feeling of tremendous anger and wondering if he had ever loved me or if our entire marriage had been a romance novel that I had created in my head. I asked him if he had ever felt close to me, felt intimate, and he said no. I was shocked.

Then I went through a stage that must be very similar to withdrawal from any addiction. I was unable to sleep. I felt pain all over my body and I would wake up realizing he was gone. I would wait for hours; I felt so alone.

There's a tremendous attraction to me to feel like I'm playing a part in a tragic novel. I like to be under stress. I'm not sure why, but I do know that life used to depress me a lot and having conflict in it helped. This became clear when Brian left. With him around life was like a roller coaster and I hardly had to do anything to cause the crisis. But with him gone, I began to see that I looked for a crisis to focus on. It usually ended in a fight with my children that they didn't understand.

I began to try to deal with my depression instead of avoiding it. I spent months in bed. When I felt insecure and afraid and angry, I became cold and a bed made me feel warm. I still functioned for most of the day but I spent every afternoon in bed. It got to the point where my kids were embarrassed to have friends over because I was in bed all the time. I felt guilty, and that made me stay in bed longer. It wasn't until I told myself that it was okay to stay in bed – at least I wasn't drinking or taking pills – that I finally stopped doing it. Instead of the bed, I have now been able to substitute an image in my head of a warm blanket being thrown over me by someone who genuinely cares about me. When I feel that stress is draining me, I use this image to get back on track.

I had built up a lot of resentments over the years, and after I admitted I had no control over Brian's behavior I got very angry. I began going to an exercise program every morning to vent the anger. I often cried through portions of it, but the exercise really helped release that energy. I also began to realize that I ate whenever I saw Brian, and I decided to lose weight. Another motive for losing weight was to become so attractive that he'd want to come home again.

Because I didn't like being home alone, I began to do volunteer work in every area available. The funny thing is that this had an unexpected benefit. I took on projects in areas I knew nothing about, and I did them well. This helped my self-confidence, and I began to know who I was, something I had never experienced. I also found many people who were <u>my</u> friends, not <u>our</u> friends. To learn that they actually liked me, and not because I was Brian's wife, was exhilarating. Eventually I didn't need the work frenzy. I began to realize being alone was a risk I needed to take, and with time it became less painful. I found out that when I needed a best friend in times of insecurity, that best friend could be me.

When I reflect on times in my marriage when I felt incredibly insecure, I realize I wanted to connect with someone else who could make me feel better, but I never did feel better. I used to talk to Brian all night while he tried to be supportive, but he really didn't understand how I felt, and his not understanding increased my anxiety and my desperate need to make him make me feel better. I can see now that when I turn to myself for this comfort, it's there.

By far the biggest change that's happened to me is that I no longer fear abandonment from anyone I'm leaning on. I used to be so afraid of Brian's anger and disapproval for fear he would leave me, but that's not the case now. He used to come to pick up the children and he'd eat food from the refrigerator or borrow money – all things I resented but was too afraid to say no. Every time I accomplished something I wanted to let him know, hoping he would like me.

I went through a kind of purification process. I took everything out of the house that was his, and I took everything out I had bought to please him. It was a process of testing my own likes and dislikes and validating my own feelings. I would pick out an outfit I had in the closet and ask myself, what do I feel about this? To my utter surprise, all kinds of images would come to mind, such as, I bought this to please Brian and I hate it. I ended up with an empty shell of a house, and then, gradually, I filled it with things that made me feel good.

Many times I needed to talk to a friend, and I was lucky enough to have a good friend who listened any time, day or night. She has been through a divorce too and we both have kids. She likes to laugh and yet she's very supportive. She also was very skeptical about sex being an addiction. I needed that, because I was trying to convince myself that our problems were because of an addiction, not just my failings or a bad marriage. Every time I explained it to her, I became more convinced myself. This became crucial because I finally believed that Brian was and always will be sexually addicted.

I'm still working on a healthy attitude toward a sex life for myself. . . . I became celibate, and I found so much clarity in not having to be sexual with anyone. It was a real relief just relaxing at home, something I'd never done before.

Putting myself first above everyone else was something I had never done before. At first I struggled with how selfish it was until I saw how much better I felt and how my life pattern changed. I had to say to myself and my children that I deserve to do things for myself.

Recovery from relationship trauma and/or coaddiction follows the same pathway as does recovery from any other addiction. There is first recognition of the problem. A "bottoming out" eventually results in a change in behavior. The bottom may occur for some of us when we can no longer deny to ourselves that our mate is having sex with other people in real life or on the internet. A particularly painful episode may make us decide that we are unwilling to take any more. For others, a crisis may occur when we threaten our mate once again with divorce and he or she decides to leave. Our change of behavior may consist of ending the relationship. A period of anger, mourning, and depression often follows. Gradually, new behavior patterns emerge as we forge a new life for ourselves. Attendance at Twelve-Step meetings and counseling with a knowledgeable therapist may facilitate the process.

Beverly has had a long struggle. A sympathetic counselor and a Twelve-Step program for families of sex addicts have given her support in her recovery. Like many divorced people whose ex-spouses maintain contact with their children, she cannot avoid interaction with him. This has been an obstacle to her recovery, but she has finally managed to detach from him and is ready to consider dating other men. She has gone through a period of grieving her marriage, anger at her husband, depression, and finally acceptance of her changed situation, and has restructured her life in a healthier way.

Another recovering single person contrasts her present life with the way it used to be:

One of the main differences in my life now, compared to before I was in the program, is I don't have the complications of a relationship. That's important because always before, a relationship got in the way of my other priorities. At this time I'm able to focus on me, I'm able to experience my feelings, and I can spend time and thoughts with my kids. I'm not exhausted to the point of just being able to hang on. I can give more quality time to my children and more positive energy to my job. I feel much better about myself because I know I can say no. That's a protection I have that I didn't have before. I was always afraid that somehow, in spite of how I felt, I'd do something once again that I didn't want to do and I'd wonder why I was doing it. At this point it seems I have more control over my behavior.

Married for many years to an unavailable and emotionally abusive man who had multiple affairs, Suzanne, 41, now lives alone with her two teenage children. In response to a query about whether she still needs a man for validation, she told me,

It's not that I don't need a man for validation; I just don't need the sexual intimacy for validation. I've come to the realization that my validation has to come from inside me, not outside. And the validation itself is different. I need to accept that I can do my best, that I'm a capable and valuable human being without having someone say he needs me. But I still like the approval and the company of men; it just doesn't have to be one man for whom I'm special. I don't have to be the best in some person's eyes. But I still do need validation.

Helene's validation now comes from her knowledge that she is doing well on the job and as a parent, and from her friendships with men and women.

Grieving

Just as recovering addicts go through periods of mourning the loss of access to the addictive chemical or behavior, so partners in recovery go through a grieving process as well. If you have ended your marriage or a committed relationship, you may well grieve its loss. You might also grieve the loss of the intense feelings you experienced in the relationship. In the past these feelings may have been your only confirmation that you were really alive and could feel. As you recall them, the tremendous highs you occasionally experienced seem to more than have made up for the more common lows in your life. Now that you may find yourself having to get along without experiencing either extreme of emotion, life may seem flat and uninteresting.

During this early time, a period of depression is common. Helene, a recovering alcoholic who subsequently recognized her propensity for relationships with addicted men, recalls that after she decided to stop seeing a sex addict she went into a serious depression. She said,

From the day I broke up with my "white knight," all I could do was get up in the morning, go to work, come home, fix a sandwich, and go to bed. For about six weeks I wasn't capable of doing anything else. I did continue to attend A.A. meetings. Gradually I was able to involve myself in more normal activities, like spending time with my daughter after I got home instead of going to bed, and talking to people in a normal sort of way.

It was as if I was in suspended animation, like there was a part of me that had died, and the other part hadn't been born yet. It was a terrible time. And then, gradually, I was able to come alive a little bit at a time. But all the way through it, I realized that getting involved with another man was not going to fix it. Just as with my alcoholism, where having a drink wasn't going to fix it. That was clear to me, so I didn't do it. This was breaking another pattern, because always before, when I was feeling low, I looked to another person to make me feel better.

Having already experienced recovery from alcoholism, Helene had the strength to go through the pain and depression of the first weeks of recovery without turning to her "drug of choice" – a man.

Making Friends

Occasional loneliness is a natural part of life for the single person. Part of the recovery process is to learn to relieve the feeling of loneliness in nonsexual ways. Making friends and going with them to movies or out to eat, joining clubs or organizations that appeal to you, doing volunteer work, attending self-help group meetings, and regularly communicating with other people via phone, email or texting often help to alleviate your loneliness.

Learning to relate to men and women as people and as friends rather than as romantic objects is an important part of recovery as single people. Many partners of sex addicts realize that they also struggle with being addicted to relationships or at least are dependent upon one person to fill those needs. A sex addiction therapist recalls, "I suggested to such a client to attend Sex & Love Addicts Anonymous meetings to learn how to see men as people and not as someone from whom she could gain a sense of 'secure' sexuality."

According to Sarah, the CPA now divorced from a man who still juggles several women at a time,

I think it's really important for women to develop and maintain close personal friendships with men. We need to learn what it's like simply to be a friend with a man, to share confidences and to learn to trust men as friends. As a single person, it's easy to become isolated. You may be working your program well by going to Twelve-Step meetings, but there may be only women at the meetings – and it ends up that you only interact with other women. I think it's very important to learn to relate to men as friends, because that's a tool you need in a relationship. Especially when we've been involved with a sex addict, we tend to get very angry with men and think that they're all bad, that we don't need them in our lives. It's important to have both male and female friends during recovery.

Before recovery, female partners may attribute enormous power to the current man in their life. They are not just men – they are the people who have control over the partner's happiness and future. Their emotions determine hers; they are the people who make the partner whole. One of partners' tasks in recovery is to learn to see men as ordinary human beings. As Sarah points out above, this is best accomplished by developing friendships with men. Similarly, male partners need to learn how to be friends with women rather than viewing them as potential romantic partners.

Working on same-sex friendships is another good project for those first months of non-dating. In our culture, this is much easier for women than for men. Women are much more willing to open up to other women about their inner thoughts and feelings. Sadly, the conversation between men is all too often limited to impersonal subjects such as sports and politics. For men, attending self-help group meetings can be a real eye-opener, as they may encounter other men who indeed have learned to talk openly about their feelings!! And the same goes for men who agree to participate in group therapy. Learning to be more open about yourself, to express your vulnerabililty, will also enhance your attractiveness to a potential romantic partner; this quality in a man is much appreciated by women.

Although many heterosexual women feel sympathy and affinity for other women and have close women friends, some see other women primarily as competition. If you are this type of woman, you are probably more comfortable surrounding yourself with male friends while avoiding women. At Twelve-Step meetings or in group therapy you will get to know other women who have gone through experiences very similar to your own, and you will probably find yourself seeing women in a new light. Several women told me, "In the past I looked at other women as competitors for men – now I suddenly have women friends."

Learning new patterns of relating to both male and female friends can form the groundwork for healthier interactions in subsequent romantic relationships. Many of us have been people pleasers, fearful of abandonment if we should reveal how we really feel about something. Through non-romantic friendships where there is not the huge emotional investment that exists in romance, we can learn that it acceptable to make our feelings known to our friends and to say no to a request that we really don't want to do. Later, once we feel more comfortable with these new patterns of relating, we can transfer them to our romantic relationships.

Developing New Interests

Another way to overcome loneliness is to fill your life with interesting activities. For some, taking a class on auto maintenance can serve the dual purpose of increasing a sense of self-competence and promoting new friendships. Reading books is an interesting pastime that also provides new topics of conversation. One partner said, "I'm reading books I wouldn't touch before, books that deal with relationships, connections, and spirituality. Before, books were boring because I had no way of connecting. I didn't have an experience or interest; my spirituality was in connecting with a man."

Many activities that in the past we thought of as couple activities can be enjoyed just as much when done alone. All that's required is a positive attitude. Darlene, a businesswoman divorced from an unfaithful husband, recalls how her attitude made all the difference in determining whether or not she enjoyed a vacation.

A few years ago I was madly in love with an exciting, unpredictable man. We planned a trip to Mexico City, but at the last minute he developed doubts about our relationship and canceled out. I had already arranged to take the time off from work, so I decided to go anyway, taking my daughter with me. I had a miserable time – all around me I saw nothing but happy couples walking arm in arm. Instead of enjoying all the fascinating things there were to see, I spent the whole time feeling sorry for myself, wishing that my boyfriend were with me. I might as well have stayed at home and saved the cost of the trip.

A year later I had an opportunity to spend a couple of weeks in Europe. I had never traveled overseas alone and the thought was a little scary. Complex travel arrangements aren't my forte, so I decided to keep it simple. I spent a week in Paris and a week in Florence, Italy. I visited museums, shops, and churches. I took long walks through each city, enjoying the sights and taking lots of photographs. I found out there are definite advantages to being a solo tourist. For example, I could spend exactly as much time as I wished at a museum or a store, and I didn't have to take into account anyone else's wishes. I was so involved in my day-to-day activities that I never felt lonely. It was one of the best vacations I've ever had. I know I could have had just as good a time in Mexico City if I'd had a better attitude.

Spiritual Growth

Since the 1930's spirituality has been an important element of recovery from addictive disorders. Many people confuse spirituality with religion, but what about those of us who consider ourselves secular rather than religious? What *is* spirituality? Here is a nice explanation that summarizes my perspective.

> People may describe a spiritual experience as *sacred* or *transcendent* or simply a deep sense of aliveness and interconnectedness. Some may find that their spiritual life is intricately linked to their association with a church, temple, mosque, or synagogue. Others may pray or find comfort in a personal relationship with God or a higher power. Still others seek meaning through their connections to nature or art. Like your sense of purpose, your personal definition of spirituality may change throughout your life, adapting to your own experiences and relationships.[1]

Spirituality is basically about *connection*. Many of us have felt an inner void that we tried to fill in the past with other people, with food or drink, or with an addiction, such as to alcohol or other drugs, food, sex, work, or gambling. Addicts and often partners have an inner loneliness, a belief that "it's me against the world," that no one but they themselves can solve their problems. The inner void may represent spiritual emptiness and may more effectively be filled by working on our relationship with our Higher Power. For secular people as well as for those who identify with some religion, meditation, taking pride in our work, helping others, and living a life of integrity can make us more spiritual and less lonely. Sarah, the CPA, describes her daily program:

If I'm working my recovery program reasonably well, I usually do a half hour of exercise a day, I read something spiritual, and I think about my relationship with my Higher Power several times during the day. While driving down the street, I may be sort of meditating. I go to a couple of Twelve-Step meetings a week. I text or get on the phone and check in with someone from the partners' group at least every other day, and if there's a problem I may be on the phone several times a day; I just may need that sort of support. I also go to church once a week.

The big difference is, I have more peace than I used to have. I am better able to let go of things. I obsess less and I lose my serenity less often. It's still hard – the old patterns are still there, but recognizing them and dealing with them faster seems to be the key to recovery for me. If I find myself obsessing, I've got the tools to deal with it.

By getting in touch with our Higher Power, we can enjoy aloneness and avoid loneliness. Accepting a Higher Power can diminish our sense of isolation and bring us closer to understanding ourselves and those around us.

For secular people spirituality can consist of a belief that you are not alone – that other people, the "world," the "universe," or nature is there with you, working for your benefit. Here is how one partner describes it:

A few years ago I went through a dark time after realizing I had to get out of a relationship with a sex addict at the same time as I was being treated for cancer. I saw a counselor and I went to Twelve-Step meetings when I had the energy to do so, but what really changed my life was when I embarked on a new practice: Every day I made it a point to notice any good thing, big or little, that enhanced my life. Some examples: seeing a beautiful sunrise; walking into my house just in time to pick up a ringing phone, at the other end of which was my son, who rarely phoned; locking the car keys inside my car – and then realizing that for some reason that day I'd thrown an extra set of keys in my purse, so that I was able to open the car door; learning that an out-of-state friend was coming to a conference in my city at exactly the one weekend that month that I was free, so that I could spend time with her. I considered each one of these a gift, and I would say (in my head), 'Thank you for looking out for me.' I began to consider every day to be a gift. I felt connected. I felt hopeful.

When You Feel Ready for a New Relationship

At some point you may feel ready to embark on a new relationship. After many years in marriage or committed coupleship, the prospect of again dating may be formidable. In the past decade, meeting and dating has increasingly been facilitated through the internet. Seeking compatible dating partners at online dating sites can be an effective, productive, and efficient way to meet new people, providing many more opportunities than meeting in bars, at parties, or through friends. But for your safety you need to choose appropriate dating websites and follow certain rules.

Today there are many online dating services, appealing to different populations, with different goals. Some websites are designed to appeal to marriage-minded singles, some are specifically for certain age groups, sexual preferences, or of a specific religion or ethnic background. Some appeal to those who are looking for a serious relationship, whereas others are designed to find a one-night stand, or to connect seekers specifically with married people who want to cheat on their spouse (avoid these!). Some popular general internet dating services are Match, eHarmony and Zoosk. Others are more specific – for people who are older, or of a particular sexual orientation, religion, or cultural background. If you're looking for a long-term relationship, state this in the profile you will write about yourself, and be sure that someone who might be of interest to you has the same goal. Be honest about yourself – it's tempting for people to understate their weight or age, or put up a photo that is years old. Of course, when you meet such a person for the first time the deception will become obvious and is likely to be very off-putting to the other person.

A problem with communication via email is that many cues about a person that would be evident in real life are missing. The less you know about someone, the more likely you are to fill the void with your imagination. The longer you communicate only via email, the easier it is to get hooked into fantasy about this person. That's why it's advisable not to spend a lot of time on emails or even phone conversation. The best way to find out whether someone is a good match for you is to meet and converse face-to-face– and the meeting should be brief and in a public place such as a coffee shop. Don't give out your home address or other information about you until you have had a chance to meet this person and decide if you feel safe with him or her. (If you are interested in learning about potential problems and scams in online dating, check out the 2014 book *Closer Together, Further Apart: The Effect of Technology and the Internet on Parenting, Work, and Relationships*, by Rob Weiss and myself).

Finding an appealing person to date is only the beginning of your journey to getting into a healthy relationship. Probably the biggest problem for the former partner of a sex addict is how to avoid another addictive relationship. Robin Norwood, author of *Women Who Love Too Much*, stated at a lecture she gave in my city, "The people with whom we can have a nurturing, trusting relationship are not the same kinds of people with whom we can feel tremendous passion and intensity." Meeting a "normal" man requires adjusting to a relationship that isn't so exciting. "Being in a relationship where the other person shows up – it *is* boring, compared to what it used to be."[2]

Accustomed to finding addicts exciting and "normal" men boring, and having already experienced the painful consequences of being in one or more addictive relationships, single persons may decide simply not to date rather than risk repeating history. Early in recovery, a period of not dating is often an excellent idea and is highly recommended. It's helpful to take at least six months of not dating, spending time with ourselves and with friends, going to meetings, and learning where our priorities are and what we want to do with our lives.

When we resume dating, we must be very aware of the reasons we are attracted to a new man. A divorced 30-year-old alcoholism counselor reports:

If I'm very attracted to someone immediately, I consider it a red flag. It doesn't mean I'll stop seeing him, but I'll be very cautious. I'll ask questions about his history, family, use of chemicals, and his previous relationships. I'm going to suspect that this is either an addict or a raving codependent. It's unfortunate, but because that is what my whole history has programmed me for, I'm most likely to be attracted to another codependent.

She has learned that instant attraction is a danger sign.

Another suggestion is to postpone sexual involvement until the new relationship has had some time to grow. Many of us tend to substitute sex for social skills. It is easier to be sexual with another person than to work at getting to know him or her. Unfortunately, a new relationship may come to a standstill in its development once the partners have begun to sleep together.

Based on her experience, the alcoholism counselor told me:

Sleeping with someone early on interferes with getting to know him. I believe that what we do is romanticize and delude ourselves when sex is involved. People are willing to sacrifice a lot of cognitive data for sex.

I also believe that really stable relationships are built on friendship, not on sex, and if you introduce sex very early you're likely to have a relationship based on sexuality rather than on companionship. I really enjoy sex, but I don't want to be in a relationship where that's all that's going on.

Postponing sex is scary for those of us who behaved in past relationships as if sex is the most important sign of love. We may fear that a man may not want to continue seeing us if we are not giving him sex. Part of our recovery process is to become involved in relationships that are not based primarily on sex. We need to learn that we are valued for ourselves and not just for what we give sexually.

Helene, the recovering alcoholic whose former husband had several affairs, contrasts her present social life with how it used to be:

When someone asks me out, I go to lunch with him or I arrange another commitment so that I can spend only an hour or so with him; that helps me take it slowly. In the past, within 24 hours of meeting someone I made emotional contact and was in bed with him. Now I've been seeing a man for two months, and we finally held hands. This is a real change for me. There's still part of me that believes there's one right person for me. But I realize that what I've sought in the past is not really "the right one," it's the connection – an emotional, sexual connection that has fireworks. I'm still attracted to that type of man, but I no longer act on the attraction. I avoid men who have an intensity that I recognize through eye contact. These folks always have some enormous problems, usually in terms of relationships. There's something about them that is not functioning in a healthy way, and it's always something I thought I could fix. When I meet such a man now I essentially interview him, looking for the broken part. I always find it – and then I run.

Before even beginning a relationship with a man she initially finds exciting, Helene tries to find out from him whether he is a man she should avoid.

Like most relationship addicts, Helene finds that healthy men are boring. She deals with this by directing her energy in other areas. She is developing more skills at work, strengthening her relationship with her children, and is become acquainted with women – a pursuit she never thought was valuable or interesting. She believes she is not yet ready for an intimate relationship.

Speaking of the problem that recovering partners may have of finding normal men boring, Robin Norwood is optimistic. She says, "When you go through the boredom, and you learn to live with it, it transforms into peace and serenity."[3]

No matter how long we have been in recovery, it is likely that certain situations will still elicit a feeling of rejection. Men with addictive personalities might continue to appeal to us and we may find ourselves hooked before we know it. We might be tempted to send texts or e-mails, make telephone calls or visit former lovers who are best forgotten. But we will probably find that with time, these situations will occur less frequently. We may not be able to prevent our initial emotional reaction, but we will more quickly recognize it for what it is. And we will be able to choose to deal with the situation in a healthier way so as to minimize the pain to ourselves.

The recovering person whose relationship has ended must in fact live through her worst fear – the fear of being alone. Like the sex addict who learns in his recovery program that sex is optional, we, having survived alone, find out that having a mate in our lives is also optional. We learn that life as a single person is not only possible, but can be enjoyable. We come to realize that an intimate relationship is a *choice*, not a necessity. Once we believe this, we are ready to make some better decisions regarding our subsequent relationships. No longer driven to connect with someone who needs rescuing, we can take the time to learn if the new person is good for *us* before committing ourselves to another relationship.

We might always be initially attracted to addictive persons, but we will not be compelled to act on those initial feelings. We will put at least as much effort into our relationship with ourselves, our children, and with our nonsexual friends as we used to put into our relationship with the "special man." No longer afraid of appearing selfish should we make our needs known, we will regularly ask ourselves what is best for *us* and make our decisions accordingly.

Finally, let's remember that decision-making is not a black-or-white matter. There is probably an addictive element in every love relationship, according to Howard M. Halpern, author of *How to Break Your Addiction to a Person*, but this is not necessarily bad. Halpern says:

It can, in fact, add strength and delight to the relationship. After all, who is so complete, so self-contained, so "healthy" and "mature" that he doesn't need to feel good about himself through a close tie with another person? In fact, one sign of a good relationship is that it puts us in touch with the best in ourselves. What makes a particular relationship an addiction is when these little addictive "I need you" elements expand to become the controlling force in your attachment. This creates an inner coercion that deprives you of several essential freedoms: the freedom to be your best self in the relationship, the freedom to love the other person through *choice* and caring commitment rather than being *compelled* by your own dependence, and the freedom to choose whether to stay with the other person or to leave.[4]

CHAPTER TEN

Final Thoughts

Helping Our Children Grow Up Healthy

The realization that sex addiction, coaddiction, and codependency are family diseases leads to the question, "How can we prevent the next generation, our children, from becoming victims of the family illness?" Too often, by the time we recognize our own difficulties and get help, many of our children are teenagers or adults and already exhibit signs of addiction or codependency. When we recognize the signs in ourselves, it becomes easier to see them in our children. The most we can do at this point is to become as healthy as possible so that the family in which our children reside is healthier. It is not helpful to bring to the child's attention his or her codependent traits; rather, we are better advised to share our experiences and what has been helpful to us. In this way our child may recognize his or her negative behaviors and make changes or seek help – years earlier than otherwise.

When we communicate with our children and encourage them to share feelings and trust in other people, we promote healthy attitudes and self-esteem. By showing interest in our children's feelings and opinions and taking their problems seriously, we help our children develop the belief that they are worthwhile people whose wellbeing is of concern to their parents. If this has not been our pattern of relating to our children, it is never too late to make a change. The older the children are, the harder it is likely to be to bring about changes in our relationship with them, but it is worth our while to make the effort.

An important lesson we can teach our children is to face problems rather than to avoid them. Dr. M. Scott Peck began his perennial bestseller, *The Road Less Traveled*, with the statement, "Life is difficult." What makes life difficult is that the process of solving problems is painful. It is tempting to avoid problems rather than to face them directly and experience the unavoidable suffering that dealing with problems entails. Discipline, according to Peck, is the set of tools we need to solve life's problems. When we teach children discipline, we teach them the necessity to face problems directly and to experience the pain involved.

There are basic principles of discipline that parents need to teach their children: delaying gratification, accepting responsibility, telling the truth, and having flexibility. The opposites of these principles – delaying problem solving in favor of immediate gratification, avoiding responsibility by saying, "It's not *my* problem," and lying – are all ways to postpone facing problems. Unfortunately, most problems do not disappear. Lying about them often only worsens the situation. For example, a child may accidentally break a dining room chair. Fearful of his mother's disapproval, he places the chair in such a way that she doesn't realize it's broken – until the evening she is having a dinner party and moves the chair. The child has postponed having to face the problem, but now most mothers are likely to be more upset at the child's deception and the inconvenient timing of the discovery than if the child had admitted the problem when it first happened.

The proper role of the parent is not to keep shielding a child from stress; rather, it is to remind the child that there is always something he or she can do about the stress, even if the only good choice is to tolerate pain for a while. Even young children have to experience some discomfort in order to grow. For example, children will not learn to walk if they are not allowed to fall, to get up, and to try again. Depending on the child's age, parents must protect them from certain stresses, but not from all. The alternative to coping with stress is to avoid it – by using alcohol or other drugs or other mood-altering behaviors. Such patterns of avoiding problems can lead to addiction in later years.

Self-discipline is the ability to withstand the pain or discomfort of pushing ahead when we really don't want to. By allowing children to accept responsibility for what they do and to experience the natural or the social consequences of their actions, we are teaching them self-discipline. Because we love our children, it is tempting to protect them from unpleasant experiences. They will grow up healthier, however, if they face both the positive and the negative outcomes of their actions.

Another feature of a healthy childhood is play. Play is fun, and it's important in a child's life. It is freely chosen and spontaneous. The play attitude allows us to enjoy what we are doing without being compulsive about it. The more dysfunctional the family, the less play there is likely to be. If our interactions with our children do not already include having fun with them, we should start now.

To become a healthy adult, the best model a child can have is healthy parents. Recovery from our own relational or childhood trauma is the greatest investment in our child's future that we can make. In understanding how to establish or re-establish a relationship with a romantic partner, we must first learn how to respect and honor ourselves. Hopefully, this book has helped you do that. To recap, some of the basic premises of this book have been:

- For some people, sexual acting out is not a matter of choice but rather a compulsive behavior similar to alcohol dependency
- Sex addicts tend to marry partners who become addicted to them
- Many partners have a history of childhood neglect, abuse, or abandonment, which has made them more reactive in their adult relationships and more likely to experience significant trauma in response to a mate's infidelity.

- Recovery from addiction and coaddiction is often best accomplished by inclusion of participation in a program based on the Twelve Steps of Alcoholics Anonymous.
- Recovery can be facilitated with counseling by a knowledgeable professional who incorporates the self-help group into the treatment plan.
- For the partner of a sex addict, divorce will not always solve the partner's problem; for many, their underlying trauma history or codependency may lead them into a relationship with another sex addict or emotionally unavailable person – unless they get therapy for themselves.
- The person whose mate is getting help for their sex addiction also can benefit from therapy for her or his own trauma and/or coaddiction.

If you have been in one or more relationships with an unfaithful mate, the best way for you to recover is to get help for yourself. A therapist can help you sort out how much of your pain is due to past as well as current relationship trauma, and how much is related to codependency. With the help of a knowledgeable counselor and a Twelve-Step program you can become a whole person who does not depend so much on another for his or her self-worth.

Recovery is a process, not a cure that can be accomplished once and then forgotten. Recovery is not a straight line, and relapses are inevitable. The Twelve-Step programs tell us that what counts is progress, not perfection. Because many of us are perfectionists who tend to be hard on ourselves, it's easy to get discouraged if we find ourselves falling back into the old behaviors. One of the goals of recovery is to learn to be good to ourselves, to be forgiving and nurturing.

There will probably always be times when you will experience an initial gut-wrenching emotional reaction to someone's words or actions that will transport you right back to the bad old days. At such times it is helpful to remind yourself that although you cannot control your initial feelings, you do have a choice about how to respond. You can examine your feelings and decide whether they are part of your old thinking and behaviors or whether they truly have relevance to your current situation; then, you can act accordingly. If you find yourself feeling frightened, insecure, panicked, and lonely, don't get discouraged nor fear that you are making no progress. These episodes are likely to occur with decreasing frequency as you continue in your recovery program. Moreover, the Twelve-Step program gives you tools for dealing with these troubling times:

- Talk with your friends or your sponsor on the phone or via email or text.
- Attend Twelve-Step meetings.
- Talk with and give help to others who are suffering – it will remind you how far along you have come in your recovery.
- See a counselor who can help you.
- Increase your connection with your Higher Power by meditating, reading spiritual materials, and seeking daily evidence of the presence of a Higher Power in your life.

As a young woman I was a needy, vulnerable person, dependent for my sense of self-worth on a partner whose own problems prevented him from being emotionally available to me. Uncertainty, unpredictability, and a roller-coaster existence was how I thought a normal relationship functioned. I felt like a victim when I learned I was not the only woman in his life. Today, when I meet other people who are at the beginning of their journey to recovery, I am reminded of the person I used to be. My own journey has taken me to a place that feels much safer and more comfortable. Along the path I have met wonderful people, I have discovered a part of myself that I never knew existed, and I have incorporated into my life a program for living (the Twelve Steps) that I believe can be of help to everyone, whether or not there is a problem of addiction in the family.

I have learned that I am not alone. Those who practice their recovery program tell us that life can be better than we ever imagined it. I believe that this promise can be fulfilled for all of us.

APPENDIX A
Definition of Terms Used in This Book

Addiction: A self-destructive relationship with a mood-altering drug or behavior. To be addicted to a behavior is to continue that behavior even though it has negative consequences. The addictive behavior becomes more important than anything else in the person's life and is continued even at the risk of losing one's family, job, or health. What defines sex addiction is not the number of sexual encounters, but rather the compulsive nature of the behavior despite the costs. Every addiction has two critical elements – a behavior disorder and a thinking disorder which denies and rationalizes the addictive behavior.

Coaddict: A spouse or significant other who becomes so involved in the life of the addict that he or she starts to participate in the thinking disorder of the addict. The coaddict's feelings and behaviors include low self-esteem, a need to control and change others, and a willingness to suffer. Coaddicts so fill their life with the relationship with the addict that they cannot tolerate the threat of losing him or her. To maintain the relationship, they join in the addict's irrational behavior and enable the addiction. Because coaddicts can be viewed as addicted to their partner, they can also be termed a *relationship addict.*

Coaddictive behavior: Behavior by which the coaddict attempts to change the addict, but which in fact may facilitate the addiction. This may refer to *any* such behavior (for example, a sex addict's spouse may avoid arguments in an attempt to be the perfect partner). It may include participating in the addict's addiction in order to control him (for example, the sex addict's partner may decide never to deny him sex, or will agree to sexual practices she doesn't like in order to prevent him from straying).

Codependency: A pattern of personality traits that *precedes* addiction and coaddiction and predisposes a person to one or the other. The primary characteristic of codependency is looking to others for one's self-worth. Codependency develops as a result of a person's negative experience in his or her family of origin, where there was a set of oppressive rules that discouraged any expression of feelings as well as the direct discussion of personal problems.

Cybersex: Any form of sexual expression that is accessed through the internet, on the computer or a mobile device. Cybersex activities include not only viewing and downloading pornography while masturbating, but also reading and writing sexually explicit emails, texts, and stories; sexting provocative photos; e-mailing to set up personal meetings with someone, or placing ads to meet sexual partners; visiting sexually oriented chat rooms; and engaging in real-time cybersex affairs, often with the use of digital cameras which transmit real-time pictures of the participants to each other. Related activities include phone sex with people met online, and online affairs that progress to real, off-line sexual activities. Although most cybersex participants are recreational users, about 8 percent are addicted. For them, cybersex is yet another form of acting out their sexual addiction.

Denial: Refusal to confront a problem directly. The denial may be done with full awareness, such as a woman pretending to her friends that she has a perfect marriage, when her life is chaotic; or it may be self-denial, as when she convinces herself that a motel receipt in her husband's coat pocket was something he happened to pick up from the floor of his office building.

Enabling behavior: Behavior that protects the addict from experiencing the consequences of his or her addictive behavior. For example, the partner who suspects an affair hides his or her pain from the mate and makes excuses to friends for the mate's behavior. By postponing the time when addicts realize their life is out of control and that they need help, enabling helps to perpetuate the behavior.

Infidelity: The breaking of trust and the keeping of secrets in an intimate relationship.

Sex addict: A person who is addicted to the sexual experience and surrounding behaviors. The behaviors can include obsessing about an actual or potential sexual partner, compulsive masturbation, excessive expenditures on pornography, compulsive use of the internet for sexual gratification, patronizing prostitutes, multiple affairs, exposing oneself, or other sexual behaviors that the addict intuitively knows are against his or her best interests. In the context of affairs, the sex addict is the person who is secretly and compulsively sexual with a series of partners, substituting sensations for feelings in a spiraling escalation of risk, without apparent regard for the destruction of important relationships with family and friends.

Resources

The Twelve-Step fellowships listed below have regular meetings for both sex addicts and partners in many large cities. Those who live in communities without such meetings can often be helped by attending open A.A. or Al-Anon meetings. Thanks to the internet, there are now many resources for information and recovery from sexual addiction, trauma, and coaddiction, as well as on-line meetings available to those who do not have local meetings.

For the Sex Addict:

Sexaholics Anonymous (SA)
PO Box 3565
Brentwood, TN 37024
(615) 370-6062
e-mail: saico@sa.org
http://www.sa.org

Sex & Love Addicts Anonymous (SLAA)
1550 NE Loop 410, Suite 118
San Antonio, TX 78209
(210) 828-7900
e-mail: fwsoffice@slaafws.com
http://www.slaafws.org

Sex Addicts Anonymous (SAA)

PO Box 70949
Houston, TX 77270
(713) 869-4902 (800)477-8191
e-mail: info@saa-recovery.org
http://www.sexaa.org

Sexual Compulsives Anonymous (SCA)

Old Chelsea Station, PO Box 1585
New York, NY 10011
(800) 977-HEAL
http://www.sca-recovery.org

Sexual Recovery Anonymous (SRA)
General Service Board

PO Box 178
New York, NY 10296
email: info@sexualrecovery.org
www.sexualrecovery.org
[This program is much like Sexaholics Anonymous, but the bottom line in SRA is no sex outside a committed relationship (vs. marriage). It is useful for singles and the LGBTQ population.]

For the Partner or Family Member:

COSA

9219 Katy Freeway, Suite 212
Houston, TX 77024
e-mail: cosa@recovery.org
http:// www. cosa-recovery.org

S-Anon International Family Groups
PO Box 111242
Nashville, TN 37222-1242
(615) 833-3152 (800)210-8141
email: sanon@sanon.org
www.sanon.org

For teenage family members of sexual addicts:

SAteen
Contact: S-Anon International Family Groups
P. O. Box 17294
Nashville, TN 37217
Tel: (615) 833-3152 (800)210-8141
email: sanon@sanon.org
www.sanon.org
http://www.sanon.org

For Couples

Recovering Couples Anonymous (RCA)
PO Box 11029
Oakland, CA 94611
781-794-1456
e-mail: info@recovering-couples.org
website: www.recovering-couples.org

Non-Twelve-Step Support Groups:

Partners of Sex Addicts (POSA)
Partners of Sex Addicts Resource Center (POSARC)
www.posarc.com
If "you're tired of being called a codependent instead of the betrayal trauma survivor you are."

Other helpful resources:

International Institute for Trauma and Addiction Professionals
P.O.Box 2112
Carefree, AZ 85377
Tel: (866) 575-6853
website: www.iitap.com
IITAP provides training and certification for sex addiction recovery

Society for the Advancement of Sexual Health (SASH)
PO Box 566
Ardmore, PA 19003
Tel: 610-348-4783.
e-mail: info@sash.net
website: www.sash.net

Sexual Addiction & Compulsivity: The Journal of Treatment and Prevention
To subscribe: http://www.tandfonline.com/pricing/journal/usac20#.VEchlufPqts
Tel: (800) 354-1420 (215) 625-8900

Adult Children of Alcoholics (ACA)
P.O. Box 3216
Torrance, CA 90510
website: www.adultchildren.com
Tel: 310-534-1815
"For adults who grew up in alcoholic or dysfunctional homes and who exhibit identifiable traits that reveal past abuse or neglect. . . brings together a diverse group of recovering people that includes adult children of alcoholics, codependents, and addicts of various sorts."

Other helpful websites:

Dr. Patrick Carnes' information web site:
www.SexHelp.com

Robert Weiss's web site
www.sexualrecovery.com

Jennifer Schneider's web site:
www.jenniferschneider.com

Suggested Reading

For Addicts: Understanding and Recovering From Sex Addiction

Augustine Fellowship Staff. *Sex and Love Addicts Anonymous*. Boston: Sex and Love Addicts Anonymous, 1986. The official book of the fellowship of SLAA.

Carnes, Patrick. *Facing the Shadow: Starting Sexual and Relationship Recovery*. (Wickenburg, AZ: Gentle Path Press, 2001).

Carnes, Patrick. *Out of the Shadows: Understanding Sexual Addiction, Third Edition*. Center City, MN: Hazelden, 2001. The groundbreaking book that explains sex addiction.

Carnes, Patrick. *Don't Call it Love: Recovery From Sexual Addiction*. (New York: Bantam, 1991.) Results of research on more than 1000 sex addicts.

Carnes, Patrick. *A Gentle Path Through the Twelve Steps: The Classic Guide for All People in the Process of Recovery*. (Carefree, AZ: Gentle Path Press, 2012).

Carnes, Patrick. *Sexual Anorexia: Overcoming Sexual Self-Hatred*. (Center City, MN: Hazelden, 1997). The flip side of excessive sexual activities is avoiding sex while obsessing about it.

Carnes, Patrick, Delmonico, David, and Griffin, Elizabeth. *In the Shadows of the Net: Breaking Free of Compulsive Online Sexual Behavior*. (Center City, MN: Hazelden, 2001). Help for cybersex addicts.

Corley, M. Deborah and Schneider Jennifer P. *Disclosing Secrets: An Addict's Guide for When, to Whom, and How Much to Reveal*.,

2012. Practical guide to getting through the most difficult part of early recovery – disclosing the sexual acting out to your spouse.

Earle, Ralph, and Gregory Crow. *Lonely All the Time: Recognizing, Understanding, and overcoming Sex Addiction, for Addicts and Codependents.* (New York: Pocket Books, 1989). Another easy-to-understand explanation of sex addiction.

Earle, Ralph, and Marcus Earle. *Sex Addiction: Case Studies and Management.* (New York: Brunner/Mazel, 1995). Good guide for therapists working with sex addicts.

Ferree, Marnie (Ed). *Making Advances: A Comprehensive Guide for Treating Female Sex and Love Addicts.* (Roylston, GA: Society for the Advancement of Sexual Health, 2012).

Ferree, Marnie. *No Stones –Women Redeemed From Sexual Addiction*, Second Editio. (Intervarsity Press, 2010). Based on personal experience, about and for women sex addicts.

Hatch, Linda. *Relationships in Recovery: A Guide for Sex Addicts who are Starting Over*, 2013.

Hope and Recovery: A Twelve Step Guide for Healing from Compulsive Sexual Behavior. (Center City, MN,1987). Modeled after the "Big Book" of Alcoholics Anonymous.

Kasl, Charlotte Davis. *Women, Sex, and Addiction: A Search for Love and Power.* (New York: Ticknor and Fields, 1989.) About women sex addicts and coaddicts/partners.

Katehakis, Alexandra. *Erotic Intelligence: Igniting Hot, Healthy Sex While in Recovery from Sexual Addiction.* (Deerfield Beach, FL: Health Communications Inc. 2010).

Laaser, Mark. *Healing the Wounds of Sexual Addiction.* (Zondervan, 2004).

Lofgreen, Connie. *The Storm of Sex Addiction: Rescue and Recovery.* (Omaha, NE: Starpro, 2012).

Maltz, Wendy and Maltz, Larry. *The Port Trap: The Essential Guide to Overcoming Problems Caused by Pornography.* 2009.

Melody, Pia, Andrea Wells Miller, and J Keith Miller. *Facing Love Addiction* (San Francisco, CA: HarperSanFrancisco, 1992).

Weiss, Robert. *Cruise Control: Understanding Sex Addiction in Gay Men.* (Los Angeles, CA: Alyson Press, 2005)

Weiss, Robert and Schneider, Jennifer. *Always Turned On: Sexual Addiction in the Digital Age.* (Carefree, AZ: Gentle Path Press, 2015).

Sexaholics Anonymous. *Sexaholics Anonymous.* (Simi Valley, CA: 1989). The official book of the fellowship of SA.

For Partners: Understanding and Recovering From Sexual Coaddiction/ Codependency and Trauma

Beattie, Melody. *Codependent No More.* (Center City, MN: Hazelden, 1987). The classic guide to understanding and overcoming codependence.

Beatty, Melody. *The New Codependency: Help and Guidance for Today's Generation.* (New York: Simon & Schuster, 2009). An updated guide to recovering from codependence.

Beatty, Melody. *Beyond Codependency.* (Center City, Minn: Hazelden, 2009). Black, Claudia. *Deceived: Facing Sexual Betrayal, Lies, and Secrets.* (Center City, MN: Hazelden, 2009).Black, Claudia and Tripodi, Cara. *Intimate Treason: Healing the Trauma for Partners Confronting Sex Addiction.* (Las Vegas, NV: Central Recovery Press, 2012).

Carnes, Patrick. *The Betrayal Bond: Breaking Free of Exploitive Relationships.* (Deerfield Beach, Fla. Health Communications, 1997). How childhood trauma influences adult relationships.

Carnes, Patrick. *A Gentle Path through the Twelve Steps.* (Carefree, AZ: Gentle Path Press, 1993).

Carnes, Patrick. *A Gentle Path through the Twelve Principles.* (Carefree, AZ: Gentle Path Press, 2012).

Carnes, Stefanie (Ed) *Mending a Shattered Heart: A Guide for Partners of Sex Addicts, Second Edition.* (Carefree, AZ: Gentle Path Press, 2011).

Carnes, Stefanie, Lee, Mari and Rodriguez, Anthony. *Facing Heartbreak: Steps to Recovery for Partners of Sex Addicts.* (Carefree, AZ: Gentle Path Press, 2012).

Conquest, Wendy. *Letters to a Sex Addict: The Journey through Grief and Betrayal*, 2013.

Covington, Stephanie. *A Woman's Guide Through the Twelve Steps.* (Center City, MN: Hazelden, 2000).

Herman, Judith. *Trauma and Recovery.* (New York: Basic Books, 1992).

Kaplan, Debra L. *For Love and Money: Exploring Sexual & Financial Betrayal in Relationships.* 2013,

Larsen, Earnie. *Stage II Relationships: Love Beyond Addictions.* (San Francisco: Harper & Row, 1987). The importance of rebuilding relationships after Stage I recovery.

Levine, Peter A. *Healing Trauma.*

Levine, Peter A. *Waking the Tiger: Healing Trauma*Mellody, Pia, with Andrea Wells Miller and J. Keith Miller. *Facing Codependence.* (San Francisco: HarperSanFrancisco, 1989).

Norwood, Robin. *Women Who Love too Much: When you Keep Wishing and Hoping He'll Change.* (Los Angeles: Jeremy Tarcher, Inc., 1985). The classic book about women who get involved with addicts and how they can heal.

Maltz, Wendy and Maltz, Larry. *The Porn Trap: The Essential Guide to Overcoming Problems Caused by Pornography.* 2009.

S-Anon International Family Groups. *S-Anon Twelve Steps.* (Nashville, TN: S-Anon, 2000).

Schaef, Anne Wilson. *Escape From Intimacy: The Pseudo-Relationship Addictions: Untangling the 'Love' Addictions: Sex, Romance, Relationships.* San Francisco: Harper San Francisco, 1990.

Schaef, Anne Wilson. *Codependence: Misunderstood/Mistreated.* (Minneapolis, MN: Winston Press, 1986).

Schaeffer, Brenda. *Is It Love or is it Addiction?* 3rd ed. (Center City, Minn. Hazelden, 2009). Useful for understanding healthy versus unhealthy relationships.

Schneider, Jennifer, and Corley, M. Deborah. *Surviving Disclosure: A Partner's Guide for Healing the Betrayal of Intimate Trust.* 2012.

Schneider, Jennifer, and Burt Schneider. *Sex, Lies, and Forgivness: Couples Speak on Healing From Sex Addiction.* Third Ed. (Tucson, AZ: Recovery Resources Press, 2003). A guide for couples who seek to rebuild their relationship.

Spring, Janis Abrams. *After the Affair: Healing the Pain and Rebuilding Trust When a Partner Has Been Unfaithful.* (New York: Harper Collins, 1996). No matter what the cause of the affair, this book describes how each party feels and how to recover.

Spring, Janis Abrams. *How Can I Forgive You?* (New York: Harper, 2004).

Steffens, Barbara and Means, Marsha. *Your Sexually Addicted Spouse: How Partners Can Cope and Heal.* (New Jersey: New Horizons Press, 2009).

Subotnik, Rona. *Why Did He Cheat on Me: The Truth Behind Why Men Stray.* (Avon, MA: Adams Media, 2010).

Subotnik, Rona and Harris Gloria. *Surviving Infidelity: Making Decisions, Recovering from the Pain.* (Holbrook, MA: Adams Publishing, 1994.)

Healthy Sexuality

Barbach, Lonnie Garfield. *For Each Other: Sharing Sexual Intimacy.* (Garden City, NJ: Anchor Press, 1982).

Blumstein, Philip, and Schwartz, Pepper. *American Couples: Money, Work, Sex.* (New York: William Morrow, 1983). This research-based book describes behavior norms for American couples.

Covington, Stephanie. *Awakening Your Sexuality: A guide for Recovering Women.* (Center city, MN: Hazelden, 1991).

Hastings, Anne Stirling. *Reclaiming Healthy Sexual Energy.* (Wellness Institute, 2000).

Hunter, Mic. *Joyous Sexuality.* (Minneapolis, MN: CompCare Publications, 1992).

Katehakis, Alexandra. *Erotic Intelligence: Igniting Hot, Healthy Sex with in Recovery from Sex Addiction.* (Deerfield Beach, FL: Health Communications, Inc. 2010).

Laaser, Mark. *Talking to Your Kids About Sex.* (Colorado Springs, CO: WaterBrook Press, 1999).

Maltz, Wendy; Peacock, Molly; and McCarthy, Barry. *Passionate Hearts. The Poetry of Sexual Love.* (Novato, CA: New World Library, 1996).

Maltz, Wendy. *The Sexual Healing Journey: A Guide for Survivors of Sexual Abuse, Third Edition.* (San Francisco: Harper Collins, 2012).

Gay and Bisexual Men

Berzon, Betty. *Permanent Partners: Building Gay and Lesbian Relationships that Last.* (Los Angeles: Plume Books, 1990).

Gochros, Jean: *When Husbands Come Out of the Closet.* (New York, NY: Harrington Park Press, 1989). How wives deal with their husbands' homosexuality.

Kort, Joe. *Is My Husband Gay, Straight, or Bi?: A Guide for Women Concerned about Their Men.* 2014.

Weiss, Rob. *Cruise Control: Understanding Sex Addiction in Gay Men, Second Edition.* (Carefree, AZ: Gentle Path Press, 2013).

For Couples

Bercaw, Bill and Bercaw, Ginger. *The Couple's Guide to Intimacy: How Sexual Reintegration Therapy Can Help Your Relationship Heal,* 2010.

Carnes, Patrick; Laaser, Debra, and Laaser, Mark. *Open Hearts: Renewing Relationships with Recovery, Romance & Reality.* (Carefree, AZ: Gentle Path Press, 2009).

Collins, Paldrom Catharine and Collins, George N. *A Couple's Guide to Sexual Addiction: A Step-by-Step Plan to Rebuild Trust & Restore Intimacy.* (Avon, MA: Adams Media, 2012)

Gottman, John M and Silver, Nan. *The Seven Principles for Making Marriage Work.* (New York: Three Rivers Press, 1999).

Hatch, Linda. *Relationships in Recovery: A Guide for Sex Addicts who are Starting Over,* 2013.

Hendrix, Harville. *Getting the Love You Want.* (New York, NY: Holt, 1988).

Kasl, Charlotte. *If the Buddha Dated* (New York: Penguin Group, 1999).

Kasl, Charlote. *If the Buddha Married.* (New York: Penguin Group, 2001).

Levine, Stephen and Levine, Ondrea. *Embracing the Beloved: Relationship as a Path of Awakening.* (New York: Random House, 1995).

Magness, Milton S. *Hope and Freedom for Sexual Addicts and Their Partners.* (Carefree, AZ: Gentle Path Press, 2009).

Recovering Couples Anonymous. *Recovering Couples Anonymous: A Twelve-Step Program for Couples, Fourth Edition.* (Oakland, CA: World Services Organization of RCA, 2013)..

Recovering Couples Anonymous. *Step Up to Love: A Twelve-Step Guide for Couple Recovery.* (Oakland, CA: World Services Organization of RCA, 2009).

Schneider, Jennifer and Schneider, Burt. *Sex, Lies, and Forgiveness: Couples Speaking on Healing from Sex Addiction, Third Edition.* (Tucson, AZ, 2004).

Footnotes

PREFACE

1. *Alcoholics Anonymous: The Stormy of How More Than One Hundred Men Have Recovered from Alcoholism* (New York: Works Publishing Company, 1939)
2. *Journal of the American Medical Association* 113(1939): 1513.
3. Corley, MD, Schneider, JP, and Hook, JN. Partner reactions to disclosure of relapse by self-identified sexual addicts. *Sexual Addiction & Compulsivity* 19:265-283, 2012.

CHAPTER ONE: LIVING WITH SEX ADDICTION

1. "Sexaholic: Addict of Infidelity," *Arizona Daily Star* (5 May 1985) Section H. Reprinted with permission of the Arizona Daily Star.
2. Alfred C. Kinsey, Wardell B. Pomeroy, and Clyde E. Martin, *Sexual Behavior in the Human Male* (Philadelphia: W. H. Saunders Co., 1948), 585.
3. Shere Hite, *The Hite Report on Male Sexuality* (New York: Alfred A. Knopf, Inc., 1981), 142.
4. Robert A. Johnson, *We: Understanding the Psychology of Romantic Love* (San Francisco: Harper & Row Inc., 1983), xii.
5. Tennov, Dorothy (1979). *Love and limerence: the experience of being in love*. Scarborough House. ISBN 978-0-8128-6286-7. Retrieved 12 March 2014.

6. *When Your Happily Ever After Isn't* (Denver: Raj Publications, 1981), 3.

7. Ibid., 12.

8. Weiss Robert & Jennifer Schneider,, 2014 Closer Together, Further Apart. Carefree, AZ: Gentle Path Press, 2014.

9. Gail Lyle, email of 6/24/12.

10. Staci Sprout, email of 6/25/12.Permission granted on 11/2/14

11. Connie Lofgreen, MSW email of 6/25/12

12. Andrew L. Erdman, LMSW. Email of 6/25/12. Permission granted on 11/2/14

13. Nancy Jarrell O'Donnell, Email of 6/25/12

14. Francine Klagsbrun, *Married People: Staying Together in the Age of Divorce* (New York: Bantam, 1985).

15. Ibid., 23.

16. Morton Hunt, *The Affair* (New York: New American Library, 1973), 39.

17. Ibid., 33.

18. Ibid., 46.

19. Catherine Johnson, "The New Woman Infidelity Report," *New Woman* (November, 1986), 73.

20. Morton Hunt, *Sexual Behavior in the 1970s,* (New York: Playboy Press, 1974) 268.

21. Kay, Director of Sexaholics Anonymous Office, personal communication, 1/5/15.

22. Patrick Carnes, "Counseling the Sexual Addict" workshop in Tucson, Ariz., 1986.

23. Alfred C. Kinsey, Wardell B. Pomeroy, Clyde E. Martin, and Paul H. Gebhardt, *Sexual Behavior in the Human Female*(Philadelphia and London: W. B. Saunders Co., 1953), 444.

24. Hunt, *Sexual Behavior in the 1970s*, 269.

25. Patrick J. Carnes, BA Green, LJ Polles, Stefanie Carnes, MS Gold. PATHOS: A brief screening application for assessing sexual addiction. doi: 10.1097/ADM.0b013e3182251a28. Reprinted

with permission from the International Institute of Trauma and Addiction Professionals (IITAP).

26. Internet Filter Review, http://internet-filter-review.toptenreviews.com/internet-pornography-statistics-pg6.html. Accessed 1/17/15

CHAPTER TWO: THE TRAUMATIZED PARTNER

1. Patrick Carnes, *Out of the Shadows: Understanding Sexual Addiction* (Minneapolis: CompCare Publications, 1983), 92, 98. Originally published as *The Sexual Addiction*. p.124.
2. Op cit, p.4.
3. Robin Norwood, *Women Who Love Too Much* (Los Angeles: J.P. Tarcher, 1985), 185.
4. Patrick Carnes, "Counseling the Sexual Addict" workshop in Tucson, Ariz. 1986.
5. Carnes, *Out of the Shadows*, 105-114.
6. Jean Harris, *Stranger in Two Worlds* (New York: Macmillan Publishing Co., 1986), 147.
7. James and Peggy Vaughan, *Beyond Affairs* (New York: Dialog Press, 1980).
8. Norwood, *Women Who Love Too Much*, p.130.
9. Ruth Maxwell, *The Booze Battle* (New York: Ballantine Books, 1976), 45.

CHAPTER THREE: THE FAMILY CONNECTION

1. Bill W., letter quoted in *The Grapevine*, January 1958.
2. Robert Subby, *Co-dependency, An Emerging Issue* (Hollywood, Fla: Health Communications, Inc., 1984), 26.
3. Ibid.
4. Claudia Black, *It Will Never Happen to Me* (Denver: M.A.C. Printing and Publications Division, 1981).

5. Subby, *Co-dependency*, 36.
6. Arthur and Cynthia Koestler, *Stranger on the Square* (New York: Random House, 1984), 170.
7. Subby, *Co-dependency*, 39.
8. Lou Ann Walker, *A Loss for Words* (New York: Harper & Row, Inc., 1986), 21.
9. Ibid, 22
10. Ibid, 104
11. Ibid, 181-183
12. Ibid, 187.
13. Patricia Love. *The Emotional Incest Syndrome.* New York: Bantam Books, 1990, p. 1
14. U.S. Census Bureau, American Community Survey Data, http://factfinder.census.gov/faces/tableservices/jsf/pages/productview.xhtml?pid=ACS_13_5YR_DP02&prodType=table
15. "Four –in-Ten Couples are Saying "I Do" Again. http://www.pewsocialtrends.org/2014/11/14/four-in-ten-couples-are-saying-i-do-again/
16. U.S. Bureau of Labor Statistics, BLS Report, Report 1049. www.bls.gov, 2014.
17. Sharon Wegscheider-Cruse, *Another Chance: Hope and Health for the Alcoholic Family* (Palo Alto, Calif.: Science and Behavior Books, Inc., 1981), 84.
18. Black, *It Will Never Happen*, 53
19. "Ask Al", *Arizona Daily Star* (2 January 1987) Section C,2.

CHAPTER FOUR: SEX ADDICTS

1. American Society of Addiction Medicine, *Definition of Addiction.* http://www.asam.org/for-the-public/definition-of-addiction Accessed 1-17-15
2. Erich Fromm, *The Art of Loving* (New York: Harper & Row, Perennial Library Edition, 1974), 8-10.

3. Stanton Peele. *Love and Addiction.* (New York, New York: New American Library, 1975).

4. James C. Dobson, *Love Must Be Tough* (Waco, Tex.: Word Books, 1983), 122.

5. Valerie Voon, Thomas B Mole, et al, Neural correlates of sexual cue reactivity in individuals with and without compulsive sexual behaviors. *PLOS One*, July, 2014. DOI: 10.127/journal. pone.0102419.

6. American Society of Addiction Medicine. *Short definition of addiction.* http://www.asam.org/for-the-public/definition-of-addiction Accessed 3-4-15

7. Patrick Carnes, statement on the Phil Donahue Show, 7 January 1987.

8. Patrick Carnes, *Out of the Shadows,: Understanding Sexual Addiction* (Minneapolis: CompCare Publications, 1983), pp. 82-85

9. Richard R. Irons and Jennifer P. Schneider, *The Wounded Healer: Addiction-sensitive Approach to the Sexually Exploitative Professional.* (New Brunswick, New Jersey: Jason Aronson Publishers, 1999).

10. Louis McBurney, "Avoiding the Scarlet Letter," *Leadership* (Summer 1985).

11. M. Deborah Corley and David Delmonico. Closing the gap: Results from the Women's Sexuality Survey on female sex and love addicts. Presentation at the Society for the Advancement of Sexual Health Conference, La Jolla, CA, September 2011.

12. Women Sex Addicts. http://sash.net/?q=women-and-sex-addiction-0/ accessed 11/17/15

13. Robert Weiss and Jennifer Schneider, *Always Turned On: Sex Addiction in the Digital Age.* Carefree, AZ: Gentle Path Press, 2015., p 66

14. Jennifer P. Schneider, Effects of cybersex addiction on the family: Results of a survey. *Sexual Addiction and Compulsivity 6* (1999):31-58.

15. Weiss and Schneider, 2015, p. 17.

16. Patrick Carnes, 1997. *Sexual Anorexia: Overcoming Sexual Self-Hatred.*, p. 1

17. Roger Pulvers, "Reversing Japan's Rising Sex Aversion May Depend on a Rebirth of Hope." Japan Times, April 29, 2012, http://www.japantimes.co.jp/text/fl20120429rp.html/

18. Philip G Zimbardo and Nikita Duncan, The Demise of Guys: Why Boys are Struggling and What We Can Do About It. (Amazon Digital Services, 2012).

19. Weiss and Schneider, 2015, p. 56

20. Gary Wilson, "What experts tell guys suffering from ED http://yourbrainonporn.com/what-experts-tell-guys-suffering-from-ed. Accessed 6/3/14

21. Arnold Washton, Cocaine may trigger sexual compulsivity. *U. S. Journal of Drug and Alcohol Dependency* 13(1989), 8.

22. Carnes, P.J., Murray, R. E., and Charpentier, L., 2005. Bargains with chaos: Sex addicts and addiction interaction disorder. *Sexual Addiction & Compulsivity* 10:79-120.

23. Debra Kaplan, *For Love and Money: Exploring sexual and Financial Betrayal in Relationships*, 2013.

CHAPTER FIVE: LIVING WITH SEX ADDICTION

1. Jean Harris, *Stranger in Two Worlds* (New York: Macmillan Publishing Company, 1986), p.61

2. Linda Hatch, *Relationships in Recovery: A Guide for Sex Addicts Who Are Starting Over*, 2013.

3. Debra Kaplan, *For Love and Money: Exploring Sexual & Financial Betrayal in Relationships.* 2013

4. Omar Minwalla, "What about me and my sexuality?" in Carnes, Stefanie, Editor. *Mending a Shattered Heart, Second edition*, Carefree, AZ: Gentle Path Press, 2011.

5. Jennifer P. Schneider, Effects of cybersex addiction on the family: Results of a survey. *Sexual Addiction and Compulsivity 6* (1999):31-58.

6. Ruth Maxwell, *The Booze Battle* (New York: Ballantine Books, 1976), 41-43.

7. Jennifer Schneider, Robert Weiss, and Charles Samenow,. Is it really cheating? Understanding the emotional reactions and clinical treatment of spouses and partners affected by cybersex infidelity. *Sexual Addiction & Compulsivity* 19:123-139, 2012.

8. Schneider, Weiss, & Samenow, p. 136.

9. GT Ray, JR Mertens, and C Weisner. The excess medical cost and health problems of family members of persons diagnosed with alcohol or drug problems. *Medical Care* 45:116-122, 2007.

10. Richard Irons and Jennifer Schneider. When is domestic violence a hidden face of addiction? *Journal of Psychoactive Drugs* 29:337-344, 1997.

11. Arthur Koestler and Cynthia Koestler, *Stranger on the Square* (New York: Random House, 1984), p.228

12. Koestler & Koestler, p.115

13. Koestler & Koestler, p. 179.

14. Koestler & Koestler, p.108.

15. Ann Wickett, "Why Cynthia Koestler Joined Arthur," *Hemlock Quarterly* (January 1985), p.4

16. Koestler, *Stranger on the Square*, p.150.

17. Ibid., p.225

18. Ibid., p.14

19. Jean Harris, *Stranger in Two Worlds*, p.122.

20. G. Thomas Ray, Jennifer R Mertens, and Constance Weisner. The excess medical cost and health problems of family members of persons diagnosed with alcohol or drug problems. *Medical Care* 45:116-122, 2007.

21. Judith Thurman, *Isak Dinesen, The Life of a Storyteller* (New York: St. Martin's Press, 1983), 149.

22. http://www.cdc.gov/std/treatment/2010/hepc.htm accessed 3/5/15)

23. http://www.cdc.gov/std/herpes/stdfact-herpes.htm

24. www.niaid.nih.gov/factsheets/aidsstat/htm, [accessed 1/15/05

25. McFarlane, M, Bull, S.S., and Rietmeijer, C.A. The Internet as a newly emerging risk environment for sexually transmitted diseases. *Journal of the American Medical Association* 284(2000):443-446.

26. Katherine M. Stone et al. Primary prevention of sexually transmitted diseases. *Journal of the American Medical Association* 255(1986):1763-1766.

27. Robert Weiss. Special populations: Treatment concerns for gay male sexual addicts. *Sexual Addiction & Compulsivity* 4:323-334, 1997.

28. David Frederick and Melissa Fales. Upset over sexual versus emotional infidelity among gay, lesbian, bisexual, and heterosexual adults. *Archives of Sexual Behavior,* 2014. doi 10.1007/s1058-014-0409-9, accessed 1-17-15.

29. Jennifer Schneider and Burt Schneider. *Sex, Lies, and Forgiveness: Couples Speak on Healing from Sex Addiction, 3rd Edition.* Tucson, AZ: Recovery Resources Press, 2003.

30. Marnie Ferree. *No Stones: Women Redeemed from Sexual Shame.* Fairfax, VA: Xulon Press, 2002. (Updated in 2010).

31. Robert Weiss, 1997,*Op Cit*

CHAPTER SIX: THE ELEMENTS OF RECOVERY

1. Patrick Carnes, *Don't Call it Love: Recovery from Sexual Addiction.* New York: Bantam Books, 1991.

2. Stefanie Carnes and Cara Tripodi. "Is This Going to Get Better?" in Carnes, Stefanie (Editor), *Mending a Shattered Heart: A Guide to Partners of Sex Addicts.* Second Edition. Carefree, AZ: Gentle Path Press, pp 41-62.

3. Stefanie Carnes, Mari A. Lee, and Anthony D. Rodriguez, *Facing Heartbreak: Steps to Recovery for Partners of Sex Addicts.* Carefree, AZ: Gentle Path Press, 2012.

.

4. American Psychiatric Association, *Diagnostic and Statistical Manual of Mental Disorders, Fifth Edition*. Washington, DC: American Psychiatric Pubishing, 2013.

5. T.L. Cermak, *Diagnosing and Treating Co-Dependence* (Minneapolis: Johnson Institute Publications, 1986), 3.

6. Cermak, pp.9-10.

7. Robin Norwood, *Women Who Love Too Much* (Los Angeles: Jeremy Tarcher, Inc., 1985), 184.

8. PERMISSION FROM SAA

9. Robert A. Johnson, *We: Understanding the Psychology of Romantic Love* (San Francisco: Harper & Row, 1983), 52.

10. Johnson, p. 55

11. Shere Hite, *Women and Love* (New York: Alfred A. Knopf, 1987), 501.

12. Hite, p.495.

13. Johnson, *We*, 55.

14. Robert A. Johnson, *She* (New York: Harper & Row Perennial Library, 1977), 32.

15. Lewis B. Smedes, *Forgive and Forget*. New York: Harper & Row, 1984. Updated 2007.

16. Janis Abrahms Spring, *How Can I Forgive You? The Courage to Forgive, the Freedom Not to*. New York: Harper & Row, 2004.

17. Erich Fromm, *The Art of Loving* (New York: Harper & Row, 1974), 22.

CHAPTER SEVEN: PROFESSIONAL HELP

1. Stefanie Carnes and Cara Tripodi, "Is This Going to Get Better??" in Carnes, Stefanie (Ed), *Mending a Shattered Heart*, pp.61-62

2. Ruth Westheimer, "Ask Dr. Ruth," *Arizona Daily Star*, 22 June, 1987, Section C3.

3. Shirley Glass, *Not "Just Friends*," 2003.

4. M. Deborah Corley and Jennifer P. Schneider, *Disclosing Secres: When, to Whom, and How Much to Reveal.* (Wickenburg, AZ: Gentle Path Press, 2002).

5. M. Deborah Corley and Jennifer P Schneider. Disclosing secrets: Guidelines for therapists working with sex addicts and coaddicts. *Sexual Addiction and Compulsivity* 9:43-67, 2002.

6. Emily M. Brown, *Patterns of Infidelity and Their Treatment* (New York: Brunner/Mazel, 1991).

7. Frank Pittman, *Private Lies.* (New York, NY: Norton, 1989)

8. N. Gartrell et al, Psychiatrist-patient sexual contact: Results of a national survey, I. Prevalence. *American Journal of Psychology* 143:1121-1126, 1986.

9. J. Herman et al, *op cit*

10. Richard R Irons and Jennifer P. Schneider, *The Wounded Healer: Addiction-Sensitive Approach to the Sexually Exploitative Professional* (New Jersey: Jason Aronson Publishers, 1999).

11. Richard R Irons and Jennifer P. Schneider, *The Wounded Healer: Addiction-Sensitive Approach to the Sexually Exploitative Professional* (New Jersey: Jason Aronson Publishers, 1999).

12. Stephanie Brown, *Treating the Alcoholic* (New York: John Wiley &Sons, 1985).

CHAPTER EIGHT: RECOVERY AS A COUPLE

1. Gabrielle Brown, *The New Celibacy* (New York: Ballantine Books, 1980), 33.

2. Brown, *The New Celibacy*, 167.

3. *Sexaholics Anonymous* (Simi Valley, Calif.: Sexaholics Anonymous Literature, 1984), 87.

4. *Hope and Recovery: A Twelve Step Guide for healing from Compulsive Sexual Behavior* (Minneapolis: CompCare Publications, 1987), 97.

5. Anne Wilson Schaef, *Co-dependence: Misunderstood/Mistreated* (Minneapolis: Winston Press, 1986), 42.

6. James C. Dobson, *Love Must be Tough* Waco, Tex.; Wood Books, 1983), p. 56.
7. Dobson, p. 122.
8. Erich Fromm, *The Art of Loving* (New York: Harper & Row, 1956), 103.
9. Deborah M. Corley, Jennifer P. Schneider, and Joshua N. Hook. Partner reactions to disclosure of relapse by self-identified sexual addicts. *Sexual Addiction & Compulsivity* 19:265-283, 2012.
10. Jennifer P. Schneider and Burt Schneider, *Sex, Lies, and Forgiveness: Couples Speak on Healing From Sex Addiction, 3rd Edition* (Tucson, Ariz.: Recovery Resources Press, 2003), 168.
11. Claudia Black, Diane Dillon, and Stephanie Carne, Disclosure to children: Hearing the child's experience. *Sexual Addiction & Compulsivity* 10 (2003):67-78.
12. Deborah Corley M.D. and Jennifer Schneider, Sex addiction disclosure to children: The parents' perspective. *Sexual Addiction & Compulsivity* 10 (2003):291-324.
13. Jennifer P. Schneider, "Sexual Problems in Married Couples Recovering from Sexual Addiction and Coaddiction," *American Journal of Preventive Psychiatry & Neurology,* 2:16-21, 1990.
14. Recovering Couples Anonymous, *Recovering Couples Anonymous: A Twelve-Step Program for Couples, Fourth Edition,* 2013. World Service Organization (WSO) of RCA: Oakland, CA., p. 6

CHAPTER NINE: RECOVERY AS A SINGLE PERSON

1. http://www.takingcharge.csh.umn.edu/enhance-your-wellbeing/purpose/spirituality/what-spirituality Accessed 12/20/14.
2. Robin Norwood, lecture in Tucson, May 1986.
3. Norwood, 1986.
4. Howard M. Halpern, *How to Break Your Addiction to a Person* (New York: Bantam Books, 2003, P. 9.

Index

Addiction(s)
Definition 31, 87-88, 90-91, 94
Models of 196-200
AIDS (See HIV)
Alcoholics Anonymous xxiv, 28
Twelve Steps of (see Twelve Steps)
Beattie, Melody xxii
Black, Claudia 78, 81
Brown, Emily 248-249
Brown, Gabrielle 262, 268
Brown, Stephanie 254
Candida (see vaginal yeast)
Carnes, Patrick xxii, 22-23, 118, 120, 193, 233
Carnes, Stefanie 193, 237
Cermak, Timmen xxii, 200
Chlamydia 167-168
Coaddiction) xxviii-xxxii, 29-30
Definition 333,334
Codependence xxviii-xxxii, 29-30, 39, 51-52, 60-61, 73
Versus trauma xxviiii-xxxi, 29-30
Corley, Deborah xxxiv, 246, 261, 269, 289, 297
Counselor/Therapist
Attitude on concealed affairs 245-248
Gender of 251-252
How to choose 231-241
Sex with client 252-2254

Suggestions for 241-255
Couple recovery 225-226, 257-308
Abstinence 262-269
Effect of length of marriage 258-259
Effect on partner 139-143
Effect on sexual relationship 304-307
Rebuilding trust 285-288
Relapse 289-294
Cybersex
Cybersex addiction xxvi, 139-143
Is cybersex cheating? 146-149
On mobile devices xxvii
Recreational users xxvi
Dinesen, Isak 162-163
Disclosing secrets 269-304
Positive outcomes 247-248
What to tell children &parents 294-304
What to tell about past sexual behaviors 269-277
Dobson, James C. 90-91, 283
Dysfunctional family 61-85
Children's roles 78
Family rules 62-71
Emotional incest 71
Family, healthy 71-72
Ferree, Marnie xxxiii, 27, 186
Forgiveness 220-224
Fromm, Erich 88-90, 227

Gardnerella vaginitis 175
Gaslighting 157
Genital warts 173-174
Gonorrhea 165-167
Halpern, Howard 325-326
Harris, Jean 36-38, 123-1224, 155-156,188
Hatch, Linda 125-126
Hepatitis 168-170
Herpes 170-173
HIV/AIDS 175-178
Hunt, Morton 18-19
Infidelity 20-22
Infidelity costs 20-22, 149-180
    Resentment 149-150
    Emotional abuse 150-156
    Physical illness 157
    STDs 159-180
Intimacy 13-18, 106, 116, 257, 262, 267
    without ever meeting 14-17
    versus intensity, 34, 305, 307
Johnson, Robert A. 217-219
Kaplan, Debra 121, 135-136
Kasl, Charlotte xxxiii
Katehakis, Alexandra 242
Kinsey, Alfred 22
Klagsbrun, Francine 17-18
Koestler, Arthur & Cynthia 64, 152-155, 188
Kort, Joe 27
Levinson, Barbara 250-251
Limerence 12

Love, Patricia 71
Marriage
    Long term, characteristics 17-18
Maxwell, Ruth 17-18, 45, 144
McBurney, Louis 106-107
Minwalla, Omar 138
Norwood, Robin xxii, 34, 45, 67, 322
Partner or coaddict xxviiii-xxxi, 29-55
    Blamed for mate's behavior xxiii
    Choice of mate 53-55, 124-131
    Confusion of sex with love 48-49
    Controlling the addict 44-48, 144-146
    Core beliefs 35-53
    Effects of mate's addiction 123-143
    Enabling the addict 52, 227
    Family of origin 32-33, 40-41, 57-85
    Fears of abandonment 40-41, 124, 277
    Female partner of gay male 26-27
    Gay male partner 187-88
    Life with sex addict 123-189
    Male partner xxxii-xxx-iv, 9-10, 41-42, 27-28, 180-187

Need for excitement 32-35, 124

Overlap with sex addiction 51,139

Physical illness 52-53, 158-159

PTSD xxix-xxxi, 238

Relational trauma xxxi, 54

Resentment 149

Sexual trauma 136-143

Tolerates emotional abuse 150-157

Peck, M. Scott 328

Peele, Stanton 90

Pelvic inflammatory disease(PID) 165-166

Recovering Couples Anonymous 307-308

Recovery 193-229, 257-326

    Counseling in 231-255

    Choosing a therapist 231-241

    Elements of 193-229

    Forgiveness 220-224

    Helping our children 327-329

    Role of Twelve Steps 201-203

    Setting limits 277-285

    Spirituality in 216-219, 319-321

    Stages of 193-197

    Tools for Recovery as a single person 309-326

    Avoiding another addictive Relationship 322-325

    dating 321

    developing new interests 317-318

    fear of being alone 325

    grieving 314-315

    making new friends 315-316

    spiritual growth 319-321

Recovery of partner in a couple-ship 257-308

    Abstinence 262-269

    Disclosing secrets 269-277

    Establishing boundaries 277-285

    Fear of living alone 228

    Stay or leave if mate is still unfaithful 226-229, 278-281, 289-294

    Tendency to monitor 260

    Tendency to control spouse 144-146

Relationship trauma 54

Romantic love 11-17, 217-219

Salpingitis (See pelvic inflamma-tory disease)

Schaef, Anne Wilson xxii, 277

Sex addict/sex addiction 22-25, 87-121

    Addictive cycle 97

    Behaviors of 23-25, 95

    Beliefs 96-97

    Brain studies 94

    Choice of partner 124-126

    Concurrent addictions 95-96, 119-121

Core beliefs 96-97
Family of origin 105
Female addict 27-28, 111-116
Financial and job problems 134-136
Guilt & shame 122
In both partners 225-226
In clergy 105-107
Intimacy disorder 116, 118
Loss of control 25
Multiple addictions 119
PATHOS screening test 23
Prevalence 27
Progression of 97-101
Recovery from 225
Reluctance to marry 115-118
Role of fantasy 91-92, 95, 122
Sexual abuse in childhood 111
Sexual dysfunction in 118-119
Sexual anorexia 118
Sexually transmitted diseases 159-180
Smedes, Lewis 220

Society for the Advancement of Sexual Health (SASH) 201, 238-239, 242
Spirituality 216-219, 319-321
Spring, Janis Abrahms 220-221
Subby, Robert 60, 65
Syphilis 162-165
Tarnower, Herman 36, 123-124, 155-156
Tennov, Dorothy 12-13
Trichomonas 175
Twelve Steps Program 203-216, 249, 254-255, 330-331
   The Twelve Steps 203-216
Vaginal yeast infection 174-5
Vaughn, Peggy 42
Walker, Lou Ann 67-71
Wegscheider-Cruse, Sharon 78-82
Weiss, Robert xxvi-xxvii, xxiv, 14, 27, 147, 187, 240
Westheimer, Ruth 240
Wilson, Bill 59-60

ORDERING THIS BOOK

You can order *Back from Betrayal: Fourth Edition* on amazon.com. To obtain quantity discounts for multiple copies, email me.

HOW TO REACH ME

If you would like to contact me, you can email me at:
jennifer@jenniferschneider.com

Additional information is available on my website:
www.jenniferschneider.com

About the Author

Jennifer P. Schneider, MD, PhD, is a physician who has researched the effects of sex addiction and infidelity in relationships for more than twenty-five years. In 2007, she earned the SASH Award for her lifetime contributions to the sex addiction field. These have included thirteen books, various chapters, and many articles for professional journals. For over 20 years she has been Associate Editor of the journal *Sexual Addiction and Compulsivity: The Journal of Treatment and Prevention*.

Dr. Schneider coauthored three books with Dr. Deborah Corley: *Disclosing Secrets: An Addict's Guide for When, to Whom, and How Much to Reveal* and *Surviving Disclosure: A Partner's Guide for Healing the Betrayal of Intimate Trust*, and *Embracing Recovery from Chemical Dependency*. She also coauthored two books with Robert Weiss: *Closer Together, Further Apart: The Effect of the Internet and Technology on Parenting, Work and Relationships*, and *Always Turned On: Sex Addiction in the Digital Age*.

Her earlier works include *Sex, Lies & Forgiveness: Couples Speak on Healing from Sex Addiction*, written with Burt Schneider, and *The Wounded Healer: An Addiction-Sensitive Approach to the Sexually Exploitative Professional*, with Dr. Richard Irons. She has also appeared on numerous television and radio shows.

Made in the USA
Coppell, TX
20 April 2021